# THE
# EVERYTHING

**PARENT'S GUIDE TO**

## TEENAGE ADDICTION

Dear Reader,

My heart is with you as you consider the different ways to deal
with an addicted teenager. In my experience, nothing com-
pares to the close bond between a parent and child. After all,
you raised your child, teaching him to be tender and loving,
encouraging him to walk, talk, and ride a bicycle. You pro-
tected him from spiders, mean dogs, and bullying classmates.
As your child grows, so do your hopes for your child's
future—you may even have visions of what he will choose as
a profession, and how many grandchildren he will have.

Then substance abuse and addiction rear their ugly heads
and everything changes. Your child becomes someone you
don't recognize, and you sink into pits of despair. The bond of
caring between parents and their child is unshakeable, but in
order for you and your child to survive the agony of addiction
and substance abuse, your relationship may need to change.

This book is written to help you relate to your child in new
ways, ways that includes the silent partner of addiction—an
unwelcome, but very much present, guest in your family. I wish
you peace, serenity, and harmony as you creatively forge new
truths and realities for the health of you and your teenager.

With hope,

*Ellen*

# Welcome to the EVERYTHING® Series!

These handy, accessible books give you all you need to tackle a difficult project, gain a new hobby, comprehend a fascinating topic, prepare for an exam, or even brush up on something you learned back in school but have since forgotten.

You can choose to read an Everything® book from cover to cover or just pick out the information you want from our four useful boxes: e-questions, e-facts, e-alerts, e-ssentials. We give you everything you need to know on the subject, but throw in a lot of fun stuff along the way, too.

We now have more than 400 Everything® books in print, spanning such wide-ranging categories as weddings, pregnancy, cooking, music instruction, foreign language, crafts, pets, New Age, and so much more. When you're done reading them all, you can finally say you know Everything®!

PUBLISHER Karen Cooper

MANAGING EDITOR, EVERYTHING® SERIES Lisa Laing

COPY CHIEF Casey Ebert

ASSISTANT PRODUCTION EDITOR Alex Guarco

ACQUISITIONS EDITOR Hillary Thompson

DEVELOPMENT EDITOR Eileen Mullan

EVERYTHING® SERIES COVER DESIGNER Erin Alexander

Visit the entire Everything® series at www.everything.com

# THE EVERYTHING®

## PARENT'S GUIDE TO

# TEENAGE ADDICTION

A comprehensive and supportive
reference to help your child
recover from addiction

Edward Lynam, MD and Ellen Bowers, PhD

Avon, Massachusetts

The Everything® Parent's Guide to Teenage Addiction *is dedicated to the memory of my father, Dr. G.D. Bowers, who instilled in me a love of books and ideas. I still hold warm images of him, sitting in his favorite chair in the kitchen, reading newspapers and books, every night. —E.B.*

An Everything® Series Book.
Everything® and everything.com® are registered trademarks of F+W Media, Inc.

Published by
Adams Media, a division of F+W Media, Inc.
57 Littlefield Street, Avon, MA 02322. U.S.A.
*www.adamsmedia.com*

Contains material adapted and abridged from *The Everything® Guide to Cognitive Behavioral Therapy* by Ellen Bowers, PhD, copyright © 2013 by F+W Media, Inc., ISBN 10: 1-4405-5671-7, ISBN 13: 978-1-4405-5671-5; *The Everything® Guide to Coping with Perfectionism* by Ellen Bowers, PhD, copyright © 2013 by F+W Media, Inc., ISBN 10: 1-4405-5160-X, ISBN 13: 978-1-4405-5160-4; *The Everything® Parent's Guide to the Strong-Willed Child, 2nd Edition* by Ellen Bowers, PhD, copyright © 2012, 2005 by F+W Media, Inc., ISBN 10: 1-4405-3342-3, ISBN 13: 978-1-4405-3342-6; *The Everything® Parent's Guide to Positive Discipline, 2nd Edition* by Ellen Bowers, PhD, copyright © 2011, 2004 by F+W Media, Inc., ISBN 10: 1-4405-2850-0, ISBN 13: 978-1-4405-2850-7; and *The Everything® Health Guide to Addiction and Recovery* by Linda L. Simmons, PsyD, copyright © 2008 by F+W Media, Inc., ISBN 10: 1-59869-806-0, ISBN 13: 978-1-59869-806-0.

ISBN 10: 1-4405-8297-1
ISBN 13: 978-1-4405-8297-4
eISBN 10: 1-4405-8298-X
eISBN 13: 978-1-4405-8298-1

Printed in the United States of America.

10   9   8   7   6   5   4   3   2   1

*This book is available at quantity discounts for bulk purchases.*
*For information, please call 1-800-289-0963.*

# Acknowledgments

I gratefully acknowledge the encouragement and assistance of my editor at Adams Media, Hillary Thompson. Her patience and vision for the book, as the process moved from concept through to publication, made it all possible. Also, I am grateful for the other editors who had a part in shaping the book, for my coauthor and first reviewer, and for the ongoing personal and professional support of Janet, Jeanine, Fay, and Ingrid. I also want to acknowledge those gracious individuals who generously gave their time for conversations, which became personal anecdotes for Appendix A: Those Who Have Been There. Sometimes it truly does take a village. —E.B.

# Contents

## Chapter 5: Why Does My Child Act That Way? . . . . . . . . . . . 66

## Chapter 6: Prevention Methods. . . . . . . . . . . . . . . . . . . . . . 80

## Chapter 7: The Normal Teenage Brain versus the Addicted Teenage Brain . . . . . . . . . . . . . . . . . . . . . . . 95

## Chapter 8: The Substance Addictions . . . . . . . . . . . . . . . . 109

# Introduction

Unfortunately, many parents today have to raise their children in a drug-filled world. Legal or illegal, recreational or medicinal, found in your bathroom cabinet or in your garage, sold in the drugstore or on the street—mood- and mind-altering substances can be found just about anywhere. It's no secret that the adolescent years are ripe for experimentation with these drugs.

So, what are you as a parent supposed to do? Since you can't change the world, does that mean you are helpless to protect your child from the dangers of alcohol and drugs? No! You can't actually control your child's choices when it comes to alcohol and drug use, but you can definitely affect those choices by giving her the best information and understanding you have. You can inform your child about the nature of the problem, about the risks involved, and about staying safe if she does indeed decide to experiment with dangerous substances.

According to Mark Gold, psychiatrist and eminent scholar at the University of Florida College of Medicine, lifestyle habits formed during the teen years are likely to be present for the rest of your teen's life, as the adolescent's brain is still developing. Those who smoke as teens are likely to smoke as adults. Those who binge-drink in adolescence are likely to abuse alcohol in later years. Those who misuse prescription medications are likely to abuse pharmaceuticals, and so on.

Addiction is a serious health problem in the United States, and many of the attitudes, policies, laws, and approaches to this ever-present issue are clouded with denial and confusion. Holding on to opinions that addiction is a moral issue or something a person just has to "white-knuckle through and stop" can get in the way of deliberate, rational understanding and action. Add shame and guilt to the mix, and parents can easily become paralyzed in the tangled, twisted road to understanding addiction in teenagers.

It is a very human reaction to blame yourself; however, as you may have already discovered, it is not good to stay in that state of mind. It is true that you have to look at personal responsibility and choices, but a lot of what results in addiction is simply out of your personal control. Accepting your lack of control can make deciding what you need to do somewhat more manageable.

In today's world, drug use has become so widespread that news of a celebrity going into rehab isn't shocking. No one bats an eye at a politician, corporate official, or famous athlete going into rehab. It's almost like a badge of acceptance into the fast-paced world of entertainment. There is even a kind of mystique attached to the relationship between artistic gifts and addiction, making figures like Jimi Hendrix, Janis Joplin, Kurt Cobain, Michael Jackson, and Heath Ledger into icons of sacrifice, something strangely positive.

Drug use is different now, compared to one or two generations ago. The boomer generation who dabbled in drugs as a part of the '60s and '70s experience is shocked at the heroin use and alcohol abuse among youths today. Because of complex social forces, drug use is rampant. This type of cultural climate makes it a challenge for a parent who discovers that his teenager is using or behaving addictively. However, the challenge is not insurmountable. This book can help you negotiate the unique situations you may encounter as a parent of a child who struggles with addiction. With the proper education, information, strategies, and a bit of personal unlearning and re-learning, you will be able to navigate your way through the labyrinth of coping with teenage addiction.

At the conclusion of this book, you'll find an appendix featuring interviews and case histories of people who have traveled a road similar to yours. The names have been changed and identifying details altered in order to protect the anonymity of those whose stories are told. You'll also find a wealth of additional resources to further assist you and your teen as you move out of the grips of addiction and into recovery.

# CHAPTER 1

# Understanding Addiction in Teens

Addiction and substance abuse can take many forms. There are multiple levels of drug and alcohol use, ranging from occasional experimentation to full-blown addictions. It's incredibly important to first determine the level of your child's dependency before you decide how to proceed. What if your teenager's drug use and behavior is just a passing phase instead of a complex addiction? This is an important distinction to make, as it may affect how you deal with the problem at hand and what type of treatment you choose for your teenager. It is also important to remember that dependence involves physiological changes that may lead to an addictive process. Repeated abuse of substances and addictive behaviors can develop into rigidly set habits, and either abusing or being dependent upon a substance or pursuit can diminish your teenager's ability to fully participate in and enjoy everyday life.

## Defining Addiction

The American Society of Addiction Medicine (ASAM) notes that addiction is characterized by "the inability to consistently abstain, impairment in behavioral control, craving, diminished recognition of significant problems with one's behaviors and interpersonal relationships, and a dysfunctional emotional response. Like other chronic diseases, addiction often involves cycles of relapse and remission. Without treatment or engagement in recovery activities, addiction is progressive and can result in disability or premature death."

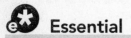 **Essential**

One distinction between abuse and addiction is that a person with addiction rarely has breaks from using the substance or practicing the addictive behavior. Severe consequences do result, and the only break from the addiction is arrest or some other catastrophic occurrence. Abusers get into trouble as well, but their use tends to be more sporadic.

Other definitions emphasize that the user continues to use the destructive substance despite knowing that it is causing harm. An important component of addiction is that the addicted behavior (drinking, etc.) becomes the primary focus of the addict's life. Work, significant relationships, and former enjoyable hobbies fall by the wayside, as the most important aim of the user is to keep the substance or behavior available. Two important hallmark elements are present with addiction—denial and the inability to stop. Most substance abusers or those who are addicted to destructive behavior will swear that they do not have a problem, and that they can stop at any time. This attitude makes it quite challenging for the addict to seek help and treatment, as she does not think she needs it. Why she is unable to stop using the substance or performing the troublesome behavior is a mystery, even to the addict. Sometimes she remembers her first drink of the day, for example, and then everything else is blank.

Addicts will commit to taking only one drink or gambling only $20, and hours later find they are in deep trouble. Nonaddicts are consistently baffled by these seemingly nonsensical parts of addiction. After all, a sane, logical person would want to stop and would not deny the seriousness of the situation.

**Fact**

Writer Jane Velez-Mitchell indicates in her book *Addict Nation* that people can become addicted to anything—plastic surgery, tattoos, or texting. People can be addicted to sugar, alcohol, violent movies, meat, exercise, or diet soda. Quite often, when an addict gives up one addiction, another soon replaces it. This seems to indicate that addictions are symptoms of the reward circuitry of the brain being hijacked, which is more of a risk if addictive chemicals are the cause.

## Consider a Historical Perspective

Addiction didn't come out of a vacuum. Alcohol and tobacco have been part of American culture since colonial times, and they are both deeply entrenched in the rituals of particular ethnic groups and the economy. Early settlers from Italy and Ireland expected to be able to drink alcohol in their new home, and those from England re-created their fondly remembered pubs. In addition, large acreages in the South were solely devoted to growing tobacco.

Furthermore, patent medicines were popular in the United States from as early as the 1600s. Of course, there were no regulations for the various concoctions that promised a quick fix for a whole range of health problems. Such potions were usually a mixture of ground vegetables, alcohol, morphine, opium, and cocaine, sure to make a person feel better, regardless of the difficulty. Patent medicines were heavily advertised and marketed on the streets and at public events.

As settlement of the United States pressed westward in the 1800s, one of the first businesses to be established in each new town was the saloon. The early pioneers, ranchers, and cattlemen worked hard and expected to play hard at the conclusion of cattle runs. Isolation also led to many women becoming addicted to patent medicines as their husbands became alcoholics via the local saloon.

Both alcohol and tobacco were points of interest in politics and the economy. For example, according to a National Institute of Health (NIH) article by Dr. Lawrence Brown, tobacco was issued to troops during the Civil War. In fact, tobacco was issued to troops all the way up to the Vietnam War. Even today, cigarettes are a virtual underground economy in the U.S. prison system. It's important to note that alcohol and tobacco have been taxed during most periods of American history, and have been important sources of revenue for the government.

### FDA Takes Hold

While the Food and Drug Administration (FDA) was not known by its current name until 1930, in 1906 the FDA passed the Pure Food and Drugs Act, a law that prohibited interstate commerce of misbranded food. The FDA also passed the Meat Inspection Act in order to better control the conditions in the meat packing industry.

### ⓔ Essential

The Food and Drug Administration arose to protect the American people from the random nature of patent medicines. However, in present times, many question the hand-in-glove relationship between the FDA and large corporations and pharmaceutical companies. The boom in prescription painkiller use over the past decades was accompanied by aggressive marketing by Big Pharm, with little restraint from the FDA.

As the industrialization movement changed economic patterns and forced more workers into cities, those still living in rural settings became gung-ho for prohibition and began pushing harder for prohibition, which resulted in the legal ban of alcohol during the Prohibition Era, the years between 1920 and 1933. However, as illustrated by stories from this time such as *The Great Gatsby*, liquor was still a booming business, and a portion of the income from the underground bootlegging economy was paid to the government. But the 16th Amendment allowing a federal income tax was passed in 1913, before the 18th Amendment for Prohibition in 1920. Prohibition came to an end because the illegality of drinking spawned crime and the cost-benefit was reassessed.

## Addiction and Twentieth-Century Wars

Dr. Scott A. Teitelbaum, the author of *Addiction: A Family Affair*, notes the profound relationship between addiction and war. World Wars I and II, the Korean War, and the Vietnam War led to military use of tobacco and drugs (just watch *Apocalypse Now* to see the desperation of young soldiers and their yearning for escape with drugs). Alcohol, in the forms of rum and beer, was rationed to both sides of the conflict during the First World War. Vietnam was the first war where recreational drugs played a major role. The military attempted to police the situation, arresting up to 1,000 soldiers per week. In many cases, the servicemen mostly policed their own people, making sure that the soldier was able to function before going into flight or battle.

## Addiction and Modern Conflicts

Unfortunately, subsequent wars in Kuwait, Afghanistan, and Iraq have resulted in many addicted veterans. For some veterans, injuries and war wounds are very severe and are usually managed with the drugs oxycodone and hydrocodone. These drugs can be addictive, but can certainly help many patients when taken properly. This drug use, coupled with a high incidence of post-traumatic stress syndrome, creates a challenge for the Veterans Health Administration, which is responsible for helping veterans.

## Teen Drug Culture: From the 1960s to Today

In the 1960s, a distinct teen culture emerged, with specific music, language, clothing, films, and attitudes. This occurred, in part, because of greater affluence. It takes money to buy alcohol, cigarettes, and drugs. Teenagers began to have some economic independence and part-time work, creating the means to acquire illicit and legal drugs. It's important to recognize that parallel with the emerging teen culture, lobbyists started working in Washington to protect the interests of the alcohol and tobacco industries. Also during the 1960s, advertising became prominent in offering pills to solve every viewer's inconvenient health problem.

Today's teen culture includes major pressure to succeed. In addition, since many adults now work long hours to earn a living, in some families there is less of a parental presence in the home. This leaves teens by themselves more of the time. This makes them more vulnerable to peer influence, a normal aspect of the adolescent years. Too often, if the promise of a friendship or romantic relationship comes with the price tag of joining in risky behaviors that have potential for addiction, the relationship will win out. Most adults addicted to nicotine began smoking as a young teenager in order to fit in with friends. It is also true that when teenagers are under the influence of drugs and alcohol, they are more likely to commit crimes, assault other people, and participate in risky sex.

The National Survey on Drug Use and Health (NSDUH) notes that, "In 2012, an estimated 23.9 million Americans aged 12 or older were current (past month) illicit drug users, meaning they had used an illicit drug during the month prior to the survey interview." This includes marijuana, cocaine, heroin, inhalants, and prescription drugs used nonmedically. Among the age group of twelve to seventeen, the percentage of illicit drug use is about 9 percent. Among young adults between eighteen and twenty-five, the rate of drug use is 21 percent (mostly marijuana). Overall, in today's teen culture, boys are more likely to use addictive substances, and their use is slightly increasing. The use of such substances by girls remains stable.

Youths today may think that using over-the-counter substances addictively, such as Robitussin, NyQuil, Vicks, and Coricidin, is relatively safe, when, of course, it is not. Also consider the abundance of sleep aids, motion sickness medication, and diet pills, and you find you have a lot to think about concerning your adolescent.

A major part of this challenge is the fact that a teenager can buy these substances legally.

### Preventing Drug Use

Positive family relationships are helpful in preventing addictions in children and adolescents. A lack of connection between teenagers and parents and very little supervision are contributing factors to the development of addictions in youth. You can take positive steps to build connections with your teen, thus reducing the risk that he will be tempted to engage in risky behaviors.

## Making Sense of Teen Culture

Today's teenagers aren't very different than past generations. They want to exist peacefully, be happy, and get along with others. There are some differences, though. For example, teens today are more accustomed to cultural diversity, and are completely comfortable with electronic devices. Some even are quite adept at making audio and video, such as "haul" girls. These teens spend vast amounts of time shopping and creating videos for YouTube, which show the results of their spree, tastefully and artistically. The amount of time teens spend texting and instant messaging means they have lot of interaction with one another, but this does not necessarily mean they will have great social skills. You've probably witnessed a group of teens in the mall or at a restaurant that are glued to their phones instead of speaking to one another.

 **Alert**

According to a 2011 SAMHSA survey of adolescents between the ages of twelve and seventeen, 14.7 percent of teens polled used alcohol during the last month, 10 percent used illicit drugs, and 8.9 percent smoked tobacco.

## New Generation, New Problems

It seems that this generation is somewhat passive. Some teens are uninterested in work and studies, preferring to be online or on their smartphone most of the time. Unlike various subgroups of the 1980s, today's teenagers are somewhat indistinguishable in terms of fashion or style. They have vast amounts of information at their fingertips, but do not have the maturity or context to make sense of it. They question authority, and want to know the reason for everything. The Internet, media, and the speed of technology make today's teenagers want an answer the second they come up with a question. In addition, the constant presence of advertising shapes teens' wants, wishes, and longings.

Today's adolescents are unlikely to subscribe to "the American Dream" because they have seen people close to them lose jobs and their homes. There is anxiety about war, global warming, and what the future holds. Faith in the usual social systems and institutions has faltered. Some youths spend a vast amount of time online, crafting identities and images, and changing them at a whim. Some look to the past to create a viable self, shopping vintage, going organic and green, and becoming an expert on an obscure topic. This generation is mostly left alone by authority figures, so the element of rebellion that shaped past generations is not present. With so much stimulation, some teenagers are somewhat numb, retreating to television or games to structure their time. Many are numb to the extent of being uninterested in school or work.

## ⓔ❓ Question

**What are the dangers of cyber-addiction?**
What could be harmful about teenagers spending hours texting or scrolling through Facebook? People of any age who are constantly online are not engaging in truly intimate conversations with other people. A real live social life requires that one be in the company of other people, face to face with cell phones turned off.

In today's cultural climate, teenagers' attitudes toward drugs are more positive than negative, in spite of efforts to change this. The 2012 Partnership Attitude Tracking Study, conducted by the nonprofit organization The Partnership at Drugfree.org, found that many teenagers believe that being high feels good and that their friends generally get high at parties. An astonishing 75 percent of those questioned reported those attitudes, and almost half of those questioned said that they did not see a great risk in getting drunk daily. Hazelden, a renowned addiction treatment center for children and adolescents, has seen in recent years that children are using stronger drugs at an earlier age and coming in for treatment further along in their addiction, some showing symptoms that one would expect in an adult who has been addicted for years.

# Recognizing Demographics: Addiction Does Not Discriminate

Earlier research on adolescent drug abuse focused on lower socio-economic groups. However, recent studies show that teenagers from well-to-do families are equally at risk. Addiction is a disease that does not discriminate. There are factors, biological and environmental, that contribute to whether a teen user becomes an abuser. (These factors are discussed in Chapter 4.) But for now, you should delete the stereotyped image of an addict being a destitute person. She could just as easily be your neighbor or the teenager who babysits your children.

## Addiction in Special Populations

A 2011 National Survey on Drug Use and Health notes that among Hispanic adolescents, marijuana and prescription drug use is increasing, and cigarette and alcohol use is decreasing. Hispanic boys use drugs to a slightly greater degree than Hispanic girls.

**Alert**

Pregnant teenagers are a particularly vulnerable group, for if the adolescent mother does not understand the effects of drug and alcohol use on her baby, there are long-term consequences for several lives. Innovative programs such as the Nurse-Family Partnership of California, organized as a public health program, offer education and support to very young mothers, helping them to take care of themselves and their babies, striving for healthy self-sufficiency without drugs. Some of these girls come from families with no emotional warmth and need to learn how to form healthy bonds for themselves, as well as warmly nurture their babies. Factual information is provided so that the teenager understands the effects on her new family of using or not using. Sometimes the teenager does not tell the health practitioner the truth about her drug use, but at least the practitioner can plant a seed for the teenager to consider.

## Is There a Cure for Addiction?

Most professionals in the recovery field say that addictions can be arrested but not cured, although there is research looking at vaccines against specific drugs of abuse. The mechanism is that by inducing antibodies, which bind the drug, there is insufficient quantity left to give a high. This would not be possible against small molecules like, for instance, alcohol. In other words, the addicted person is somewhat different biologically from a nonaddicted person, and that does not change over time. The addicted person, regardless of age, can learn and unlearn specific behaviors and patterns of thinking in order to be freed from the effects of substance abuse or behavioral addictions. Most addictive persons require the support of groups or those in the helping professions. Such assistance is readily available in most communities in the United States, and even those who live in remote areas can find online groups for discussion and help.

### Fact

Although there may be no magical cure for addictions, there are thousands of nationwide groups accessible in person and online. If you want to kick fast food, there are vegans who can keep you company. One enterprising person started a group for cutting down on materialism, the 100 Thing Challenge. He and his club members aspire to own no more than 100 items.

Seasoned people with years of recovery from addictions sometimes say that the desire to use or drink has gone away, but those who are successfully sober generally stay in close touch with others of the same experience. Sometimes life's stressors—loss of a job or a relationship, or the death of someone important—can bring the addiction or a different addiction to the forefront.

The most effective ways to manage addiction include the components of personal responsibility, education, facts about the consequences of continued addictive behaviors, and involvement of the entire family. Your child's addiction problem didn't fall out of the sky or arise in a vacuum; the complex nature of teenage addiction requires that everyone involved receive support and education. Sometimes it seems that your teenager is doing her new pastime to get at you or to make you mad. But she's just doing it because that is the nature of the disease, and as the parent, you have choices about how to respond intelligently and deliberately.

# Is Addiction a Disease or a Moral Issue?

In the past, addiction was labeled a moral failing. It was believed that people drink or use drugs on purpose and can stop at any time. At the present time, you can still encounter this mindset—people who view substance use a weakness.

Many in the addictions professions, however, subscribe to the belief that addiction is a disease, and there's nothing moral or immoral about it. You wouldn't judge a person who has diabetes or pneumonia, and a similar stance can be taken when thinking of the addict as a person who has a disease. For family members, the disease concept can be tremendously helpful, as it removes, at least somewhat, the guilt and futility that often accompany efforts to control or help the troubled person. The stigma may slightly remain, but less so, especially if families of addicts meet with each other and discuss the specific related issues that arise.

 **Essential**

As with other diseases, alcoholism, drug addiction, and behavioral addictions result in changes in brain activity. Over time, those who continue to practice addiction lose certain brain functions, and the neural pathways are changed to accommodate the addiction. Such changes can be seen on MRI scans.

Today, the American Psychiatric Association states that addiction, or more currently referred to as "substance use disorder," is a chronic and relapsing illness. In other words, it may have started with a simple desire for a temporary buzz or a relief for boredom, but with repetition, the brain chemistry changes, and the disease is in place. It becomes involuntary rather than voluntary, a difficult idea for a nonaddict to grasp.

# CHAPTER 2

# What Causes Addiction?

Growing evidence about addiction points to coexisting factors, rather than distinct cause and effect. It's never a clear-cut black-and-white situation. And individual personality and character can change the trajectory of the disease, even if all the risk factors are there. Addiction is complex, with genetic and environmental components that interact in somewhat mysterious ways. Some people believe that alcoholism is a spiritual malady, and the only way to overcome it is to develop a spiritual life and be of service to others. Combinations of many different forces and factors cause addiction, not any one thing.

## Predisposition

A predisposition toward addiction means that circumstances can interact in such a way that the likelihood is great for addiction to appear in a certain individual. The biological wiring of a person and his character traits can combine to create a proclivity for use and abuse. Sometimes you can even recognize a likely candidate for addiction. A person you know may have an "over-the-top" personality, and no one is surprised by news that he is in trouble with drugs and the police. Another individual might have a short fuse and short attention span, and decide to bypass the normal career path and make a profession of meth production.

Learned behavior may be an aspect of predisposition. It is typical for children to admire and to copy the behaviors of those in their family, extended family, and friends of the family. If the child sees people using addictively, he understands this to be a desirable and normal thing to do. If the child sees people escape their emotions and life problems through substances, he will be inclined to do the same thing, as that is what is strongly modeled in the environment.

Likewise, if children grow up with addicts, it is highly possible that basic needs are often unmet. The child is anxious most of the time about food, clothing, and shelter, not to mention consistency in human relationships and the comfort of a safe routine. The child becomes accustomed to a high level of anxiety, and this becomes the norm carried into adult years. The highly anxious young person and adult is more likely to turn to substances and addictive behavior to manage the anxiety that has become an ongoing part of life.

# Genetic Factors

It is commonly said that addiction runs in families. What does that mean exactly? It means that those certain individuals have a genetic and personality makeup that causes drugs and alcohol to be metabolized. The brain chemistry might even be different between the two types of people in those families where there are an inordinate number of alcoholics and addicts. The classic Stockholm Adoption Study concluded that genetics plays a major role in development of alcoholism. The biologically vulnerable had a greater risk than the environmentally vulnerable. Those vulnerable in both ways had an even greater risk.

It is difficult to tease out specific factors, although scientists have begun to isolate the genetic tendency to addiction to certain chromosomes in the human body. As you can imagine, it is unethical to do research on human beings that might put them at risk, so a lot of the research on addiction is performed on animals, especially rats.

### Essential

Drug and alcohol abuse releases dopamine in the brain's pleasure center, setting up a desire for increasing amounts of the rewarding pleasure. The body's natural system of releasing dopamine is disrupted, as the addiction releases up to ten times as much dopamine. The person is an addict at that point, at the mercy of the drive for more and more pleasure. Recent evidence shows that addicts continue to use just to feel normal again, as their dopamine reward mechanism is damaged so that they have a muted reward from normal day-to-day stimuli. The brain cooperates in the dysfunctional quest.

Biologically, some people seem to be put together differently. Some adults in support groups for alcohol or drug cessation recall being given as a child small amounts of alcohol at family gatherings, and they would go around drinking the last of every glass that was set down for a few minutes. This could be at age three or four. Not every child behaves this way. Children can display addictive tendencies in other ways—needing to finish off all the chocolate cake or have every example of a Matchbox car collection.

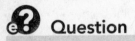 Question

**Why are adolescents especially vulnerable to the development of addictions?**
The prefrontal cortex is the final region of the brain to develop, leaving children and adolescents without a mature context for making decisions about cause and effect, indulging and facing the consequences. If the pleasure circuits are chemically stimulated at a young age, they can dominate future actions.

Alcoholism does tend to run in families, seen more often in the males of the family, sometimes skipping a generation. It is not uncommon to see other addictions clustered along with the alcoholism. People in seemingly addictive families might tend to change jobs a lot, cheat on their spouses, use drugs along with alcohol, or accrue a large amount of debt, perhaps getting out of it with several successive bankruptcies. These types of clusters help a person to see that all these behaviors are symptoms, and it does no good to force the cessation of one addiction because the addict will pick up another one or find a way around the first one.

Author David Sheff says that people who tend toward addiction are different *before* they become addicts, not *because* of the addiction. Research shows that the fibers connecting the different parts of the brains in predisposed individuals are less efficient, especially in those areas associated with self-control. In other words, the braking system is weak. The "enough" message may get through, but too slowly to prevent trouble.

# Compulsivity

Being unable to stop a behavior is an aspect of addiction of any kind. Alcoholics often promise to have only one drink but are constitutionally unable to have only one drink. One sober alcoholic said that he realized that he had a problem when it seemed that every time he had one drink, he woke up in jail in another state. Much of his life before recovery was in a blackout, following that one drink.

Compulsivity can show up in needing to earn straight As, have a better car than the neighbor, or have more stamps on the passport. It could mean finishing an entire bag of Oreos when intending to eat only two or feeling that life will come to a standstill without thirty minutes at the gym every day. The key is that the person feels that the behavior *must* be done in a certain way in order to feel safe and in control. Even that particular latte before starting work could veer into compulsion if the individual fears that something bad will happen without it.

It seems that there is no scientific proof that there is a set type of addictive personality that leads to substance abuse problems. In essence, not all personality traits lead to addiction. At the same time, there are traits that tend to accompany the presence of addiction. Some of these are as follows:

- Negative self-talk—self-blame, catastrophic thinking, perfectionism, and rationalization
- Sensation-seeking behavior
- Difficulties with delayed gratification
- Nonconformism, criticizing the normal achievements and ideals of society
- Antisocial behavior, not caring about the effects on one's actions on others
- High anxiety
- Manipulation of others
- Dependency on others

The compulsive person has a drive to see something through to the end, and not necessarily in a positive way, such as finishing a degree or meeting a sales quota in a new business. He may feel the need to argue with someone until the relationship is completely shattered, break all the china in a fit of rage instead of just one plate, or fail all of his classes at school rather than just slightly slipping in one or two.

**✅ Fact**

A nonaddicted person experiences a balance between the pleasure centers of the brain and the prefrontal cortex, which helps the individual reason out the consequences of a behavior. The addicted person has no such inner monitor and "goes for broke," with little or no interest in the long-term outcome.

Compulsivity can be seen in a teenage girl weighing herself every day and not feeling okay until she hits a magic number. It can mean eating only one or two foods for an extended period of time in order to lose a few pounds, or working out excessively at the gym because of a barely distinguishable soft roll around the belly. It can mean feeling anxious if a text is not answered right away or from getting a few days behind with friends' Facebook posts. One feels afraid of missing out on something important, often dropping what is truly important in order to do something compulsive.

Most addicts are both impulsive and compulsive, to varying degrees. Those who are high on both measures are particularly impaired.

## Immaturity

Of course, teenagers are, by their very limited number of years, somewhat immature. It's to be expected, as they are lacking in life experience. In general, addicts tend to have a short attention span and want what they want when they want it. Some very honest members of Alcoholics Anonymous and other programs for various addictions admit that their bottle or cigarette was actually a kind of pacifier.

For those who start their addictions in their teens, their emotional development generally stops at that age, creating the anomaly of an individual who has the chronological years of an adult but the emotional maturity and impulse control of someone twelve years old, or even younger. An addicted individual often shows immaturity across the board, displaying an inability to commit to viable relationships and struggling to get along with people on the job, sometimes quitting without having any other plan but to never see his boss again.

## 🅴❗ Alert

Dennis C. Daley in his book *Addiction and Mood Disorders* describes a formula for the causes of addictions: Biology + Psychology + Family Influences + Social Influences + Alcohol/Drugs = ADDICTION.

You may observe a sense of entitlement and lack of patience in your child. The teenage addict is unable and unwilling to methodically build up experience and resources to accomplish a desired aim. It is likely that goals are short-circuited and plans quickly change, as a new person or opportunity appears. Impulsivity seems to make the addict or alcoholic extremely vulnerable to external (or internal) stimuli, simply reaching for the next hit because it's there. You might expect to calm and admonish a two-year-old in the supermarket with, "No, we don't need that right now. We have some of that at home." It might help to imagine that kind of susceptibility in the mind and body of the grown or almost grown addict.

# Defining Important Terms

It is helpful to understand exactly what each terms means when referring to substance abuse issues. The following are some of the most commonly used expressions and their meaning:

**Substance Abuse:** The use of a substance without a prescription, in a way other than as prescribed, or for the experience or feelings elicited.

**Substance Dependence:** When an individual persists in the use of alcohol or other drugs despite problems related to the use of the substance, substance dependence may be diagnosed. Compulsive and repetitive use may result in tolerance to the effect of the drug and withdrawal symptoms when use is reduced or stopped. This along with substance abuse is considered a substance use disorder.

**Substance Use Disorder:** The newest classification of addictions, encompassing the previous substance abuse and substance dependence definitions, and rated by clinicians as mild, moderate, or severe.

**Addiction:** A chronic, relapsing disease characterized by compulsive drug seeking and use, despite serious adverse consequences, and by long-lasting changes in the brain.

**Physical Dependence:** An adaptive physiological state that occurs with regular drug use and results in a withdrawal syndrome when drug use is stopped. This often occurs with tolerance. Physical dependence can happen with chronic—even appropriate—use of many medications, and by itself does not constitute addiction.

**Tolerance:** A condition in which higher doses of a drug are required to produce the same effect achieved during initial use; often associated with physical dependence.

## Use, Abuse, Tolerance, and Withdrawal

A tolerance for alcohol and drugs tends to develop over time, which means that the addicted individual passes through certain predictable stages. It might be helpful to define a few terms before moving through the stages.

The first stage is occasional use and experimentation. At this level the person can generally stop with no difficulty. Trying new things is a natural, healthy part of the adolescent testing her wings. It may not be desirable, but it is not necessarily dangerous at the experimental stage.

The next stage is abuse, where one uses the substance more regularly, needing the drug or alcohol to a greater degree but still able to function normally in most aspects of life. Tolerance begins to build, and the person needs more and more of the drug in order to experience the desired buzz or euphoria. The body needs the chemical in order to feel normal, and the person experiences withdrawal symptoms when she is not regularly using the substance. Withdrawal symptoms cause her to use the substance more.

 **Fact**

In quantitative terms, the *Diagnostic and Statistical Manual of Mental Disorders, Fifth Edition (DSM-5)* describes abuse as a pattern of use over a year's time, during which the person experiences clinical distress, misses school, fails to meet obligations, engages in reckless behavior, is arrested, or faces legal troubles. The person continues to use, in spite of these negative consequences. The guide has no distinction between abuse and addiction, offering instead a continuum from mild to moderate to severe.

Then the person reaches addiction, where her life revolves around keeping the abused substance available at all times. Other parts of her life fall by the wayside, as the highest priority is using the substance first thing in the morning, upon awakening. At this stage, the addiction is firmly set. The addicted person spends most of her time seeking the substance or behavioral situation she is addicted to. Other enjoyable aspects of life have deteriorated.

As drug or alcohol use increases, tolerance increases, which precipitates more use in order to achieve the same intoxicated effect. The nervous system changes, and the body seems to reach a state of requiring the substance. The withdrawal symptoms are powerful, and the user will do anything to stave them off. The person's biology compels her to use and continue using. The brain requires the drug or other addictive substance in order to function normally. However, there is hope that the brain can eventually compensate without the drug, though it remains vulnerable to the neurobiology reasserting itself.

## Signs of Addiction

David Sheff, author of *Clean*, offers the following helpful list of addiction criteria. In most cases the addict will show many of the following behaviors:

1. Is preoccupied with getting high
2. Limits friendships to people who are similarly addicted
3. Spends an increasing amount of time talking about drugs and getting drugs
4. Follows rituals of drug use in social interactions
5. Routinely lies, steals, and is violent
6. Seems to have no will power
7. Shows withdrawal symptoms
8. Shows a high tolerance for the abused substance

It is suggested that none of these indications is a higher priority than any other. The key is to simply count and notice *how many* of the indicators are present. The more indicators present, the higher likelihood that the person is an addict.

**Alert**

Anna David, former executive editor of the Fix, an addiction and re-covery site, relates how she progressed from drinking, which alleviated her teenage insecurities, to pot and cocaine. She was high-functioning, keeping up good grades at school, but lived for the weekends when she could party. In her twenties she snorted cocaine all night, took Ambien to sleep, and went to work high, still high-functioning. She admits that becoming an addict "snuck up" on her.

## Situational Triggers

Some situations seem to precipitate addictive behavior. These can vary according to individual background and experience. Just as a Thanksgiving dinner invites overeating, meeting friends in a bar creates an atmosphere for drinking. The flashing lights and constant noise in a casino make people want to gamble. It might be a habit to light up a cigarette after making love. High-stress work might trigger a craving for caffeine and sugar.

A person becomes conditioned by the experiences of life, sometimes starting in childhood. The Super Bowl is not the Super Bowl without drinking beer. A birthday is not a birthday without massive amounts of sugar. A marriage is not a marriage without lots of fighting and making up.

**Alert**

At least one study revealed that stress is one of the reasons teenagers turn to drugs. Stress seems to melt away when one is high; however, major stress can set up a need for more and more of the substance in order to achieve the desired goal. Stress changes the chemistry of the body, somewhat blunting the normal responses to the environment. This combination of factors can lead to addiction.

Someone with an addictive personality might notice a relationship between stress and his desire to use something addictively. Perhaps a huge stack of bills or an unwanted phone call precipitates an eating binge. Having something to celebrate, such as a promotion, bonus, or coveted business deal, provides an excuse to shop or drink to excess. Visiting a difficult relative means a reward of a few hours at a casino.

The response an addicted person has to certain triggers is conditioned over years of practice, making it quite a challenge to react differently. Any kind of disappointment—end of a relationship, loss of a close friend or relative, not getting the job or special date, even an admired political candidate losing an election—can mean a retreat into addiction. Death is especially jolting to the addicted person, as the American culture is not skilled in or comfortable with the grief process. Those with addictive tendencies may instantly start a bender of some kind. Even old-timers in Alcoholics Anonymous share openly about the miracle of getting through unemployment or the death of a family member without picking up the bottle.

In regard to stress and celebration, the desire to alter one's brain chemistry artificially seems to be strongly influenced by one or the other. So the addict must find ways of dealing with stress apart from relapse. In addition, the addict must find a means of celebrating life without chemical intoxication.

Even a fragrance, a particular style of fashion, or a physical location can set off a craving. Holidays are known triggers for many addicts and alcoholics. Those in recovery are encouraged in their support group meetings to stay away from triggering places and people and to carefully structure their time and activities with like-minded people around times and days that are likely to be emotional or sad.

# CHAPTER 3

# The Cultural Context of Addiction

In our media-driven society, your teenager is bombarded with images every day, many showing glamorous, entertaining people using alcohol, cigarettes, and other addictive substances. Addiction stories are everywhere, and the process of rehab is somewhat glamorized. In actuality, true addiction might not be that pretty. In the United States, many self-destructive behaviors have become so widespread that they are considered normal—overeating, overspending, overdependence on pharmaceutical drugs, working long hours, having too many plastic surgeries or unsatisfactory relationships, and living beyond one's means. The best thing you can do for your teenager is to educate them about the dangers of addiction.

## The Addicted Society

Being wasteful seems to have become a norm in the United States. The United States is able to create material wealth, but so much of that wealth is discarded. The need to consume creates laws that prevent restaurants from donating leftover foods to shelters and others who might need it. Natural resources are plundered for the profits of corporations, and everyday news often includes reports of a prominent person caught padding expenses or using public money for personal use. Americans seem to be afflicted with the disease of "I want more, more, more."

**Fact**

Addiction is expensive. The National Institute on Drug Abuse estimates that substance abuse in 2000 cost the United States $484 billion annually, more than cancer and diabetes combined. These statistics refer to the health-care expenditures, lost earnings, and costs associated with crime and accidents only. Beyond these costs are the human costs of a neglected child, a damaged friend, a problem marriage, and a family bogged down with confusion and grief. While there is heartbreak and terrible loss associated with cancer and diabetes, these are seen with greater sympathy and effective treatments are more accessible. Addiction is truly expensive.

Addiction is progressive. Like ripples on a pond, the substance abuser's problem moves out like a tidal wave. Innocent people are killed by impaired drivers, devastating families. Children are born with fetal alcohol syndrome, needing institutional care all their lives. Prisons are filled, families are torn apart, as all society is warped by the social costs from addiction. These contribute to a stigma and angry reactions not seen with diabetes or cancer. Indeed, addiction is progressive like a tsunami.

**Alert**

The pressures to conform to societal constraints can be hard to ignore. For example, you may have felt that when a neighbor asks you when you are going to get a new car, commenting that his new SUV is safer for the family, he is implying that anything smaller and hence less gas-guzzling would be unsafe, and therefore irresponsible. Teenagers are especially susceptible to the pressure of needing the latest upgrade to their gadgetry. When the iPad came out, in cities across America, lines formed at Apple Stores long before opening time.

Overconsumption is an attempt to fill a void, regardless of the age of the shopper or consumer. If a woman is in a sad, loveless marriage, she might feel that several pairs of designer shoes will make her feel attractive and important. A man in a similar position might seek out porn to fill the emptiness. Teenagers are not immune to experiencing the same spiritual void, only they are not mature enough to name the difficulty. If everyone in a teen's family relies on consumer goods to fill a void, it makes sense for the teen to do the same thing. So he looks for the next song, item of clothing, or catch phrase that will pump him up momentarily. A sad situation can become dire when adolescents turn to drugs, alcohol, and other addictive behaviors in order to substitute for a spiritual longing.

### Essential

It is a universal human need to experience meaningfulness in life. As a parent, you can strengthen your teenager's lack of interest in abusing addictive substances by fostering self-awareness and encouraging her to explore hobbies, interests, and various types of community service. Find the activities that help your child feel self-actualized.

## Media Pressures

The media's coverage of how to achieve the right look, the right background, and the right possessions and lifestyle often makes people feel insecure—especially teens. Most people feel as though they need to live up to a certain standard to be happy. For example, if you aren't able to fit a family vacation into your budget for the year, you may feel deprived and angry at other families who can. The media tells you that you *should* be able to take a cruise with your family, and when you can't, you feel insecure. This is how your teen may feel as well when trying to fit into peer culture.

For example, one fascinating aspect of a drug pusher's marketing is the use of "free samples." It appears that in many situations, younger teens can get cannabis from dealers for nothing. It is best to be aware of this pattern, and to warn your teen to avoid the lure of the "free sample."

According to Velez-Mitchell, many Americans are at the mercy of consumerism and media following. It's so pervasive that it's somewhat impossible to fully acknowledge. They are powerful forces, but it is important to try and follow your own path despite what the media says. Your teen will see that you do not buy in to the world of consumerism and grandeur, and follow suit.

## Want and Need

It helps to pause for a moment and think about the distinction between want and need. If a family has two young children who play outside all the time, a washer and dryer is probably a need. A want would be something desired, but not entirely necessary, like expensive detergent. The American culture of consumption is based on what the media says and tends to ramp up the wants into the need category. A teenager truly feels that he needs to have a certain cell phone in order to be a part of his favored group. He needs to have certain games, certain music, and certain clothing. It is quite difficult for a vulnerable teenager to see that these things are wants, rather than needs. It helps if the parents are well grounded and not too quick to jump on the latest commercial bandwagon. Also, if the teenager is encouraged to work and earn money for his particular wants, he might be able to sort them out a bit more dispassionately.

**Fact**

It is estimated that 80 percent of the opioids consumed each year are done by Americans.

# The Celebrity Factor

It seems that American culture promotes celebrities to almost god-like status. The media has to cover everything from fashion on the red carpet, who is marrying whom, who named their baby what, who got arrested, and who is going into rehab and where. There are even reality shows available on each of these themes, and social media sites like Twitter provide constant updates on celebrity life.

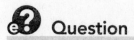 **Question**

**Why are details about Paris Hilton and Lindsay Lohan newsworthy?**
They aren't. Millions of viewers follow reports of arrests and revolving-door rehab for prominent figures. These viewers may know, rationally, that there are greater issues that could merit attention—global warming, abuses in agribusiness, and murky ethics in elections. However, there seems to be some sort of perverse pleasure in seeing how Paris looks in orange and listening to a summary of Lindsay Lohan's relapses.

Celebrities control public opinion to a high degree, deciding which foods and restaurants are cool and what kind of clothes to wear from season to season. With drug and alcohol rehabilitation so extensively in the public eye, the process can be strangely glamorized, shaping a vulnerable teen's opinion that it might be a positive thing to get so out of control with drugs and alcohol that one could stay in a posh Pacific Palisades resort for a time, noshing on organic food and receiving one-on-one time with a very kind counselor. It is confusing when the idolized person is thrown off a popular television show for bad behavior or a grizzled mug shot goes viral around the Internet. The young mind wonders what is real and if the arrest and mug shot are a part of an act.

In addition, prominent athletes are sometimes featured in alcohol ads or other products for the consumer. Although sports figures are closely monitored for drug use, sometimes one escapes the system and then pops up in the public eye with an embarrassing drug charge. Such a dichotomy is confusing to a teenager who looked up to such a person, thinking of him as a role model. It is tempting to smooth out the discrepancy by emulating the drug and alcohol habit while continuing to admire the person.

 **Fact**

A YouTube video that garnered over 15 million views shows a three-year-old girl crying because she loves Justin Bieber and wants him to love her back. The phone rings, the child smiles for the first time, and she exclaims, "It's Justin!" The video's popularity shows how celebrities influence American children starting at a young age.

Talented performers who are able to create something new with a confidence attract a huge following and emulation. Madonna and Lady Gaga motivate many thousands of fans to imitate their clothing and habits. Even Lady Gaga's meat dress showed up as Halloween costumes the year she wore a garment made from a slaughtered animal. For the present generation, a performer doesn't need to have a solidly developed career or discipline, such as music, dance, or theatrical performance, to become popular. Winning a reality show countdown or marrying an elderly billionaire is sufficient to achieve celebrity status. Even criminals who orchestrate school shootings or other public destruction become models for impressionable adolescents. A generation ago, no one had ever heard of school shootings, and now they are in the news every month or so.

## ⓔ✱ Essential

Anyone can be paparazzi, as the advent of cell phones with video and audio capability makes the man on the street a possible source of breaking news about a celebrity's public mishap, racist comment, drunken altercation, or breakup with a spouse. Such relentless availability increases consumption of news about celebrities.

The average person has opinions about Michael Jackson's death, Whitney Houston's death, John Edwards's out-of-wedlock child, and Tiger Woods's infidelities. Writer Jane Velez-Mitchell surmises that the American addiction to celebrity details is a way of numbing out, like any other addiction, allowing people to sidestep otherwise disturbing news of tsunamis, international civil wars, and, closer to home, the day-to-day decisions of creating a satisfying life. Many people are much more excited about voting for their favorite idol or dancer on television than voting in an upcoming election. Adolescents in particular are vulnerable to such undue distraction, as they have little life experience and no context as to what is normal and what is completely dysfunctional.

##  Fact

In his book, *The Mirror Effect: How Celebrity Narcissism Is Seducing America*, Dr. Drew Pinsky says that when stars are exhibiting dysfunctional, high-risk behavior, such as posting sex videos, losing a large amount of weight in a short time, publicly getting drunk, and using drugs, they are in effect modeling that behavior for others. It would be helpful for teenagers if the consequences of such behavior were reported.

A mature, seasoned person understands that all people are created equal. Those who are on a pedestal are usually there more or less by circumstance and for arbitrary reasons. It is also helpful to understand that all humans are interconnected with a variety of strengths and weaknesses. Limiting your child's exposure to the media can help guard against this obsession with fame. Young people who spend a lot of time watching television and browsing the Internet are more focused on celebrities and often want to emulate them. Spending face-to-face time with your children and limiting screen time is a great way to teach them the value in real relationships.

## Advertising

Advertising works well because, just as with addiction, it appeals to the pleasure senses. Author Linda Simmons notes in *The Everything® Guide to Addiction and Recovery* that it seems no accident that teenagers get credit cards at about the same age that they are able to legally drink and go to casinos. Casinos are advertised as places of great fun with free food and drinks and lots of entertainment. No one mentions that there are no clocks in casinos, and the décor and ambiance are designed to keep the customers gambling. Some high schools have a Casino Night as a part of their entertainment, complete with blackjack tables, poker, and other Vegas-type trappings. The sponsors may find this to be a lighthearted school function, but what does it teach the students?

 **Fact**

Howard Bragman, author of *Where's My Fifteen Minutes?*, believes that as many as 20 to 25 percent of teenagers want to be famous, but are not sure what they want to be famous for. He comments that twenty years ago, that same percentage wanted a master's degree in business.

Many stores and displays are targeted to young consumers, providing discounts for multiple purchases and even greater deals if the teenager uses a new credit card. Stores and clothing lines hawk the newest trends, knowing that adolescents are hungry for approval, fitting in with their chosen crowd. Electronic fads are powerful, as well, as so much of the teen culture depends on communication via cell phone or computer. There are often strong tie-ins with the entertainment industry and food industries.

Advertisers want to create an emotional response to their ads. For example, when the gigantic Marlboro Man billboard towered over Sunset Boulevard in Los Angeles, how many drivers along that thoroughfare believed that was a positive image, not to mention those of television and magazine ads, combining Wild West lore with the appeal of a handsome cowboy? Many ads downplayed the dangers of smoking. Therefore, young people could look at the ad and only see a positive, when in reality there were a lot of negative parts of smoking the ad did not highlight. Explaining to your teen how advertising works may help him feel less inclined to go out and buy the latest gadget just because a TV commercial says he should.

## 🔔 Alert

A study found that smoking was present in 64 percent of Disney's youth-oriented movies from 1999 to 2006, eliciting a Disney response that the company would no longer allow smoking in those movies and would discourage smoking in Touchstone and Miramax movies, also owned by Disney.

## The Impact of Sports Ads

Beer is often strongly advertised at nationally televised sports events. It seems that everyone in the stands drinks whatever beer has the most prominent sponsor backing. Young people who love sports and watch with excitement may learn that drinking beer is a part of the enjoyment. If they also observe that in their own houses all the men are drinking beer while watching the game, they may come to believe that in order to enjoy sports and be a good fan, they have to drink beer. If you watch sports with your child, don't make alcohol a part of the game.

## Ads Promise Solutions—No Matter the Cost

Advertising tends to prey on viewers' insecurities while at the same time offering a particular product or activity as the remedy for a sense of inferiority or inadequacy. Insecure about fitting in? Then buy this car and you will instantly be a part of the important crowd. Having a hard time keeping up financially? Then get this black card and create more debt. Feeling sad, blue, or fearful? Talk with your doctor about this drug and ask him to prescribe it for you. Young people who watch a lot of television are subjected to thousands of these insidious messages. One solution for teenagers—and people of all ages—is simply to watch less television, decreasing the number of hours of exposure to the advertising messages.

 **Fact**

A writer in the new field of neuromarketing, Martin Lindstrom, comments in his book *Buyology* that research studies show how branding and logos precipitate brain responses. It is his belief that much of what is called advertising is an effort to reach the consumer's subconscious mind. Actual brainwaves have been studied, showing how people react emotionally to particular ads and products.

Velez-Mitchell suggests that at the moment you want to buy something, stop for a moment and think about what the purchase is intended to create—a fantastic date, sexual potency, acceptance into a sought-after group? Rationally, you can see that those things are not really for sale. In her book *Addict Nation*, she suggests that people think about what values might replace the addiction to having and owning material things—spending time in nature, developing personal spirituality, and being of service to others. This idea of taking a pause can be taught to your teenager if he is in the earlier stages of experimentation. Help him to ask those questions of himself and decide whether there might be another way to achieve those aims and possibly develop some more satisfying life values.

## You, the Parent, Can Have a Positive Influence

Adolescents who observe their parents making deliberate choices rather than automatic, reactive responses are at an advantage when it comes to deciding what to do and what not to do in their own lives, including whether or not to accept an offer of drugs or marijuana. If your child listens to you or your partner graciously decline an invitation or resist pressure to do something or to buy something, you'll help him to learn to diplomatically respond in a similar way. "Yes, I'd love to hang out with you, but I'll pass on that. Thanks." No big speech is required, nor a lecture on the evils of the activity or substance.

# Seeking an Identity

A healthy developmental milestone of adolescent years is forming a separate self from the parents—a distinct identity. This process is emotionally difficult for the youth and the parents, even under the best of circumstances, as there is so much love and shared experience. Both sides perceive the change as a loss, sometimes holding on too much and sometimes wanting to completely break away in despair.

The pressures of advertising and the media confuse the issue, causing the teenager to reach out externally, trying to form a self from the random bits and pieces that are thrown at her every day. Your teen may have faced a similar situation. Such a bombardment of information and stimuli creates an impossible maelstrom of possibilities, perhaps none truly relating to the essence of the evolving person. A young adolescent has no context for evaluating so much data. She's almost numb from trying to keep up with it, and there's no time to truly reflect on who she is and what she wants.

Peer groups that offer drugs and alcohol provide an easy way out of the laborious task of forming a separate identity. There it is, ready-made, and adolescents without a firm foundation of more wholesome values are ripe for moving into a drug culture, as the drive for identity is quite strong. Such a move instantly satisfies several needs—identity, belonging, rebelling against the parents and other authority figures, and a high degree of sensory pleasure.

## Ethnic Pressures and Distractions

The United States has been called a melting pot, but sometimes the pieces cluster instead of melt. Distinct groups form that don't blend in, as it is natural for ethnic groups to desire to keep their customs and practices, even within another country's culture. For example, in some Native American groups, it has been an important part of spiritual rituals to use peyote and other culturally accepted hallucinogens. Unfortunately, such substances are illegal under the laws of the United States. This inconsistency makes it very difficult for youth of those groups to become integrated as a people.

Some cultures are strongly family oriented and would believe that an addicted person is an embarrassment, someone to be hidden and explained away. There may be overtones of believing that the difficulty is a moral issue, a strong test of faith and will power. For example, in some Native American cultures, the peyote stick is important as a peacekeeping symbol, an aspect of life that induces the supernatural, inviting the individual to unite with the large Other, the Universal. This usually is done in the group setting. The fact that peyote is considered illegal does not stop the people from using it.

# CHAPTER 4

# Factors in Teenage Addiction

A lot of research has been done on the various correlations between heredity and environment in adolescent addiction. It is important, however, to think clearly and not confuse the word "correlation" with "cause." It is healthy and more productive for parents to focus on characteristics that can be changed. This is more helpful than throwing your hands up in despair and blaming your teenager's substance abuse on your Great-Uncle Arthur, who was a lovable wino. Still, it is helpful to be informed about those related indicators that heighten the likelihood of adolescent addiction.

## Parental Addiction

A family history of addiction increases the possibility that the adolescent will fall into the same behaviors. If a parent or other close family member is a user, the child may see that behavior as normal. It becomes particularly sticky if the parent has a very close relationship with the child, as the using rituals become associated with intimacy and warmth. Practically speaking, children who are around drug users may be unconsciously taking in information about possible contacts for the future—who uses, who supplies, and who is willing to be a runner.

**Fact**

> Human beings are social animals who want to belong. If belonging to a family means drinking, drugging, and brawling, the children raised in such families will learn to do so. A child who breaks away or tries to break away can feel enormous pressure to stick with the pack. In order to counter such forces, a teen has to find a new group of people who are not self-destructive.

The American Academy of Child and Adolescent Psychiatry says that children of alcoholics are four times more likely to become alcoholics themselves. When you consider that one in five Americans grew up with an alcoholic parent, it is clear that there is a large number of people with a very great likelihood of following their parents' footsteps.

## Single-Parent Families

Studies show that single-parent families are much more common among addicted teenagers than two-parent families. This statement is not meant to point an accusing finger at single-parent families, but merely to highlight an indicator to watch for. It is also important to note that children who have close relationships with their same-sex parent are less likely to become addicted to substances.

There are always exceptions to the norm. If you are a single parent with a teenager struggling with addiction, remember to focus on what you can change. Usually a single-parent family has a somewhat lower economic status than a double-parent family.

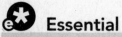 **Essential**

> Students who are forced to attend poor schools in poor neighborhoods are shortchanged in terms of marketable skills. Getting into using and dealing drugs becomes a viable option to earn a living.

# Poverty

Studies are somewhat contradictory in terms of socioeconomic status and teenage addiction. In fact, a study in London in the mid-1990s revealed that the highest group of drug and alcohol users is among the wealthy. It is good to be open-minded and not too stereotyped in one's thinking. Practically speaking, teenagers from wealthier families can better afford substances to abuse. Both genders in high-income families are found to be at high risk, especially if other factors are present that precipitate addiction.

David Sheff, author of *Clean,* says that people living below the poverty level are 50 percent more likely to use and 100 percent more likely to abuse or become addicted than those who are above the poverty line. Drugs admittedly are present everywhere, but in a poor environment there may be fewer alternatives for diversion. In some communities drugs are the norm. The exact relationship between poverty and drug use is unclear, and a researcher at the RAND Corporation (*www.rand.org*) believes that some people space out with drugs in order to cope with poverty and depressing surroundings.

# Peer Influence

The types of friends and the number of friends who use and behave addictively have a great effect on teenagers. It is normal for a teenager to want to be cool, but if being cool means going to a rave at an illegal location and using ecstasy all night, the result cannot be positive. Pay close attention to the people your adolescent associates with, and notice, especially, if there seems to be an air of secrecy about friends, times, and locations. You, as the parent, have a right to know what is going on, even if your child is establishing independence. Keep a line of communication open with your child, just in case she gets in trouble and wants to call you at 3:00 A.M. for a ride home after a party turned dark and dangerous. Threading this needle is often difficult for parents today. Being an effective monitor is always good, but having some authority to set limits is necessary. Too much authoritarianism, and you might find heightened secrecy with your teen and a lack of asking for parental help. Too much leniency, and the child ends up needing a probation officer to set any limits, which often is too little, too late. Just remember, you don't want her to feel intimidated or afraid to reach out to you for help.

 **Alert**

The power of peer influence extends even into the jail and prison system. While parents often want to have their child "scared straight" by having incarceration happen early on, it is often better to have legal consequences emerge from a lack of response to parents and treatment providers in a progressive fashion. If a teenager gets into serious trouble, ends up in juvenile detention, and progresses through to prison, he is forming a social network all along the way. When he is out, it is highly likely that he will tap into contacts made while incarcerated, continuing the addiction lifestyle with a wide network of support.

## Getting Control over Peer Influence

At least one study (Ravenews, 2012) showed that students who participate in drinking, smoking, and partying feel more popular. (Of course, your child wants to be popular, so be very aware of who she's with, so you can help determine the components of being popular. You might be able to encourage more wholesome associations— music, sports, arts, or environmental efforts.) Further, some research suggests that the *perceived* positive effects of drugs on socialization and artificial feelings of well-being end up swamping the negative effects of drug and alcohol use. If your teen perceives that she will have a positive social experience when using drugs or alcohol, she may be more likely to use, regardless of the consequences.

It is important to have open discussions with your teen about managing the pressures of using drugs and alcohol in social situations, whether these situations are stressful or celebratory. Provide context for your teen, and discuss any possible social outcomes of avoiding drug and alcohol use. If your teen is aware that these pressures may arise in social settings (like parties or school trips), and has practice avoiding them in healthy ways, she will be better able to avoid negative choices while on her own in these settings.

 **Fact**

The need to belong is so great that adolescents can be led to participate in hurtful group activities, such as cyberbullying. The Institute of Cyberbullying (*www.cyberbullyinginstitute.org*) reports that as many as one in five middle-school students bears the brunt of bullying on social media sites. Teenagers feel brave as they anonymously taunt and abuse their peers, sometimes driving the victim to suicide.

If your adolescent is in a group of peers who downplay the present and long-term effects of drug abuse, she can be swayed to try it and use habitually, especially if everybody in the desired group is a user. It is important to remember that teenagers deeply crave acceptance in a peer group. It's a universal human need, according to psychologist Abraham Maslow. Adolescents go through a time of forming a separate identity from their parents, and aligning with peers is a natural part of the process. Maslow describes the hierarchy of needs in his book *Motivation and Personality*. The needs of the profile of humanity go according to the hierarchy of human needs in his book. Forming a separate identity while aligning with others is about half way up the post of human needs.

## Violence in the Environment

Is the home or neighborhood a war zone? This kind of chaos and danger causes a teenager to want to escape. Domestic violence, fierce arguments among neighbors, and even watching too much violence on television creates a need to find peace, even if it's through drugs and alcohol. Exposure to violence sets up a need to feel numb, which may mean going to a different place where things aren't so bad, even if the different place is a gang or crack house with all that accompanies those conditions.

You may have to cope with your teen losing a peer to substance abuse–related death. You may be wondering how you should open up the topic with your teen. Is it best to avoid estranging your teen by sounding judgmental? Should you convey concern about your teen's safety despite your teen feeling invulnerable? Should you help your teen with self-blame for the death? In short, yes. Nearly every family and teen has experienced this in his or her community. There is a real irony in that drugs and alcohol are turned to as a coping strategy for violence, yet produce more violence in the end. Keep an honest dialogue with your teen no matter the circumstances.

## ❓ Question

**Is there a way out of the violence?**
Some suggest that if children who are subjected to violence in the home or neighborhood are taught anger management at school, the power of that variable might be diminished. Such programs as peer-directed mediation and negotiation could be highly beneficial in working out more productive ways of solving conflict and meeting one's needs.

### Reacting to Abuse and Chaos

If a person is abused as a child or teenager, it becomes easier for that young person to abuse himself in the future, because that is what is taught and learned—that one's physical self is not really important, and it's okay to do harmful things to the body. Such youth may have painful, locked-in emotions, and addiction is a way of escaping them. Stress is one of the precipitators of using and drinking, and previous harm to the body can sometimes cause extreme stress. For example an incest survivor may have need to precipitate the original sin, especially if not acknowledged as an adult. The teenager may not have the time, interest, or maturity to investigate past reasons for today's turmoil, and simply turns to drinking or drugs.

If a home is chaotic for a teen, drugs and alcohol can become a way to cope with conditions that are out of control, creating some semblance of control, or at least tolerable escape. A study at the National Institute on Alcohol Abuse and Alcoholism (NIAAA) found a high incidence of childhood trauma among adult alcoholics. Of the alcoholics studied, more than half had some kind of serious childhood trauma.

## ⓔ❗ Alert

Velez-Mitchell cites a horrific example, showing the relationship between poverty and addiction as well as how too many of these factors lead to numbing out. In the 1990s, there was a news story in which a fifteen-year-old girl took her seven-year-old stepsister to a crack house where the older sister prostituted herself for cash and, for more cash, handed over the seven-year-old, who was raped by a group of men ranging in age from thirteen years old to their twenties. To a nonaddicted person, these actions are incomprehensible. Everyone involved in this incident was a victim of neglect and abandonment.

## The Impacts of Trauma

Gabor Maté, an addiction physician at the Portland Hotel in Vancouver, a residence for people experiencing homelessness, says that addiction is an attempt to smooth over a deep childhood pain. Some loss or trauma is deeply imprinted on the child's brain, and some kind of addiction is the only way to make it go away. Addiction is an attempt to achieve a positive state of mind from a negative situation that happened in the past.

Divorce is one such trauma that can precipitate teenage drug use. Although very common in today's shifting relationship landscape, such an occurrence can be a psychic earthquake for a child, completely breaking up his sense of any kind of security in the world. He may seek an escape in order to cope with so many new uncertainties. Divorce often brings along with it relocations, changing schools, loss of friends, less contact with a parent, diminished financial resources, and new mates for one or both parents. All of this can be quite difficult for an adolescent. The very foundation for personal security seems to have changed or disappeared.

## Role Models

It cannot be said often enough that children copy what they see, know, and admire. You are the most important person in your child's life, regardless of what he says otherwise. An example speaks much more loudly than words and lectures. If you live a clean, addiction-free life, you are miles ahead of the game.

Notice with a clear eye who your teenager admires. Listen to what he says about that person. Is it a positive influence? Be very aware of what and who is shaping your teen's identity. Listen when your adolescent talks about a favorite musician or movie icon, and inform yourself about that person. What do the lyrics say? What is the message of the movie?

One of the highest predictors of addiction is the presence in the home of an addicted individual. One in the immediate extended family, such as a close family friend, an uncle, or a grandparent, would also have a powerful influence on the young person. If that person is deeply loved, the association becomes almost unshakable, as the teenager fondly remembers the rituals, fragrance, humor, and affection of the treasured relationship. It becomes a primitive desire to re-create that in one's own life and possibly in the choice of a life partner.

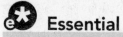 **Essential**

In addition to the example set by significant people in their lives using or abusing substances and behaviors, children and youth see the modeling of escape as a viable way to handle problems, rather than dealing with discomfort or challenges in a constructive way. Escape is an acceptable norm in this kind of background.

The power of these strong associations defies logic. Someone who grows up in a family with a loved, addicted person may find a normal, nonaddicted individual boring and unattractive. If Daddy and Grandpa smoked, it is likely that a child in that household could find smoking a comfortable habit and have nothing against a life partner who smokes. The deep, primitive associations and emotional memories are stronger than any information about the dangers of tobacco and the excruciating progression of emphysema. The truth of the matter is that everyone wants to be loved, and if love is perceived as present in the person who has an addiction, that will override any intellectual, rational objection.

## Is There a Genetic Factor?

Addiction does tend to run in families, a mixture of the influences of environment and heredity. It is impossible to tease out what exactly is the extent of each aspect of cause. Biology shows that alcoholism and other addictions tend to be passed down more through the males in a family, and sometimes it skips a generation. Of course, you do not choose your relatives, but it is good to be aware of family patterns, just in case suspicions arise that another one is continuing the legacy.

Some scientists believe there is combination of several genes, a whole constellation of biological traits and tendencies that increase the likelihood that those related to alcoholics and addicts have a higher chance of going in that direction. The actual addiction can be hidden, as with an elderly aunt who dies leaving caches of hidden bottles all over the house, or whose autopsy results show addiction to prescription drugs, surprising everyone in the family.

## Predisposition

Researchers are cautious about naming clear causes and effects with addiction. The word *predisposition* is much more commonly used. This indicates that a person is more inclined to go a particular direction or make certain choices. Those inclinations could be biological or environmental. Author David Sheff in *Clean* cites the following case of a young boy's introduction to addiction: The twelve-year-old boy had an opportunity to drink alcohol at a friend's house for the first time. When they began drinking, the friend gagged and stopped drinking, and the twelve-year-old drank as much as he could, vomited, and blacked out. He loved the taste on his lips and the feeling of being cool. The boy came from a poor family and suffered from low self-esteem. He didn't feel that he fit in anywhere. Drinking made his self-consciousness go away.

After that night, he drank when he could and started smoking pot. When his parents saw him smoking pot, they shrugged it off, believing that kids experiment as a part of growing up. He began to deal the drug in order to be able to afford to drink and use.

Ecstasy was his drug of choice, along with alcohol. He also used cocaine, meth, and pills. He began high school on scholarship at Sonoma Academy in Santa Rosa, California, feeling out of place because he came from a poor family. He was amazed by the mansions his classmates called home and felt that he couldn't accept an invitation from such affluent peers.

He became known as the party kid, and used weed and ecstasy every day, starting in the morning, and then dealing the drugs with other students. He hung out with the older students, even though he was a freshman. He didn't want anything to do with anyone who wasn't buying from him or willing to use with him. He almost got caught on one occasion when some students told their parents, who then spoke with the dean. However, his stash was well hidden in various disguised containers in his locker, so he was not caught.

When he went home, he found that his parents were divorcing but couldn't afford to live in two different residences, so they simply split the space in the house and continued to cohabitate, yelling and fighting much of the time. During the break from school, the young man smoked weed the entire time and inhaled gasoline from the lawnmower.

## ✴ Essential

Author Jane Velez-Mitchell confesses that a part of her predisposition toward alcohol was growing up with an alcoholic father. Having someone in the home who is drunk seems normal, and one is inclined to seek out and repeat what seems normal from the baseline of childhood experience.

## Specific Stressors

Loneliness, insecurity, and stress are precipitating factors for addiction. Any of the factors discussed in this chapter contribute to the higher likelihood of turning to drugs or alcohol, especially when several of the conditions are combined. For example, if a teenager comes from a poor, single-parent family where the same-sex parent is not involved in her life, and there is also a mental illness, trauma, or a close relative who is an addict present, the likelihood is high that such a girl would turn to the comfort of drugs or alcohol.

### LGBT and Questioning Teens

An adolescent's raging hormones can cause considerable confusion, even under the best of circumstances, but add the further isolating situation of homosexuality, and the stage is set for a higher chance of using addictively. Teenage sexuality is powerful, and if a young gay person cannot find healthy, thriving role models, it is possible that addiction might provide that elusive loving relationship.

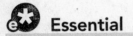 **Essential**

Psychologist Abraham Maslow cites the human need to belong as one of the strongest human drives, slightly less than the basic physical needs. Gay, lesbian, bisexual, and transgendered youth have more difficult challenges in finding peers, simply because there are fewer of them, and the prejudice and stigma sometimes require remaining closeted. If a desperate youngster finds a new gay friend who uses drugs or alcohol addictively, it would be no surprise that soon both would be using.

Children who question the orientation of their sexuality or seem inclined toward transgender desires may feel terribly alone. They may not know anyone who shares their particular path. A teenager is not mature enough to work out a way of being at peace while still feeling ostracized or different. He may know that he is different, but have nowhere to turn. Children are sometimes quite sensitive and realize that even their parents would judge them harshly if they yearn to become the opposite sex. Boys especially experience strong cultural measures to "be a man" and would be censured in various subtle and obvious ways if they dressed up in mom's clothes and played with dolls.

## Marginality
The experience of being marginalized is quite isolating and painful, regardless of the forces or reasons behind them. Any of the factors discussed in this chapter inherently include the result of being marginalized. Perhaps a teenager is a recent immigrant, struggling fiercely with language and pop culture. It is so awkward as a teenager not to fit in.

Perhaps the adolescent is handicapped in some way, whether mentally or physically. Gifted and talented students sometimes have challenges in finding their tribe. Add this factor to other precipitating factors of addiction and the potential Mozart or Kahlo might turn to addiction for solace and comfort.

## Prejudice

It is human to vehemently deny the presence of prejudice in oneself, but the fact of the matter is that it is human to hold deeply held attitudes for or against certain types of people. It shows up in politics, entertainment, business, and everyday social relationships. Who has not laughed at a rerun of *King of the Hill* in which the residents of Harlan show despicable ignorance and prejudice toward their new neighbors from Laos or shared humor about the deep Southern accent and figures of speech of someone in public office? When President Carter was in office, it was no surprise that there was a bestselling book titled *How to Talk Southern.*

 **Fact**

Seven percent of black children have a parent who is incarcerated, as compared to 1 percent of white children. Children with a parent in prison suffer from shame and stigma. Every day, they are aware that someone critical to their existence is considered unworthy to be a part of general society.

One might protest that "some of my best friends are" and fill in the blank with the criticized group of the day, but still, as long as people are alive and breathing, prejudices have a part in attitude and behavior. Such stereotyped attitudes and manners affect teenagers. A specific group of teenagers might be treated differently at school, along with those of other cultures. If something negative happens in the news, such as a 9/11 epic disaster, those of the associated ethnicity go through horrors of prejudice and ostracism. For teenagers, it can be excruciating, as they have little context for placing such cruelty into some kind of meaningful response. It would be quite human to turn to drugs, alcohol, and risky companionship when social conditions are especially tough.

## Mental Illness in the Family

A federal SAMHSA study shows that there is a strong association between mental illness in the family, mental illness in an individual, and addiction. The list of possibilities is long—obsessive-compulsive disorder, depression, bipolar disorder, anxiety disorders, and schizophrenia. It is shown that six out of ten addicts have one or more disorders of other kinds. Those who have mental health issues are more likely to turn to drugs than those who do not, as these mental conditions cause emotional turmoil and anguish. Escape of any kind is welcomed and sought, even if the end result is rationally known to be negative. Addiction becomes a kind of "self-medication," giving a false sense that the mental illness is improved, when things are worse than ever. Using is a way to ease depression or anxiety, and if an adolescent sees this example in the family, it is natural to want to re-create it. Those with mental illnesses long to feel normal, even if the avenue is drugs or alcohol. Author David Sheff notes that his own son, diagnosed with bipolar disorder and depression, said upon using methamphetamines, "If only I'd been breastfed on this." According to Sheff, methamphetamines gave him the feeling he'd looked for his entire life, a sense of being soothed. Drugs are an escape from the frustration, confusion, and pain of mental illnesses. The user is not especially interested in the long-term effects of drug or alcohol use, because he or she is seeking the short-term alleviation.

A nonaddict can see that using something addictively is not a permanent solution, but the addict does not think in those terms. It has been shown that depressed people who drink alcohol, smoke marijuana, and use stimulants feel better temporarily, but experience worse, deeper, and more frequent depression in the long term. The addiction solution to mental illness is like sealing a gaping wound with dung. Temporarily the bleeding stops, but now the person has introduced a far worse problem of infection, and the wound may start bleeding anytime. Better to deal with mental health problems in the accepted manner than to rely on addictive substances, which merely complicate the picture.

## Question

**Is there a cause-and-effect relationship between mental illness and drug problems?**
Writer and researcher David Sheff says that there's a two-way street between mental illness and drug problems. A 2007 *Lancet* study showed a relationship between using marijuana and various psychotic conditions, including schizophrenia. The study showed that people who smoked pot experienced the onset of mental illness years earlier than those who did not. And those who had a mental condition and stopped smoking felt better.

The link between smoking pot and mental illness is strongest among the youngest users, those between the ages of twelve and fifteen. Of course, it is good to recognize that the majority of pot smokers never develop a mental illness, but of those with mental illnesses in adult years, many trace the roots back to using marijuana as teenagers. Still, one has to keep a clear head about the difference between *cause and effect* and *correlation*, the coexistence of two factors or conditions. The distinction can be confusing, but important to keep in mind. Cause and effect indicates that if one thing happens, the other should probably follow. Correlation indicates that the two factors exist at the same time but not one being caused by the other.

## CHAPTER 5

# Why Does My Child Act That Way?

Adolescence is that ten- to twelve-year process of growth that begins when your child separates from childhood around age nine to thirteen and finally graduates into early adulthood in his or her early to midtwenties. It is a long process of transformation that manages to turn a dependent child into an independent young adult by the end. Adolescence is not a punishable offense. It is part of life. Therefore, do not punish teenagers for the process, but do hold them accountable for how they manage it.

## Suspicious Behaviors

During the adolescent phase of parenting, you may wonder who that alien is in your once-loving child's bedroom. In adolescence, to some degree, your child will try to push against your authority (opposition), pull away from your company (separation), and get around your rules (manipulation).

### Normal Behavior and Warning Signs

Adolescence takes the magic out of parenting. As a parent you will likely become more and more disenchanted with the abrasive teenager, and your teenager may feel the same about you. This is how it should be—conflict over freedom wears down the dependence between the two of you until by the end of adolescence you are each willing to let the other go.

It takes parental vigilance to help children remain drug-free, so parents need to know what signs of substance use to watch for. There are general and specific indicators that are worth keeping alert for as your child makes the journey through adolescence.

### ☑ Fact

According to a 2011 study by the American Psychological Association, 70 percent of high-school students have tried cigarette smoking, 25 percent before the age of thirteen; 81 percent of high-school students have tried alcohol, 32 percent having their first drink before the age of thirteen; and 47 percent of high-school students have tried marijuana, 11 percent of whom tried marijuana before the age of thirteen.

Some of the general indicators have to do with your teenager making decisions that seem uncharacteristic or inconsistent with her established history and true character as you know her to be. In each case, substance use takes the user from a caring to a noncaring (freedom from normal caring) mental frame of reference. Here are some common examples.

- A normally honest child starts lying.
- A normally smart child starts making unwise decisions.
- A normally motivated child starts becoming apathetic.
- A normally well-performing child starts failing.
- A normally obedient child starts getting into social trouble.
- A normally even-tempered child starts becoming explosive.
- A normally confiding child starts avoiding communication.
- A normally responsible child starts acting irresponsibly.
- Drugs and alcohol become essential to having fun.

Always be on the lookout for atypical changes in your teenager as she journeys through adolescence. None of these general changes by itself is a sure sign of substance use, but three or four of them together should cause you to question whether alcohol or drug use may be disorganizing your teen's life. Keep in mind that denial is an aspect of addiction. It may seem as if your teenager is blatantly lying, but to her, perhaps not. It can be baffling.

Risk-taking behavior may increase. Adolescents believe that they are invincible, above the laws of nature and society. They might think they are better drivers than those of the previous generation, even under the influence of a couple of beers. Long hours of partying might lead to sleep deprivation, which further increases the likelihood of poor judgment in all kinds of situations—sexual behavior, driving speed, and choice of companions.

It is the nature of the young to think that they are on top of things, and it can be quite difficult to even get the attention of a youngster highly motivated to continue using, let alone have a serious conversation about the patterns you observe.

### Parental Influence Matters

Parents' values matter. If the mother and father take dangerous risks, the teenager sees this as an example and a norm. If the atmosphere in the home is one of health and caring for the body, the adolescent is impacted by that context, especially if the parents live out those beliefs in their own lives, not just talk about it.

Some parents wonder if allowing children to drink or do drugs at home is a viable compromise to "keep them safe" while they are experimenting. It's not worth it. This practice is illegal, and the parents can be held responsible if someone in the group is allowed to drive drunk or high and has an accident.

# Disappearing Money or Valuable Possessions

You may discover that certain pawnable items from your house are missing—computers, other electronic devices, music equipment, power tools. It's difficult to face, but the addicted teenager will go to any lengths to keep the supply of substance flowing into his life. This first priority alters his behavior to the extent of stealing from those who love him most. It may seem, too, that your child is more affluent than usual, with no apparent source of income, such as a job or an allowance. This could be an indicator that your teenager has begun dealing in drugs in order to afford them.

### ✅ Fact

You may be completely shocked and feel deeply betrayed by the mere thought of your child stealing from you or the household. The behavior is not personal. It's simply a repercussion of the power of addiction. The first priority of the addict is to keep the supply of the substance available. Other important relationships slide down the list in terms of importance. This can be quite painful to accept, but it is a part of the disease.

Your adolescent may ask for money more often, sometimes with a plausible need. Check your instincts. If the reason seems somewhat vague, the money may be going toward drugs or alcohol. Usually a teenager will not ask for large amounts of money, as that would arouse suspicion in the parent. The requests will more likely be for small amounts but will be somewhat more frequent than usual. Remember that drug dealers often give out "free samples" and that alcohol is very often stolen from homes or stores and shared.

## Lower Grades in School

Even good students show faltering grades when substance abuse comes into the picture. Your straight-A student may bring home reports of C or lower, and if she is an average student, you may see some failing grades and receive calls from the school guidance counselor or teachers. Lower grades are an unfortunate indication that your teenager's priorities have changed, and schoolwork is no longer at the top of the list.

 **Alert**

> The trait of lying becomes more evident as the adolescent shifts into more serious abuse and addiction. At first some excuses may seem plausible ("The teacher said we don't have any homework this week"), but your instincts may tell you differently as the lying escalates. Don't allow yourself to become confused, as the teenage addict may twist what you said or rewrite history quite differently than what you recall. Stay very clear-headed, even if you have to write things down, as the teen's manipulation can easily derail you.

You may discover weeks or months after the fact that your teenager has missed school and is still ditching classes to an alarming degree. You fear for her ability to complete her requirements and graduate. You never envisioned yourself as being the parent of a dropout. Conversations about college are no longer of interest, and there's no enthusiasm for anything in the future—work, career, or school.

## Sudden Change in Choice of Friends

You may notice that your teenager's friends are no longer the affable ones that comfortably hung around with your family. He's in with a new crowd, and the change seems to have taken place rather quickly. The new crowd does not want to come into your house, and your teenager does not introduce you to his new friends. He and his friends meet in various places that you don't know. You may not know the parents of these new friends, unlike your teenager's previous group.

**Fact**

People in Alcoholics Anonymous speak of the tendency to "seek lower companions" as the disease progresses. This is a predictable aspect of the addiction.

It becomes very difficult to keep up with your teenager, as you often do not know where he is or whom he might be seeing. Whatever agreements were in place for calling at certain times, leaving the cell phone on, etc., are forgotten, eluded, or excused away. Prepare yourself. An addict can be quick-thinking and smooth-talking in order to keep the practice going, once the use has shifted from abuse to addiction.

## Changing Manners: A Rude Awakening

Your formerly courteous daughter has turned into a tattooed, pierced, gothic creature who utterly disdains her parents. A certain amount of rebellious behavior is to be expected as a teenager separates emotionally and psychologically from the family. A separate identity can take the form of obnoxious music and strange clothing even in normal, healthy, well-adjusted adolescents. But an addicted teenager takes this pulling away much farther.

She speaks to you with disdain and derision. You might see erratic, even irrational behavior, especially if she crashes from time to time, going through a slight detox process before starting up again in order to alleviate the discomfort of withdrawal. It may seem that she realizes that there is a problem but is genuinely unable to stop.

Chores are ignored, and agreements that you had in the past are laughed off. You might find that a clever girl can trick you in confusing arguments about what was said and not said. Be careful not to let this drive you crazy. Keep your own head and memory straight, and accept the fact that, in some ways, you're dealing with a stranger who has some resemblance to the daughter that you knew and loved before the addiction took over.

## Mood Swings

Mood swings may become evident in your teen. You may find that you never quite know what to expect and find yourself uneasy, walking on eggshells. Your teenager may miss curfews and become hostile, sullen, hyperactive, or withdrawn, and she may avoid eye contact. She might become deceitful and lethargic. She might seem even sneaky, locking doors, becoming secretive about conversations with others and vague about how her time is spent. Her employer at her part-time job may call and ask about missed work, which you probably knew nothing about. Her principal may ask to see you about her multiple unexcused absences.

Keeping an eye out for mood swings can be tricky, as even under the best of circumstances teenagers are going through raging hormone changes. Even well-behaved, nonaddicted adolescents can be volatile and unpredictable. This is normal. Keep your radar out there and trust your own judgment about whether the situation is within the parameters of typical teenage angst, or something quite different or more extreme. It is also helpful to network with others parents, attend gatherings where parents are updated about teen patterns, or seek consultation with a professional.

## Whether to Confront or Not

By the time you observe many of these symptoms, it may be too late to actually prevent substance use or abuse. However, it is possible that a well-timed conversation can turn your teen away from addiction. Notice the reaction when you bring up the topic of concern about too much drinking or using (or any at all). If the teenager mumbles and changes the subject, as in many other conversations, it is possible that there is not really a problem. The key thing to watch for is a quick, angry reaction when you mention your concern. This is an indication that the addiction is in place, and your teenager starts to see you as a threat to her continuing the behavior that has become integral to her life. Try not to react to that anger. Just notice it. It's a clue to how far the addiction has progressed.

## My Teen Just Wants to Be Alone

Isolation is a factor in addiction. The addicted person often simply wants to be by himself in order to participate in the chosen addicted behavior or substance. Your formerly friendly adolescent retreats behind a closed (even locked) door, and you wonder what really goes on during those hours of retreat. He possibly is in touch with others in his new world via text or computer, or he may simply be doing his drug or behavior in the peace and quiet of his own den.

 **Fact**

Addiction may lead to a feeling of isolation from other students and from the school. Diminished ability both academically and in sports creates a feeling of futility and extreme loneliness, and furthers the use of the substance that seems to make the pain go away, at least temporarily.

Sometimes substance abuse is combined with other addictive behaviors—playing games for hours and connecting with Internet contacts that share the same interest. Hours can go by and nothing has been accomplished, except countless online or text conversations with people who are a part of maintaining the substance supply or fellow gamers.

His grooming may deteriorate, and you'll see physical changes in his appearance. There's no time for washing his hair or pressing a shirt. Usually teenagers are quite appearance-conscious, wanting to have just the right clothes and look. This need diminishes as the desire for the substance or addictive behavior moves to the forefront. He may act secretive and make a lot of trips to the restroom, basement, or other isolated places where his behaviors won't be observed. He may seem exhausted, depressed, and hopeless much of the time.

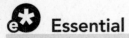 **Essential**

As substance abuse becomes more prominent in the adolescent's life, other latent conditions may appear—depression, panic attacks, and anxiety disorders. If you suspect that your teenager is seriously using, become watchful for other psychological challenges.

You might observe sleeplessness and loss of interest in former pursuits, loss of weight, sickness, and the disappearance of your over-the-counter prescriptions and alcohol. A teen using amphetamines may require very little sleep, and those on marijuana may want to sleep to excess. Be diligent and watch for changes in his sleep patterns. You may also notice that his participation in sports, church groups, and family functions has become sparse. This can be due to the shifted priority to obtaining the substance, or it can be due to a desire to keep the addiction secret. Your teenager might start skipping meals, saying that he is on the run with no time to eat.

Some of these changes can be subtle. You might notice slight changes in the tone and color of your adolescent's skin. Posture may change to a more slouched, hunched-over style. You have to trust your instincts. If something seems off, it probably is. Do you suspect that your adolescent is drinking or using first thing in the morning? One clue is his starting a set, rigid ritual early in the day that excludes you; this could point to substance abuse that has become more addictive, requiring an early first hit or drink in order to function.

## Should I Go Through His Possessions?

You have to figure out for yourself and within your own conscience how much or how little to invade your addicted teenager's space. You may normally respect the privacy of your child's room, especially if he shows signs of growing responsibility and independence. However, with an addicted adolescent, a betrayal has occurred, and basically all bets are off. The rules have changed because he has shifted into dishonest, secretive behavior. In such cases, you may decide that you are within your rights to search his room for paraphernalia or other incriminating material.

 **Alert**

Any inclinations you have had to be a pal and friend to your teenager have to be released. You cannot be a buddy and still police the environment for signs of drug use. It's more appropriate to be friends with your own peers and concentrate on being the rational adult as you pursue your suspicions that your teenager is becoming involved in drugs.

Be prepared for loud, belligerent protests, as nobody likes to go backwards in terms of freedom and independence. Ignore this wall of fury, if possible, and do what you need to do. Truthfully, the bottom line is: as long as your teenager lives with you, you have the ultimate authority, especially when illegal or harmful activity is involved. You are the grownup. Don't forget that. Remember the toddler years when you had to deal with public tantrums? The tantrums of an insulted teenager can be equally furious. Just look at him with love, and imagine that he's two years old, and you're doing what you need to do to be in charge of the situation, especially when his well-being is at stake.

Your child is almost like two people living in the same body at this point: One of them is addicted, and the other clings to what things were like before. You can appeal to the "before" personality to ally against the addictive pattern. Accountability is key. Monitor everything with increased scrutiny: Do spot inspections of their stuff, be sure they know they need to be home when expected, that they know they can only go where you have told them they are allowed, and try getting them back into normal activities while desisting from the sneaky actions. They can earn their privileges back once they prove they are being responsible. Even try vocalizing your concerns, saying, "I'm here for you in battling this problem, but I know there are times when you will not realize that. We can agree to disagree, but I care so much about you that I will never stop doing what I need to do."

## A Helpful Checklist

It will be difficult to persuade a teenager to consider answering questions about abuse and addiction indicators. Usually, the addict is the last one to see his addiction. However, a checklist such as this one, adapted from the Alcoholics Anonymous Twenty Questions and a federal guideline of what to observe in an addicted teenager, could be helpful:

1. Do you often talk and think about drinking?
2. Are you drinking more now than in the past?
3. Do you need a drink to relax?
4. Do you like to drink alone?
5. Do you forget things that happened while you were drinking?
6. Do you keep a hidden bottle for a quick pick-me-up?
7. Do you have to drink to have fun?
8. Do you need a drink in the morning to alleviate a hangover?
9. Is drinking affecting your finances and work?
10. Is drinking affecting your closest relationships?

If your teen answers "yes" to even a few of the questions, it could indicate that a serious problem is developing.

In most cases with teens, it might be best to explore these in conversation one at a time. For example, open up the issue of how much time they and their friends think about drinking or drugs. Is this something they perceive as an "extra," that is, they get together to listen to music and dance, and the alcohol is just something they like, or does it appear that the drug is the whole reason for getting together, as in, "Jake got some really good weed, so he invited us over to smoke him out"? However, don't expect honest answers, and fill in the gaps with what you otherwise know to be true based on what you've observed.

## Scuffles with the Law

Along with bad manners and an unfortunate decline into deviant behavior, you may find that your teen is having trouble with the law. This could take the form of petty theft, driving under the influence of alcohol, violent altercations, or possessing and selling illegal substances. Your first inclination may be to bail her out, as you know that she's a really good kid and that this is a temporary phase. Be careful that denial is not at the forefront of your decisions about what to do in the case of arrests and breaking the law. It may not be in the best interests of your child to protect her from the consequences of her behavior. A few nights in a cold cell or some community service might be the wake-up call your child needs to face the seriousness of the presence of addiction in her life. She might "hear" from a judge what she cannot hear from you.

A probation officer can be a great in helping to connect your teen to effective interventions in the community and enforcing her attendance in treatment. The problem with teens is that they often will not go to treatment when a parent alone wants them to go.

**Fact**

> It is not unusual for teenagers to want to do what is forbidden. To a certain degree, this is a normal part of becoming a separate individual, creating an identity that is apart from the parents. But some activities, such as shoplifting, tagging, and graffiti, are extreme and illegal. Some serious drug users progress into burglary or credit card theft.

Nobody likes to get that phone call bringing news that a child is in jail or juvenile detention. You will feel mortified, especially the first time. Keep in mind that if you let yourself become a financial buffer to the consequences of addicted behavior, there may be many more phone calls and bail-outs. Jail or prison isn't really what you would want for an adolescent, but sometimes such environments can put the young person in contact with rehab programs and groups for support in overcoming drugs and addictive behavior. Sometimes the experts know how to "get to" a kid better than you do.

This result of a child's illegal activity is no reflection on you. At these times it becomes imperative that you envision your teenager as truly a separate person, growing and evolving on her own path, however irregular and surprising. A detour to jail and other self-imprisonment can sometimes be enlightening to a young person, and help that person get back on a straight path.

Even if your teenager is a high-functioning addict, a DUI—and certainly several DUIs—is a clear-cut warning sign. She may even be arrested for underage drinking or possession of an illegal, controlled substance. Your teenager might be getting into fights, physical altercations serious enough to require police intervention. She may engage in shoplifting, either for another thrill or as a way to get more items to sell for spending money. Parents of children who have dealt with your child's growing aggression might be calling you. If and when you receive calls from the school or other authorities, try to listen carefully to what is said. Watch for your tendency to make excuses for your child, explaining away any thing that could be a real reflection against you. Truly listen to what authorities are telling you.

Watch for your own tendency to go into denial and make excuses for your adolescent. This measure doesn't serve your teenager's best interests in the long run. It's very difficult to accept the reality of the seriousness of addictive behavior. After all, this is the child that you raised from the cradle. It's quite challenging for a parent to shift gears into the watchful mode of noticing symptoms and deciding whether it's possibly a serious problem of addiction. Don't gloss it over, thinking it's a one-time thing, especially if an infraction requires that you bail the child out financially. It's more helpful to an addict of any age to fully experience the consequences of any substance abuse.

 **Fact**

In an effort to alleviate clogged court systems and prevent the accumulation of a police record, some states have drug diversion programs that allow first offenders to take classes to learn about drugs and their effects. Attendance is mandatory, usually paid for by the participants. Classes cannot be missed, as the alternative is jail.

# CHAPTER 6

# Prevention Methods

One of the most important parts of prevention is simply being aware of what is going on in your adolescent's world today, particularly in terms of which substances are popular to abuse. For example, according to Dr. Scott Teitelbaum, today's teens have shifted from illegal substances to a greater use of over-the-counter medications. These medications are legal and teenagers can easily buy them. The Internet has tons of information about how to mix various over-the-counter medications to create mixtures for getting high. Adolescents tend to think that these drugs are safer than illegal drugs, but they are not.

## Communication Matters

Having a friendly, trusting relationship with your teenager lessens the likelihood of your teen participating in addictive behaviors. But how can you foster such conversations when your teenager seems so mysterious and far away? Johnny Patout, who writes for the online magazine *Addiction Professional,* suggests that parents not try too hard to be hip, and respect that it's normal for teenagers to want to be private, closer to their peers, and independent. Too much pressure to be your teen's pal will alienate your adolescent. He suggests the following points to facilitate positive communication:

- Don't try to use teenage jargon. By the time you learn a new word, it is probably out of fashion, and you will have many opportunities to see your adolescent roll his eyes.
- Speak honestly. Even as teenagers try on various identities, they actually crave a secure anchor, someone who cares about them and will tell the truth. You can be that person.
- Be conservative about physical contact. You may have been highly affectionate with your child during the growing-up years, and you see your son roughhouse with friends. However, a side hug across the shoulders may be all that a teenager wants. Remember that adolescents are forming an individual identity, and that requires a certain amount of pulling away, even physically.
- Don't tell too many of your own war stories. If you start your sentences with "When I was your age . . ." you will likely be tuned out. In later years, your teenager can see some parallels between generations, but not now. In many ways times are different now, and you may not really know what experiences are like these days. Listen to find out.
- Don't say that these are their best years. A child who is experiencing drastic physical and emotional shifts, catastrophic disappointments in friendships, and severe uncertainties about the future does not want to think that this is the best it's going to ever get. He always wants the hope that somehow things will improve. Reassure him that there are no particular best years, that each stage of life has its rewards and challenges. This balanced message is much more encouraging and true.
- Let him have his favorite thing sometimes. Your teenager may be obsessed with a particular piece of clothing or jewelry, a special ritual, or a favorite food. Let that be the case. Adolescence is an insecure experience, and if one thing makes him feel better, let him have it. Adults are really no

different, starting the day with a particular latte from a particular barista and reading jokes from a special Facebook group before work sets the tone for the day. It's human.

- Help your teenager think for himself. Critical thinking and problem-solving is needed at every stage of life. If you do your part to hone those skills, your adolescent has a precious lifelong skill. Help him explore consequences of various choices and brainstorm various avenues of exploration. Be careful not to have your own agenda. Truly let him think about the range of actions and choose one that fits his preferences and desired consequences.

- Don't ask questions your teenager is likely not to answer. This sets up a negative mode from the get-go, which is not what you want. Also try to avoid topics that may elicit lying. What you want is to build the bridges that are positive, shying away from the aspects of life that your teenager wants to keep close to his heart.

## ⁇ Question

**Is it permissible for me to ask my teenager how easy it would be for her to get drugs, even particular, specific drugs?**
Yes, but be ready to hear the answers. You could make a chart of the substances you wonder about and rate each one as easy, not too hard, or impossible. Be aware of your own resistance to this information. It is real and a part of your child's world.

## Question Everything: Required Reporting

If you discover your adolescent is lying and covering things up, it is time to shift gears and stop giving her the benefit of the doubt. She may loudly protest that you don't trust her, but that is the truth—you don't trust her because she has already broken the trust that was there. From this point on, especially if you suspect substance abuse, you'll need a tighter rein on the teenager's activities, and stringent communication and reporting in. The child needs to tell you where she's going, when, and with whom. Her cell phone should be on much of the time, so you can check in, and she needs to follow through with you about homework and chores. Be prepared for loud complaints and much eye-rolling, but stay your course, as the increased structure will provide a protection for your child in the long run. Try and link together responsible behavior with achievement of more privileges. So a good "yes" response to monitoring from your teen allows for more "yes" responses from you when she requests to do things (that are safe). In addition, if you are in a shared custody situation, you must find a way to agree on how to monitor your teen, or the child will manipulate things so she can go to whichever parents provides the least supervision.

## Recognize Early Warning Signs

One of the best ways to stop an addiction before it starts is to recognize early warning signs of unhappiness. Other sections of this book provide helpful lists of things to watch for in your teenager to determine how bad her addiction is. This list will show you what to look for to help prevent an addiction before it starts.

- Your child seems to lack solid friendships with peers.
- Your normally motivated child becomes apathetic.
- A usually mild-tempered child becomes explosive.
- A teenager who usually confides in you becomes secretive and silent.

**Fact**

It is an American trait to want more and get it faster. Watch for this factor in yourself and in your teenager's personality. Try some behavior modification games to teach him to wait and to develop some delayed-gratification skill. Make the reward something completely meaningful for having some patience—a special shared activity with you, tickets to a coveted concert, or something connected with a strong interest, perhaps a savings account toward a musical instrument.

### "But All My Friends Are Doing It . . . "

Your teenager may plead with you and exert considerable pressure to get you to approve something that doesn't seem right. This is where you have to remember that you're not a friend to your adolescent—you're a parent. This is the first important step in preventing an addiction. There may have been times in other phases of her childhood when the two of you enjoyed each other's company as friends, but those times are over, especially if you suspect that addiction might be creeping into the picture. If you are part of a two-parent family, elicit the support of your partner in drawing the line in terms of what is allowed and what is not.

Be prepared for your teenager to pull out all the stops with plaintive refrains about the other, cooler parents letting the group stay out late, have a sleepover with both sexes present, drive the family car, or any number of things that are more or less designed to make you feel inferior and defensive. Don't buy into it. You undoubtedly have done a good job raising your child up until this time, and that doesn't change overnight. Sometimes you can stop that behavior by saying you will call the other parent to verify that that person condones the particular thing your teen is ranting about. Usually the truth is flushed out at that point, as your teenager stops you, mortified that you would invade her social space in that way. Some parents have threatened to sit in class with their teenager, supervising tests or quizzes until the teen is done. Of course, the adolescent would avoid that at all costs, and manages to complete the home-work, even after saying nothing was assigned.

### ⓔ✴ Essential

Develop a strong vigilance and sixth sense about the availability of drugs at various places your teenager might go. Spend some time on the phone with other adults who know what goes on, and feel confident about taking a strong stance that protects your adolescent. You may take the brunt of outrage when you forbid the adolescent to go to a particular event that you feel is dangerous, but you both can weather the storm.

The all-night dance that "everyone" is going to strikes you as a possible rave, and although you don't want to deny your child the social experience, you want to protect him. If you keep the com-munication lines open, there might be a compromise that works for both of you. You might require that the child take a cell phone that is left on at all times and that he call you every two hours. You agree to stay awake at those times and hold him to the agreed-upon calls, with consequences if you don't receive the calls.

If one of those calls results in a request to drive some distance and get the child at 3:00 A.M., be willing to do it with no recrimi-nations or I-told-you-so's. It would be something to celebrate if this happens, an indication that the teenager is using good judg-ment to get out of a potentially dangerous situation and trusting you to help—to perform the role of a loving parent, even if it's inconvenient.

### Family Rules

If you discover that, in fact, your child has been involved with substance abuse, you have every right to tighten up the usual fam-ily rules with protection against further abuse in mind. Some typi-cal rules might be as follows:

1. There will be zero tolerance for drugs and alcohol.
2. Random drug testing will be performed.
3. Room and backpack will be periodically searched.
4. No discretionary money will be given to or kept by the teenager.
5. Any money earned is to be turned over to you and parceled out for basic needs.
6. No driving is allowed, except to school and to work.
7. No more partying is allowed, and all social activities are to be approved by you on a case-by-case basis.
8. The teenager is required to make restitution for theft and damage due to drugs and alcohol.
9. Cheerful participation in family activities is required.

You can decide, over time as the adolescent does well with these guidelines, if the two of you can negotiate for a bit more freedom. But it has to be earned.

## Counteract the Risk Factors

One way to curtail the likelihood of your child becoming addicted is to minimize the risk factors in his life and environment. This may take considerable effort, but it is worth it to safeguard your teenager's life and well-being.

Poverty is one of the risk factors for teenage addiction. You might not be able to make a larger salary or get a different job, but there are solutions that could positively impact your adolescent. Consider such measures as taking in a roommate, starting a small business on the side, or going to school yourself to learn a different trade. Is there another adult in the family who could get a job to improve the circumstances? In extreme situations, it might be worthwhile to think about having the teenager live with a relative who can offer a more wholesome environment and healthy activities. It isn't easy to consider such a step, as pride can get in the way, but sometimes a cousin, aunt, or uncle might enjoy mentoring a youngster.

Peer influence is a given force, but you do have a certain amount of control, especially during the young years. Try to capitalize on your teenager's passionate interests, and find groups and clubs that engage in those things. It might be a jazz band, a mechanics club, or aficionados of another culture, such as ancient Tibet. One young child loved sharks, perhaps not a typical interest for a girl, and her mother made sure she went to every shark exhibit at the local natural history museum. She was encouraged during face painting parties to paint a shark face on her own face, complete with large teeth. Another child likes to make his own illustrated books, and his parents encourage him to enter a public television story contest every year. He enjoys the outlet and meets other literary students at the final reception.

 **Fact**

If there are genetic predispositions to addiction in your family, talk openly with your teenager about this, even discussing the traits and addiction history of family members who have struggled. Maintain a watchful eye in these cases, realizing that there are genetic forces in place that you have no control over. Focus on what you can do, and remain alert.

## Dealing with Violence

Violence in the home environment is a common trigger for adolescent addiction. You and others in your home can talk about this and simply agree to stop fighting, especially having interactions that veer into physical violence. Some families might find this way of being together normal and acceptable, but it doesn't have to be that way. Some anger management classes could be in order, and a new household rule can be established that says no hitting, no matter what. If you learn that a particular relative or friend is abusing your teenager or anyone else in the family, simply forbid that person to be with your children.

In addition, be clear on your policy about guns. There is always so much news about accidental shootings among children. If there are tensions in the home and potential volatile outbursts, having guns on the premises can make the dangers even worse. More than that, an atmosphere of violence creates a climate that the adolescent wants to escape, and you don't want that escape to be into drug and alcohol practices.

### ✅ Fact

The "because I say so" used by your parents probably won't fly with today's generation of adolescents. Yes, you are the adult in the situation, but realize that teenagers, especially older teens, can be very clever in getting around you and finding a way to get what they want. For example, your son's incessant communication with friends via text makes it possible for him to quickly create a backup plan, if you have foiled his original one.

Within reason, exercise care and control of your teenager's role models. You have the right to limit time with relatives who might be a bad influence and to educate yourself about the music, games, and movies that your teenager likes. In any of these aspects of his world, are drugs, violence, rebellion, and/or cruelty made out to be positive things? Take the time to learn what and who is important in your teen's world, and do what you can to nudge it in a positive direction. Even if it involves spending money on travel, lessons, experiences, or social events that place your teen in a position of status with peers, it is worth it. The greatest danger facing your teen's future is developing substance abuse, and its cost will swamp the funds you otherwise would spend even if it is a sacrifice.

## Dealing with Special Circumstances

In the areas of stresses in connection with race, marginality, and prejudice, only so much is in your control, but you can seek out groups and sympathetic people to help form positive connections to counteract the negative aspects of existence. You might find associations on the Internet that could connect your teenager to others like her or clubs connected to city recreation departments. Your example of feeling good about your ethnic background and who you are in every way is the best antidote to risk that you can give your child.

If there is mental illness in the family, do everything you can to get supportive help for each person, including the person who is challenged. This means clearly and factually looking at the extent of the difficulty and access resources to assist in the situation. Try to notice if the mentally ill person and her needs take away from positive attention to your teenager, and do everything you can to counteract that tendency in the family dynamic. Make it your business to conserve health, well-being, and happiness, even if there are problems—including serious problems—in the family.

# Clean Up Your Own Act

Example is an important influence on children, and actions truly do speak louder than words. If you want your children to be addiction-free, it will help to look at your own life and see where you might tune up your behavior. Are you someone who *must* have a new car every year? Is that daily cocktail after work the high point of your day? Do you become riveted to certain stories or news reports, blocking out everything else in your life? How well balanced are the various aspects of your life?

One by one, look at each addictive substance and behavior and see where you stand with it. It might help to do some journaling on each one, to see where you are out of control. What would make you angry or frightened if taken away or if circumstances changed your access to that thing? Could you get through the weekend without your over-the-top Mexican dinner every Friday night? Where are you with phone and Internet use? Do any of your relationships suffer because of an addictive diversion? Do you fanaticize about the lottery and buy tickets that cut into the family budget?

If this kind of housecleaning makes you uncomfortable or extremely frightened, you might want to get a professional counselor or therapist to support you as you look at your own situation with addiction. Just as denial is an aspect of your teenager's addictive tendencies, it might be present in your own struggles to find equilibrium. Remember, anything can be addictive if taken to excess—talking on the phone, collecting specific things, bingo, reading, even achievement. The key is whether or not the behavior gets in the way of your life functioning.

## Share Family Stories, Especially Skeletons in the Closet

It can be helpful to a teenager to hear stories about other family members who have been addicted and what happened with them. This technique can be a way to educate your child about the effects of addiction, but only if the discussion is held in a friendly, nonjudgmental way. If your approach is in any way dictatorial or autocratic, the adolescent will tune out everything you say.

Perhaps there's a grandfather who struggled with alcoholism and suffered great losses materially and in relationships because of the inability to moderate or stop. Tell these stories kindly, but factually, emphasizing that you understand that the addiction is a disease and not under the control of the person drinking or using. Temper the stories with information about how much you loved and admired the addicted person. Be blunt and factual about the trajectory of the disease and the impact on lives around the relative.

## Share Your Own Experiences

If you had times during adolescence of using or abusing, tell those stories as well. Relate the facts of when you started, the effect on your life, what kind of troubles you got into, and how you felt about those experiences. If you stopped, share why you stopped and how. If your addiction progressed into adult years, share as much as you can about that. Let your teenager know what types of recovery you have gone through and which aspects you still practice.

These talks won't be in the vein of preaching or lecturing, but merely telling family stories, stories from which the adolescent can learn. If you want to, talk about the genetic aspect of addiction and how people in some families tend to become addicted to substances more easily and in higher proportions than those in other families. Keep the door open for future talks and be willing to answer questions if your teenager wants to think about it and come back to you. It most likely will not be a one-time discussion.

# Encourage Normal Adolescent Developmental Tasks

The teenage years are fraught with rapid change and volatile emotions, even under the best of circumstances. It's as if you're giving birth again, and you hope the result is a mature, functional human being. The teenage years are also quite demanding for the adolescent. Sometimes he feels like a child and wants you to indulge him and take care of him. At other times he wants nothing to do with you, as he wants to be a grownup. The following is a list of developmental tasks that should be completed by the time the person is into his early twenties:

- Learn how to maintain a household
- Learn how to drive and maintain a car
- Function well in romantic and sexual relationships

- Work steadily and maintain an income
- Learn how to manage money and budget for clothing, food, entertainment, shelter, car
- Develop a trade or make significant progress toward a profession
- Develop competence and experience in hobbies and activities that bring satisfaction
- Know basic health practices—how to stop serious bleeding, what to do when someone faints, how to call 911 or Poison Control

Adolescents who are doing well with these tasks can be given more and more freedom with the hope of launching into adulthood in their late teens or early twenties. Those who need more support can get it along with smaller increments of independence. Maybe the child can manage money for clothing and school supplies, but not the car. The parents can help at each stage of the way, supporting but not bailing the child out when there's been an agreement. A teenager needs to take care of certain aspects of his life on his own.

As much as possible, help the child without accusations when things have not gone as planned. Adults mess up, too, so simply help him look at the situation and make adjustments so that everything is covered. Perhaps he forgot to budget for the prom, which can be very expensive, or he forgot to get new tires, resulting in some inconvenient flats and drastically interrupted schedules. Perhaps there's an unexpected pregnancy, and lives have to be immediately reorganized—decisions made regarding who is going to pay for what and who is going to live where with whom. It is best to approach these problems with a level head. Remember that although you want your teen to take responsibility for his own life, he is still learning and will need support along the way.

# Listen to Your Child

Be alert for teachable moments, which will probably come every once in a while over a long period of time. These small discussions on important, relevant topics are better and more effective than one big lecture, which is probably what you had as a teenager. The teachable moments could be when a friend gets arrested for drugs, there's a terrible car accident, or a peer makes a suicide attempt. Check with your teenager around these times and be available to listen. Don't try to come across as any kind of expert. Just make it very clear that you love your adolescent and are there to listen and offer support and help.

## Be Open to Change

Perhaps there's a drastic change in your own family, such as a divorce or death. Maybe the main breadwinner is laid off. Children, even very young children, can sense when something is going on in the family, and it's easier for everyone if the truth is out. If there's a financial downsizing, let the child ask questions. More than likely they will be very basic: Are we going to lose our house? Will we have to move? Do I need to get a job? The facts of a situation do a lot to alleviate anxieties and fears.

Listen attentively and learn to ask open-ended questions. Open-ended questions are those that have a whole range of possible answers, unlike closed-ended questions that are answered with a yes or no. Some examples of open-ended questions could be as follows:

1. How do you feel about Grandpa's death?
2. What is it like for you to have lost your friend?
3. How do you feel about the school shootings in the news?
4. Which aspects of your life are most important to you right now? Which expenditures are non-negotiable in terms of your happiness and security?

5. How are you doing as you weigh your different college options or work options? What are the strengths and weaknesses of each possible scenario?
6. What can you do in this distressing situation to make things better? (You can ask this with regard to such situations as bullying, discovery of domestic violence or incest in a friend's family, or serious illness of a family member or friend.)

Attentive listening requires tolerance for silence and waiting. This is not the time to jump in and offer quick answers and solutions. You provide a great gift for your teenager when you sit quietly with her, giving her the time and dignity to gradually form the thoughts into articulation. The same thing happens when a friend offers to listen to you. Keep in mind that you have more experience when working through important junctures in your teen's life.

# CHAPTER 7

# The Normal Teenage Brain versus the Addicted Teenage Brain

Once you get past the moral impact of addiction, it is easier to look at the scientific and biological truths about brain function with reference to addiction. Experienced, intuitive mothers have said for generations that the addicted child was different, even as an infant, showing more sensitivity, more reactivity, and a shorter attention span than other children of the same age. The brain is sensitive and malleable during the formative years. Researchers are now finding that traumatic experiences in the childhood years cause brain changes, making the person more predisposed to addiction.

## Addiction Impacts the Brain

The adolescent brain is not fully developed and is vulnerable to substances and processes that could alter the course of its maturation. In particular, the prefrontal lobe evolves during the teen years, creating an adult who is able to put the brakes on behaviors that could have negative consequences.

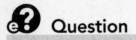 **Question**

**Why are adolescents more apt to develop addictions?**
The prefrontal cortex is the last part of the brain to develop, and so the immature brains of children and adolescents are less able to manage both the decisions involved in resisting addictions and the ability to chemically handle the addictions. Therefore, once an addictive substance is introduced into the adolescent's brain, the dopamine pleasure circuit tends to dominate decision-making.

In a well-balanced teenager, the pleasure circuits are tempered by the prefrontal cortex, the region of the brain that monitors logic, rationality, and decision-making. In addicted teenagers, the pleasure circuit overwhelms the prefrontal cortex; radiographic images even show that there are fewer than the normal number of membranes (when compared to a nonaddicted teen) connecting the various regions of the brain, making it difficult for the addicted teenager to understand when it's time to stop.

## Hijacking the Brain

The brain is hijacked when the addictive substance causes a chemical response to divert from the intended neural pathways and go directly to the pleasure receptors, especially those that produce dopamine. This occurs in the midbrain, and the behavioral result is that the person is highly motivated to get more and more of the substance. The midbrain is a less complex part of the brain than the frontal lobe; the midbrain controls responses to sensory information. The hijacking process is physical, as drugs take over the receptors, binding to them and changing the way the brain works—and not in a good way. In recovery, the brain can return to normal functioning, but it seems unusually susceptible to getting hijacked for the rest of the addict's life.

## Hallucinogens and Their Dangerous Impacts

Hallucinogens, such as LSD, alter the mental processes, distorting the perception of time and orientation, intensifying visions, and creating an exaggerated euphoria. An LSD trip may include drowsiness, numbness, nausea, trembling, and a general feeling of weakness. Promoters of LSD at raves say that the drug enhances the impact of lights and lasers. However, such enhancements can end up with a trip to the emergency room. For example, in one dreadful incident reported in Judy Monroe's book, *LSD, PCP, and Hallucinogen Drug Dangers*, a bright, funny student took LSD and decided that he could fly. His lunge from the seventh-floor dormitory window resulted in instant death.

## Alcohol's Effects

Alcohol alters brain chemistry, causing an imbalance of normal functioning, resulting in slowed speech, motor movement, and decision-making. Excessive drinking causes blackouts, when the brain acts erratically but later cannot recall what has happened normally. Serotonin is decreased with excessive drinking, creating the risk of depression and anxiety. Other chemical changes associated with drinking cause impulsivity, short attention span, and lower tolerance to pain. All these shifts in mental patterns precipitate more drinking, especially as tolerance increases.

 **Alert**

Joanna Jacobus of the Department of Psychiatry at the University of California–San Diego explains that the "go" system in a teenager's brain, the primitive brain structure, develops early but the "stop" system, the prefrontal cortex, takes longer to mature. The stop system cannot keep up with the go system in a teenager who is experimenting or moving into addictive behavior.

Alcohol affects the medulla, the section of the brain that regulates survival functions. Breathing and heart rate may become atypical. A person who drinks heavily ages more rapidly, especially males. Decreased blood flow to the medulla decreases memory, creativity, and problem solving. Death can occur from alcohol poisoning or hypothermia from alcohol intoxication, in addition to the more common accidental deaths. Overall, these mental alterations result in a less capable person, a tragedy for a teenager who is just barely starting out in life.

# The Monster on the Face

Patrick Martin, former addictions concierge at Aurora Las Encinas Hospital in Pasadena, California, describes the short-circuited response of the drinker or user who has moved into the addictions phase. "It's as if there is a monster on the face, and the monster takes over from that point." The addict is at the mercy of that force, and there is no turning back. Rationality is gone, and the only motivation is to keep drinking or using. There is no interest in consequence, even if the results are severe.

### When the Monster Takes Over

PCP (phencyclidine), also known as "angel dust," is a recreational drug that can be ingested, smoked, or injected. Users are especially vulnerable to life-threatening results, as the drug can cause violent outbursts, resulting in drowning, burns, falls, and accidents, indirect results of the effects on the body and brain. More PCP users die from their bizarre behavior than from the direct impact on the brain.

LSD has unpredictable results, and no one knows whether there will be a good trip or a bad trip. Sometimes the result is catatonia and complete detachment from other people along with repeated, nonsensical motions. Flashbacks, violence, confusion, suspicion, depression, and anxiety can be the results of LSD. Users of LSD report that the simplest tasks became enormously difficult, such as putting on shoes and socks. Students often miss classes and tests because of drug use.

### The Addiction Moves Into Highest Priority

As the addiction progresses, it takes over the brain and body, making continuing the supply the most important objective. Other important parts of the teenager's life are ignored—school, family, work, goals, and physical health. The user is more or less married to the substance.

### ⓔ Essential

A 2013 Yale University study showed that it takes at least three months of abstinence from addiction for the prefrontal cortex to return to normal functioning. Those who have only a month of rehab are at high risk for relapse.

Cocaine is especially sinister, as it can lead users to addiction after only one use. School and work are abandoned, and the only thing of importance is getting the next high. Some users move into dealing so they can afford to keep their supply moving toward them. After repeated use, more of the drug is required to reach the same level of euphoria. As the costs of the habit increase, the addict commonly resorts to theft, stealing from family and friends without remorse. The addiction has first place.

## Brain Chemistry Changes with Drug Use

The reasons so many drugs have such a powerful hold over the user is because they can actually change the chemistry of the user's brain. For example, according to David Sheff, marijuana blocks the inhibitors that control dopamine flow, making the smoker relaxed and calm. Unfortunately, the relaxation is so deep and ongoing that the person loses ambition, exhibiting what researchers call "amotivational syndrome," a condition in which the person does not have any drive to pursue meaningful activities or achievements. The average income of marijuana smokers is lower than non–marijuana users, and their IQs are eight points lower. The eight-point drop was for those who abused cannabis during and after their teen years, as measured from baseline at thirteen until thirty-eight, twenty-five years later. The drug use has altered their brain chemistry, a detriment to their health and well-being.

## Marijuana's Impacts on the Brain

Teenagers scoff at warnings that marijuana is habit-forming and dangerous. They say that everyone smokes, including good students, and that most of their friends enjoy edible marijuana in brownies, gourmet ice cream, scones, and barbecue sauce. There are even cookbooks that offer recipes for such delicacies as Ganja Granny's Smoked Mac 'N' Cheese.

Marijuana can indeed become addictive. Marijuana seems to affect the higher-level cognitive processes. One study shows impaired communication between regions of the brain, even in adolescents. The changes might be subtle, but they increase over time if the teenager continues using pot. A 2007 study done by Dr. Susan Tapert, which used children as young as twelve who smoked marijuana, compared brain function of users with a control group of nonusers. She observed changes in brain tissue, along with memory loss and a diminished ability to concentrate in those children who did smoke marijuana. Marijuana impairs attention, coordination and balance, reaction response, judgment, and the ability to organize complex information.

## Designer Drugs and Dangerous Chemical Reactions

Many new designer drugs, like "bath salts" and "pep spice," are available to teens today. These designer drugs are incredibly dangerous, and can cause different effects in the brain than other addictive substances. Many designer drugs, like bath salts, are similar to amphetamines in that they cause stimulant effects of the body. Bath salts can cause hallucinations, paranoia, heart palpitations, and nausea, and are associated with violent outbursts, heart attacks, organ failure, and suicide. Bath salts users experience reduced sensitivity to pain and accordingly can end up injuring themselves. In these extreme situations, the brain has abandoned its usual function of providing protective and useful feedback to the person.

### ✅ Fact

Education regarding the brain processes and what happens with addiction is quite helpful to those interested in stopping the addiction. Information about the parts of the brain, triggers, and the mechanics of addiction help the addict intelligently participate in the process of arresting the disease.

Pep spice, or synthetic cannabis, mimics the effects of cannabis on the body; these designer drugs are sprayed on herbs and marketed under popular brand names like K2. Spice products are also labeled as "herbal incense," and the effects of the drugs are much more potent and powerful than traditional marijuana. Severe effects can include blurred vision, hallucinations, psychoses, vomiting, seizures, high blood pressure, and heart attacks.

## Electronics Can Change the Brain, Too

Spending an inordinate amount of time playing video games also alters the brain chemistry. Generally, there is a good balance of alpha and beta waves in your brain. The alpha waves are those present when one is relaxed, perhaps daydreaming, or imagining a faraway scene. The beta waves are associated with emotion and creativity. Spending hours playing video games reduces the amount of beta waves rather quickly, and the player is almost entirely in alpha mode, almost as if hypnotized. This altered state of consciousness can induce long hours of playing, which can cause problems in other aspects of the player's life. After the session is complete, the teenager is likely to be irritable, distractible, and unable to relate well with other people. The brain does not function well when long hours of alpha activity are experienced while awake. Adolescents who play games excessively have lower levels of beta activity, even when not playing games. This aftereffect inhibits satisfying activities in other parts of life.

## ⊖ Alert

According to author Jane Velez-Mitchell, half of the teenagers today send fifty or more texts during a typical day. One-third send more than 100 texts a day, and this is while they are in school. There have been news stories of parents getting physically assaulted during attempts to take away a teenager's phone.

Although research into cell phone use is in its infancy, it is known that time on a cell phone excites the cortical area of the brain, the portion that regulates movement and language. A teenager who spends hours texting is honing into a different reality, not one that concerns his actual environment and requires eye-to-eye communication. Social skills can suffer incredibly when children spend hours texting and e-mailing instead of interacting with one another in person. It is known, as well, that the mere presence and appearance of a computer screen can put a person rather quickly into the alpha state—as quickly as within thirty seconds.

## The Pleasure-Reward System

In general, addictive substances and behaviors reward the person with the release of dopamine and serotonin in the brain. With increased use, the circuits are taken over by the pleasure neurotransmitters, and the addiction is more or less set, making turning back a challenging proposition. (Paradoxically, marijuana at first causes pleasure and relaxation, but heavier use over time increases the presence of depression, actually decreasing the pleasure experienced.)

The user perceives the high level of pleasure as a strong reinforcement (a strong reward), not realizing that increased amounts are required as a tolerance is developed. Even if warned, the teenage addict is unlikely to change her mind because of the strong feeling of reward associated with the addiction. The drugs of abuse cause lasting, severe, and drastic changes to neurocircuitry, unlike that in normal activities such as sex, love, video games, athletic competition, or music events. This kind of information is often distorted by the drug addict to rationalize his or her addiction (of course, that is expected).

 **Fact**

Dr. Pierce Howard states in *The Owner's Manual for the Brain* that the pleasure circuit begins in the amygdala, then goes to the anterior cingulum, and then to the temporal lobes. In its entirety, the pleasure circuit is called the medial forebrain bundle, or in ordinary language, the "hedonic highway" or "pleasure pathway."

## The Roles of Dopamine and Serotonin

Dopamine and serotonin are the chemicals most often associated with addiction. Dopamine is the major reward that chemically propels the user to keep on using, in spite of negative consequences. Dopamine brings such a sensation of pleasure that the addict will do anything to keep it flowing.

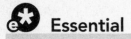 **Essential**

The human body has not caught up to the virtual age. We are designed for fight or flight, and a life lived on the screen does not provide for physical outlets for energy. The brain cannot automatically distinguish between danger on the screen and actual physical danger.

According to Linda Simmons, gaming, a popular activity among teenagers, causes a rush of dopamine, bringing on a high similar to that of any other addiction. The player wants to keep playing for longer and longer lengths of time. The teenager experiences euphoria and is unable to stop, continuing with the games again and again.

In the nonaddict, drugs cause a surge of dopamine, but the flow returns to normal and the floodgates of dopamine close after the person stops using drugs. In the addict's brain, the floodgates of dopamine open and stay open, making the person want a continued supply of the substance to instigate continuous surges of dopamine. The brain is malfunctioning at this point, and even a small amount of stimulating substance opens the floodgates, which the user perceives as a strong need for the continued supply of the substance. The receptors become less and less capable of processing the drug, tolerance builds, and damage becomes permanent.

Marijuana goes to the brain quickly, releasing dopamine, which causes the feeling of euphoria and being high. The user perceives this as a reward, although other consequences are negative, such as decreased ability to perceive sensory stimuli and the distortion of the senses. Coordinated movement is diminished, and the immune system is compromised.

Writer David Aretha notes in his book *Cocaine and Crack* that cocaine, like other drugs, releases dopamine in large quantities, creating a need for more cocaine in order for the brain to create more of the euphoria. Cocaine creates a high that lasts a long time, as the dopamine stays in the receptors after the cocaine hits. However, the high is followed by a crash—irritability, depression, and exhaustion—and the brain is unable to manufacture dopamine on its own at the needed level after cocaine distorts its processes. Methamphetamine and other amphetamines (speed) also act directly on the dopamine system, causing an intense and long-lasting rush.

 **Alert**

During the healing process from addiction, the brain's altered patterns can be rewired, as the recovering addict gains awareness of her thinking patterns that led to addictive behavior. The process is slow, but a motivated person with support can do it. This repair can be done if the addiction has not gone on for too many years.

Ecstasy stimulates the flow of dopamine and also affects serotonin, the neurotransmitter that regulates appetite, perception, sleep, and mood. LSD affects serotonin, inhibiting and exciting the part of the brain that regulates sensory perceptions, which is why LSD creates hallucinations, mood swings, and distorted perceptions.

## Permanent Damage: The Brain Is Rewired

At the stage of permanent damage after years of use, radiologists can see differences in the brain of the addict when compared to the nonuser. There are vacant spots, and the connectors between the sections of the brain are weak. These physical changes cause impaired judgment, forgetfulness, weakened cognitive function, and slower mental processing. At the earlier stages of damage, it is sometimes possible to regain function if drinking and using has stopped, but it may take months or years. With advanced stages of addiction, it is impossible to regain the earlier healthy functions. Even after such a recovery, the addict's brain is very susceptible to return to the problematic pattern that sustained chemical dependency.

### ✅ Fact

Addicts and recovering addicts are especially vulnerable when undergoing surgery. They often become re-addicted to the drugs used during the healing process. One sober alcoholic with many years of sobriety had surgery on his hands and wrists, and started using OxyContin addictively following surgery. Soon marijuana was added to the mix, and he was no longer sober.

## Lapses in Memory

According to David Sheff, addiction causes changes in the hippocampus region of the brain, the place that regulates memory. Marijuana smokers especially lose memory function and the ability to concentrate as the myelin sheath erodes away. Studies comparing marijuana smokers past and present with nonsmokers of marijuana show distinct differences in the appearance of the brain, with more "holes" and empty areas in the images of the pot smokers.

Marijuana affects reading comprehension, math ability, and the ability to recall pertinent details during problem solving. Response time is slowed, which makes riding a bike or motorcycle, rollerblading, or skateboarding especially dangerous. Pot smoking combined with alcohol increases the likelihood of car crashes. Marijuana affects the nervous system and spinal cord, increasing the chance of accidents and overdoses, especially when combined with other drugs.

Cocaine also affects memory and learning, as it works in the prefrontal cortex and amygdala, the seats of those processes.

## Poor Judgment

Susan Tapert's studies, mentioned in an earlier section, showed that heavy marijuana use in adolescents is associated with poor planning abilities, slower bodily movement, and poorer skill in general thinking. It is believed that the maturation process of the brain is interrupted by the presence of marijuana, and that tasks that should be relatively simple become demanding for the teenager, requiring more time and involvement of more parts of the brain than would be the case in a nonsmoker.

Marijuana users believe they are functioning well in their own subjective sense, while objectively they are quite impaired. Marijuana makes it difficult to accurately assess how much time has passed. Response time is affected, which is especially dangerous for driving, and some smokers may experience paranoia, anger, anxiety, and hallucinations, making rational decision-making quite challenging. Adolescents who smoke marijuana while pregnant may be surprised to find out that their infants can be born prematurely with breathing and nervous system problems, and have health and learning difficulties when older.

## Inability to Consider Consequences

Teenage marijuana smokers are more likely to quit difficult or time-consuming tasks than complete them. This inability to consider long-term consequences affects the smoker's opportunities in school and at work, because everything becomes slower and just too hard. Eventually, personal relationships suffer, as the parts of the brain that control the emotional maturation processes are arrested. Fred Holmes, who counsels teenage addicts, comments that if an eighteen-year-old comes into his office seeking help to stop marijuana or other opiates, his social-emotional development is likely that of a twelve-year-old. This difficulty creates problems with thinking things through. He doesn't have the experience of a teenager who had gone through the mastery of normal developmental tasks. He's like a child in an adults body.

**Fact**

The human brain is remarkably plastic from birth and is able to adapt to change well into the twenties, when full maturation usually occurs. It was once thought that full development happened at approximately age twelve, but now it is thought that healthy teenagers continue to mature into their twenties. Drug addiction interrupts that maturation process.

Teenagers who use marijuana and are sexually active are less likely to use protection and to remember limits for their behavior. As their response time is slowed, they may not act quickly if they find themselves in a dangerous situation.

# CHAPTER 8

# The Substance Addictions

Usually when addiction is discussed, people think of having an addiction to substances, especially alcohol and drugs. It has only been in the last few decades that behavioral addictions have gained attention, requiring a broadening of the idea of addiction. Addictive substances are ingested into the body, usually orally, although sometimes through the nose or intravenously with a needle. Of course, there are behaviors associated with the using processes, but most of the focus when thinking about substance abuse is on the substance and what it does to the body.

## Alcohol

Although your focus is understandably on the present and what to do about your teenager who drinks, it helps to realize that alcohol has been a part of civilization since thousands of years before the time of Christ. As early as 7000 B.C., China fermented rice, honey, and fruit to make alcoholic drinks. Early brewers in India made alcohol from fermented wheat, fruit, and sugar cane. By 1700 B.C., the Greeks had created a wine industry, serving it at every possible opportunity—with meals, at religious events, and for medicinal purposes.

Alcohol is probably the longest-standing addictive substance and is deeply entrenched in cultures around the world. Some

American families could not imagine a wedding or a funeral without the bar and free-flowing drinks. The following checklist, paraphrased from A.A.'s *A Message to Teenagers: How to Tell when Drinking Is Becoming a Problem*, provides some questions for the teenager who wonders if she's crossed that line:

1. Do you drink to escape problems?
2. Do you drink when you are angry?
3. Do you drink alone?
4. Are you slipping at school and at work?
5. Have you tried to cut back and failed?
6. Do you drink first thing in the morning?
7. Do you chug down your drinks?
8. Are you more forgetful than you used to be?
9. Do you cover up how much you drink?
10. Are you getting into more trouble?
11. Do you get drunk, even when you didn't mean to drink that much?
12. Are you proud of how well you hold your alcohol?

### Essential

Certain patterns of thinking may accompany excessive drinking—"I have to finish all of this since I started it," "It's important to treat everybody and stay until everyone is ready to go home," and "I can't get through this without drinking. Anyone would drink with everything I have going on in my life." Experienced people in Alcoholics Anonymous say, "Don't pick up the first drink," and joke about it being a disease of the elbow.

### Fake IDs

The age of legal drinking has gone up and down in the United States as influenced by various cultural forces. Up until the middle of the 1990s, the usual legal age was twenty-one. Changes were made around the time of the Vietnam War, as various groups protested that it was not right that an eighteen-year-old could be drafted to go into combat but could not vote or take a legal drink. Some states lowered the drinking age at that point to eighteen.

Numerous Internet sites show visitors how to make a fake ID or how to order one from them. Before the advent of the Internet, enterprising college students used to create small businesses for themselves by making IDs for others. These days the cost is up to $150 for an ID, and according to the advice given on those sites, if a bouncer or bartender raises his eyebrow, sometimes a little extra cash under the ID will smooth the way. Children and teen-agers these days are remarkably adept with scanning and photo manipulation. It's even possible to buy holographic paper online, and bitcoin payments allow completion of the transaction without a paper trail.

## Binge Drinking

Binge drinking is more prevalent among males than females, and is often associated with college students and frat parties. Binge drinking is defined as a male drinking five or more drinks during a two-hour period and a female drinking four drinks during that same time period. Most binge drinkers are twenty-six years old or older and are not actually addicted, merely choosing to binge from time to time. Driving while under the influence is highly correlated with binge drinking, and almost all of the drinking of those under twenty-six is during binge-drinking episodes.

## Periodic Drinking

Periodic drinking is somewhat like binge drinking, but the episodes are further apart. The drinker has likely moved to the addiction stage of the disease, but does not believe he is an alcoholic because he goes for long periods of time without drinking. This type of drinker goes on what is commonly known as "a bender," getting completely drunk and out of control, after going as long as several months without drinking.

 **Alert**

Food cooked in alcohol is not alcohol-free when it is served. Some of the alcohol may cook off, but the remaining traces may be enough to trigger a craving in a recovering alcoholic. Alternatives are available in a book by chef Liz Scott, *The Sober Kitchen*. Also, during holiday parties it is courteous to offer nonalcoholic drinks, as one never knows how much rum might be in Aunt Gloria's famous eggnog.

### Hazing and Rites of Passage

In recent years there have been more and more news articles about students who die from drinking rituals on college campuses. Some fraternities have been fined or closed down because of such dangerous practices, but such incidents still frequently occur. Adolescents are so bent on being accepted by their group of choice that they do unhealthy or even life-threatening acts to gain membership into the desired group.

The site *www.elementsbehavioralhealth.com* reported several terrible hazing happenings in the late 1990s. For example, two new pledges to the Sigma Alpha Epsilon fraternity at Louisiana State University lost their lives because of heavy drinking. Paramedics who were called to the scene to care for sick pledges were unable to wake four of the pledges. One of the pledges was in cardiac arrest with a blood alcohol count of .588. (This breaks down to the equivalent of twenty-one shots an hour.) Another nearly died from the alcohol poisoning that took his friend's life.

Leslie Baltz, a student at the University of Virginia, died after falling down a flight of stairs after drinking. Your teenager would benefit from hearing these reports, as they portray in clear facts what happens when too much alcohol is consumed.

# Methamphetamine

Methamphetamines are man-made drugs that are smoked, inhaled, or taken orally or intravenously. They proliferated during the 1980s, starting in California and the Southwest and progressing across the rest of the United States as users discovered how easy it was to cook the substance in their basement or garage. The ingredients are inexpensive, and the euphoria is intense. Rock methamphetamine is called "crystal meth." Injected or snorted meth takes effect as quickly as within two minutes, and the effects last up to twelve hours.

Meth labs turn into big business, as each meth user is said to teach as many as ten people how to make the addictive substance. The three primary ingredients in crystal meth are pseudoephedrine (the active ingredient in Sudafed), iodine crystals, and red phosphorus (the substance on the side of a matchbox). Numerous other substances are used to cut or extend the crystals, including Epsom salts or Ritalin.

## Question

**What are tweakers?**
Tweaking is the last phase of a meth binge, characterized by anger, agitation, paranoia, and obsessive actions. The tweaker may not have slept or eaten for days, but does not feel hungry or sleepy. Tweakers may hate everybody and become excessively violent, attacking those who annoy them, even their own children. Such tweaking might be followed by a crash, sleeping for up to three days, falling into a coma, or even death.

Meth production is dangerous to everyone involved, as the process can be explosive. When members of a meth community have small children, chances for neglect and physical injury are high. Chronic users of meth can experience auditory and visual hallucinations, violent outbursts, paranoia, and even death. In the book *Methamphetamine and Amphetamines*, author David Aretha tells the story of one anguished mother who lost three teenagers to meth use. All three had been good students in high school, but turned to meth in college. They became withdrawn and volatile around their parents and then completely ignored them. One Mother's Day was especially miserable as the mother of the adolescents drove around her city trying to find them. One was in a hospital, recovering from an overdose. Another was in jail, and a third was not found. The third one was twenty, the mother of a child of her own, and on the streets somewhere. This kind of devastation is not what any mother expects.

# Tobacco

Smoking is one of the most difficult addictions to stop, and the earlier a teenager starts, the more likely it is that the child will be a smoker in her adult years. It is only recently that advertising targeting children and teenagers has become illegal. It is possible that you remember the character of Joe Camel, who portrayed indirectly the attractions of cigarettes. Joe Camel is not so cool anymore, as the tobacco industry has somewhat been reined in by the government and the American public.

There are many reinforcements to the process of smoking—physical, psychological, and social. Almost everyone has heard stories of older people who are hospitalized for emphysema, on oxygen, and still wanting their cigarettes. It is estimated that about 25 percent of American teenagers smoke cigarettes, still responding to iconic images of movie stars of the past who made it seem sophisticated and grown-up. Who has not seen the familiar image of James Dean and responded to his look of detached savoir-faire?

Nicotine is highly addictive, and it acts as a stimulant on the central nervous system, causing smokers to feel like they need a cigarette to wake up, to calm down, or to focus on a task.

### Essential

Smoking prematurely ages the skin, causing people to appear twenty years older than their actual chronological age. Other bodily systems are harmed, including the heart and lungs, and smoking is harmful for the fetus in a pregnant woman, often resulting in a lower birth weight and other challenges.

Peer pressure plays a large role in an adolescent wanting to start or to continue smoking. If everyone in the chosen group is smoking, she will want to smoke, as well. Dr. Teitelbaum, author of *Addiction: A Family Affair*, offers the following checkpoints to think about, if you wonder whether your teenager is smoking:

- Performs poorly at school
- Does not identify with the school
- Is isolated from other students
- Performs poorly at sports events
- Has little hope of going to college
- Needs a job to support the habit
- Skips classes
- Uses other illegal substances
- Is under pressure at home and school
- Enjoys hiding the smoking habit

Nicotine is at the top of the difficult-to-beat drug list, and if you can prevent your teenager from starting or help him to stop, you might be able to prevent a lifelong addiction and an early or especially painful death.

# Marijuana

Marijuana is widely smoked among teenagers today. In some groups, it is impossible for an adolescent to fit in unless she smokes pot. Peer pressure is very real and a powerful component of risk for starting marijuana. Some research indicates that half of the students graduating from high school have used marijuana at least once. Some have become daily users.

There has been much debate about whether marijuana should be legalized, as it is so widely used across a wide age span. Some states have legalized it for medicinal purposes, setting up clinics for those who are able to get a prescription. Some signs that your teenager might be using marijuana could include the following:

- Dizziness and difficulty walking
- Acting silly for no reason
- Bloodshot eyes
- Forgetfulness
- Sleepiness
- Evidence of pipes, bongs, rolling papers
- Odors, including incense and other fragrances, in the bedroom or on clothing

Children turn to marijuana for a variety of reasons, sometimes to cope with stress, loneliness, or depression. Anger and anxiety lead teenagers to pot in search of something to alleviate the discomfort. At first it seems that getting high provides an outlet, but, of course, it's not a long-term solution to the challenges of life. As with the other addictions, role models who smoke pot and close family members who smoke pot are strong examples that precipitate teenage experimentation.

## A Word of Caution to Divorced Parents

If you and your partner have divorced, you may have differing opinions and values when it comes to marijuana use. If your ex occasionally uses or is addicted to marijuana, choose your words carefully when discussing these behaviors with your child—you should avoid sounding judgmental toward your child's other parent in order to prevent your child from feeling like a pawn. If your child is being impacted by your ex's use, if your child has access to marijuana when with your ex, or if you feel your child is in danger in your ex's presence, do not hesitate to break the silence, both with your teen and with the proper authorities. Your child's safety is your number one concern.

## 🛑 Alert

If you feel that your ex's marijuana use has become a danger to your child or family, you may be able to get a court order for testing, particularly if you are dealing with custody proceedings. Be sure to have evidence to support your claims: If your accusations are not based on truth, custody may not be granted in your favor, and you could face punishment for false accusations.

## Social Pressures for Marijuana Use

Much of marijuana abuse occurs simply from falling in with the wrong crowd. People of all ages want to belong, and if parents notice that their child or teenager is falling in with a group that uses marijuana, it is possible, at least in the early stages, to divert the likelihood of addiction simply by forbidding the child to see those people and constructively offering alternatives for a social life. This move will be met with loud protests, as every adolescent wants to be independent in every way, especially socially, but if you catch your child at such a crossroad early enough, you might successfully divert her into a better social milieu.

# Cocaine

Cocaine emerged as a popular drug in the 1970s, when it seemed to be everywhere. A subculture developed that included musicians, concertgoers, athletes, and business executives, all of whom used cocaine. It was so widely available that a status of "almost legal" became associated with cocaine, and some of the high-end users laundered drug money in real estate. One of the sad things about the cocaine popularity is the result of now older boomers who are addicted—if they are still living, considering the risks of coke.

 **Fact**

Coca-Cola appeared in 1886, and its nickname Coke hinted at the secret powerful ingredient. Coke was first sold only in drug stores. It was thought to be completely harmless, a pleasant drink that provided a refreshing lift to the spirit. Though cocaine was removed from the formula in 1903, the drug was still legal until 1914.

The shift to crack cocaine in the late '80s changed the image of cocaine, as more reports of death reached the media. Cocaine use has diminished since the 1980s.

Cocaine releases dopamine in large quantities, resulting in the effect of euphoria and changes in the brain's reward system. Tolerance develops quickly, and the user needs more of the drug to attain that initial high. It can be snorted, injected, or smoked, with each method varying somewhat in the time it takes to create the high and in how long the high lasts. Cocaine's effects on the body can include dilated pupils, coronary problems, headaches, high blood pressure, and digestive problems. Coke users are at high risk for sudden death because of cardiac arrest, followed by respiratory arrest.

# ⓔ❗ Alert

The prisons are clogged with those who have been incarcerated for crack cocaine offenses, resulting in what some criticize as racial profiling. The laws have been harsh concerning crack cocaine, which is more likely to be used by blacks compared to whites, who favor powder cocaine. Jane Velez-Mitchell says, "Hundreds of thousands of poor minorities are serving sadistically long terms in prison for low-level, nonviolent drug crimes," sometimes leaving behind families fending for themselves while the prisoner loses the prime of his life behind bars. In 2010 a Fair Sentencing Act was passed that lessened some of the disparity.

# Prescription Drugs

Prescription drug abuse is a national problem, with the number of people who have unintentionally overdosed overtaking the number who overdosed with the crack cocaine surge of the 1980s. Though prescription drugs can help manage pain for many, they can also become very addictive.

According to Dr. Teitelbaum, there are three types of prescription medicines—opioids, central nervous system depressants, and stimulants.

## Opioids

The opioids are regarded as narcotics, making a person feel better in general, especially after a surgery. The opioids are related to a chemical found in the opium poppy, which interact with the pain perception circuits in the brain. They are effective as painkillers but become dangerous if the correct dosage is not followed. The medications included in this class are Vicodin, OxyContin, morphine, codeine, Darvon, and Demerol. In recent years adolescents have increasingly used Vicodin and OxyContin. For persons with a predisposition toward addiction, using the opioids for pain following surgery can create a vulnerable situation with the temptation to use more than is prescribed or to get more than one doctor to give a prescription.

The opioids are dangerous alone and especially when combined with other substances, and it is always recommended that dosages be followed exactly. The opioids cause a brief feeling of euphoria, a sense of well-being, possible drowsiness, stomach problems, and breathing problems. Those who cook down the pills and snort or inject the drug subject themselves to a higher risk of death, as the drugs are designed to be long-acting. The quick release into the bloodstream can cause heart failure and respiratory arrest.

### 🅔❗ Alert

A teen fad called "cabinet parties" works like this: Adolescents raid their parents' medicine cabinets, looking especially for Vicodin and OxyContin, and take them to a party where they dump them all into a bowl for group consumption. The mix is called "trail mix," and the process is called "pharming." Kids dip into the bowl, taking the pills by the handful. It is recommended that medicines be locked up and thrown out when outdated. Better yet, be a good example and minimize reliance on medications for getting through life's difficulties.

Addiction to the opioids is a serious matter, and even your child having a dependency (taking more than the doctor prescribed) should get your attention. Heroin is an opioid that is easy to stay addicted to because it is not very expensive, and can be smoked or injected. Going off the opioids abruptly is not a good idea without medical supervision. Withdrawal symptoms include muscle and bone pain, sweats, cold flashes, digestive upsets, and insomnia, and are probably the worst to have to endure psychologically, causing many to relapse within days or week.

## Central Nervous System (CNS) Depressants

These drugs are commonly prescribed for anxiety, sleepless-ness, and other symptoms. Usually they are intended for short-term use, often in conjunction with therapy. Some of the CNS drugs are Nembutal, Valium, Ativan, Klonopin, Temazepam, and Xanax. Some of the newer sleep medications are Ambien, Sonata, and Lunesta. None of these should be combined with alcohol or other medications or drugs. The wrong combination can be fatal. As with the opioids, withdrawal symptoms can be severe, and the person should not stop the prescription without medical assistance.

## Stimulants

These medications are used to treat ADHD as at low-dose ranges they can help compensate for its neurologically based inat-tentive, impulsive, and hyperactive symptoms. At addictive-dose ranges, the stimulants operate by increasing dopamine in the brain, the chemical associated with attention, pleasure, and move-ment. If more is taken, addiction is likely, as the brain patterns are disrupted, creating euphoria, paranoia, and agitation.

# Heroin

Adolescents who abuse prescription drugs often progress to her-oin, as it is cheaper than prescription pills on the street. Heroin is highly addictive, with a strong potential for overdose and death. Heroin produces a sense of euphoria, loss of critical thinking skills, and a feeling of heaviness in the arms and legs. Usually the rush is followed by a period of drowsiness. The coming-down phase brings with it the desire for more of the drug. Tolerance grows, and the user wants more and more to reach the same level of high. Street heroin may be laced with contaminants that are damaging to the brain, liver, kidneys, or lungs.

Withdrawal from heroin is severe, lasting up to three days or a week, and can include the following symptoms:

- Severe craving
- Kicking motions
- Cold flashes
- Vomiting
- Diarrhea
- Sleeplessness
- Pain
- Restlessness

 **Alert**

Health conditions associated with heroin abuse are infectious diseases such as AIDS and hepatitis, lung problems, kidney disease, collapsed veins, spontaneous abortion, and death from overdose.

The terms "cold turkey" and "kicking the habit" come from the process of heroin withdrawal. Some addicts who go off of heroin experience withdrawal symptoms for months. Heroin treatment often includes therapy in which the participants learn behavioral and thought management and ways of living in a healthier manner.

## Ecstasy

Ecstasy is a man-made drug that contains the stimulant qualities of meth and the hallucinogenic qualities of mescaline. It is a dangerous drug with potentially long-term effects, lasting up to seven years. Ecstasy causes mood, appetite, and sleep disturbances. The psychological effects include confusion, depression, and anxiety. Ecstasy can cause hyperthermia, resulting in liver, kidney, and cardiovascular system failure. Death can be the result. Ecstasy is a popular party drug because it is cheap, and the euphoria it produces lasts for four to six hours.

# CHAPTER 9

# The Behavioral Addictions

It has only been since the 1980s that the behavioral addictions have been recognized as serious conditions. Since many of the behaviors are considered hobbies or pleasant pastimes in moderation, some people have difficulty accepting them as true addictions. Instead, the addicted people will say that they can stop if they want to. Some research has shown that many of the brain patterns and alterations are the same with the behavioral addictions as they are in substance addictions. Slowly, the general public recognizes that certain behaviors can, in fact, pose a threat to well-being. The important criteria are similar to those indicating substance abuse—experiencing a high (and withdrawal), deterioration of close relationships, significant loss in school and job performance, and building up of tolerance. The evidence is still preliminary and suggestive, but the parallels are useful to consider when planning an intervention.

## Internet

During his career, Steve Jobs envisioned a computer in every home. In a few short decades, that vision has become close to reality, as the average American spends three or more hours online every day. Activities for teens might include e-mailing, shopping, chatting, scrolling through Facebook, and playing games. This seems harmless enough, but when the time spent takes away from the rest of life, it could become an addiction. Linda Simmons, author of *The Everything® Health Guide to Addiction and Recovery*, suggests the following checklist to determine if you notice your teen's Internet use has crossed the line:

- Preoccupation with the Internet
- Defensiveness when someone suggests cutting back
- Jeopardizing school and work
- Isolation from real-life relationships
- Physical symptoms, such as carpal tunnel syndrome
- Lies about how much time he spends on the Internet
- Using the Internet to escape difficult emotions and situations
- Inability to cut down on Internet time
- Feelings of guilt about the amount of time spent online

The anonymity of the Internet is seductive, and many teenagers develop alternate identities and lives for their online interactions. Gathering images and telling false stories about oneself takes a great deal of time and energy, effort that perhaps could be better spent on learning how to be an adult and function in life. However, these days everyone texts (according to your teenager), and it seems so very important to the adolescent to maintain those intense conversations and keep abreast of the dramatic ups and downs of the relationships. It seems odd to an adult to see a group of teenagers walking, each of them looking down at a phone instead of talking with each other, but it is natural to them.

Cyberbullying has arisen with the advent of the Internet, and there have been sad cases of suicide in which teenagers have been so brutalized by their peers that they simply could not continue living. Some Internet users say that being online puts them in a different state of mind, much like meditation, and everything else recedes into the background. In fact, studies show that the combination of the alternate reality and the screen induce an alpha state, much like hypnosis.

## 🔔 Alert

Excessive screen time dovetails with the other addictions—shopping, gambling, partying, obsession with celebrities, and looking for pharmaceuticals or recipes for mixing drugs. As the Internet is a level playing field, there is little regulation, and almost any information is available, whether or not it might be considered healthy or desirable.

Sometimes you might forget what life was like before Google, when researchers used dictionaries and encyclopedias. Now just typing a few words or phrases into a search box brings up the desired information. The challenge with teenagers is that they lack the ability to discern the truth for themselves. They can veer wildly from "It's true because it's on the Internet" to "Nothing on the Internet is trustworthy," as there's always another equally valid opinion.

One of the most important things for teenagers to learn is how to develop relationships. The Internet creates a sense of false intimacy, and a teen can feel satisfied with his online socializing, even if there is no true interaction. Large numbers of people, not only teenagers, come home from their typical day to immediately go online and see what is happening there.

# Gaming

Video games can be an entertaining diversion and an introduction to various topics and interests, but taken to excess, too much gaming alters the brain chemistry, leading to life problems similar to the other addictions. Too much screen time places the gamer in an artificial waking alpha state while decreasing the beta activity, leaving him irritable and unable to focus, even after the computer is turned off.

Simmons offers the following checklist in order to evaluate whether playing video games has become a problem:

- Does game time cut into other life functions?
- Do thoughts about video games dominate your mind, even when you're not playing?
- Do you stay up late at night playing games?
- Do you cut classes and miss work in order to play games?
- Has gaming language seeped into your real-life conversations?
- Are you acting and thinking like your favorite gaming character?
- Do you have more online gaming friends than in-person friends?
- Have you unsuccessfully tried to cut back on the amount of time you play video games?

As with the other addictions, gaming leads to a state of euphoria, requiring more and more online time to maintain the state of high. It becomes important to play one more time, raise the score, and have one more chat about the game.

### ⊘ Fact

Writer Jane Velez-Mitchell tells of a case in Reno, Nevada, where a couple in their twenties were so consumed with World of Warcraft that their two small children were starving and near death when social workers intervened and took them to the hospital. There was plenty of food in the house; the parents were simply too involved in their games to notice that the children were hungry. The parents pleaded guilty to child neglect, and the children were placed in foster care.

There is not much research available on gambling among teenagers, but it is well known how devastating that particular addiction can be. As with the other addictions, the gambling becomes the main focus of life; jobs are lost and relationships dissolve. It has been shown that compulsive gamblers show the same types of brain activity as those who engage in any other addiction.

# Pornography

Pornography addiction begins with simple curiosity, sometimes looking at magazines and videos found in a parent's drawer. It is natural for young adolescents to be interested in sex and the opposite sex, as one of the developmental tasks for teenagers is to form healthy intimate relationships. It is natural to enjoy looking at images of sexually attractive people.

The line of danger is crossed when teens connect sexually online with adults, sometimes unknowingly. A normal sexual relationship brings all sorts of benefits that enhance every aspect of life. When pornography addiction takes over, the addicted person usually is unable to maintain a healthy in-person relationship. Fears and inability to bond come to the forefront, and the porn addict is unable to commit to a real person.

## 🅔 Alert

Pornography creates the illusion of a relationship, making the individual feel that someone is there who cares, and this substitute might seem like enough if the person comes from a family without trusting, loving relationships. A teenager who comes from such a barren background may feel unworthy of a real-life relationship.

In today's sex-laden society, it is impossible not to encounter triggers of sexuality and images of both sexes. Like food addicts, the porn addict has to learn to function in the midst of so much stimuli. For concerned parents, there are numerous computer blocks available for filtering out the types of sites that you don't want for your teenager, and there are support programs for partners and family members of the porn addict.

**Fact**

Along with porn, there are Internet predators that make it their business to create a false identity and try to form online relationships with young people, eventually luring them to an actual meeting in person. The Lifetime movie *Defending Our Kids: The Julie Posey Story* (2003) graphically tells the story of a daughter's experience with an online predator. The mother works with the police, develops a teenage persona, and engages sufficiently online and in person in order to catch the man.

Author Linda Simmons offers the following helpful checklist in order to determine whether or not pornography has moved into an addiction for your teen:

- Do sexual thoughts monopolize your thoughts and behaviors?
- Is it a struggle to stop viewing pornography?
- Have your school work and job suffered because of pornography?
- Do you spend more money on porn than you can afford?
- Do you become impatient with television or magazines that don't offer porn?
- Do you use pornography to escape difficult emotions?
- Do you keep your pornographic activities secret?
- If asked about using pornography, do you feel angry and defensive?
- Do you keep using porn in spite of negative consequences?
- Do you feel that you will never gain control of the pornography inclination?

As with the other addictions, the addict develops tolerance, requiring a progressively stronger fix. In the case of porn, the user requires more and more and more quantity, eventually moving into extremely disturbing content in order to achieve the desired state of arousal. Unlike in real life, the Internet provides unlimited numbers of sites and images, making it possible to indulge in the addiction for hours. This leads to moral bankruptcy and feelings of intense shame.

## Texting/Sexting

One of the things that teenagers need to realize is that once an image is on the Internet, it's out there forever. Sometimes in the intensity of the moment, an adolescent will not think about the ramifications of posting or texting a provocative photograph. Sometimes it will be done on a dare or to get a desired relationship. Girls are vulnerable to pressure to do sexual things in order to be loved and cherished. Just as in the old days when teenagers argued about getting to first or second base, girls today may be asked to send a certain type of revealing picture in order for a boy to decide to date her.

 **Essential**

Rapid-fire texting, with its unique language and icons, may slowly replace the nuances of in-person relating, and eventually teenagers may lose the ability to relate in person. Of course, parents have to inform their adolescents about such dangers, which is a challenge, as teenagers feel invulnerable.

It seems that too much texting removes a person from the reality of life. In the dreadful case of fifteen-year-old Josie Ratley of Florida, a texted comment to Wayne Treacy about his brother's suicide resulted in the boy driving to where she was waiting at a bus stop after school, viciously attacking her until she nearly died. His texts to friends before the attack bragged about how he was violently going to do her in. Wayne was charged as an adult with attempted first-degree murder and went to prison. One wonders whether some adult intervention and face-to-face mediation might have averted such a tragedy.

There are specific Internet sites that cater to teenagers who wish to say mean things about their peers, taunting them about what they wear or who they might want to date. This type of activity, like the mean texting, amounts to cyberbullying, which can have disastrous results. You may recall the case of the Long Island girl who committed suicide in 2010 after receiving vicious taunts. It is difficult to understand, but the taunts continued, even after her death. One follow-up posting was, "She was obviously a stupid depressed—who deserved to kill herself . . ." This almost incomprehensible detachment from the emotional/social reality of the situation is an example of what happens with an excessive amount of electronic relating and not enough in-person skill.

Writer Jane Velez-Mitchell offers some possible motivations for whipping out the iPhone and sending that next message:

1. Self-importance
2. To escape uncomfortable emotions
3. To indicate to those in the vicinity that they are not important to you
4. To feel that high of reading the next incoming message
5. To people-please by answering very quickly
6. To put off something else that needs to be done
7. To sense a connection in spite of feelings of alienation
8. To imply that you are busy and popular
9. To fill up downtime

In terms of sexting, if you suspect that your child, especially a daughter, is sending sexual images of herself, do what you can to have an honest talk with her. Of course, it can't come out of the blue. The groundwork of positive relations and good communication has to be there. Let her know that you see the many positive qualities that she has to offer to a relationship, and none of them requires taking off her clothes. This can be in the same vein of the sex talk that most parents have with their teens as they move through puberty, helping them to make intelligent decisions about what to do and not to do sexually.

 **Fact**

The most important thing is that your child values herself as a whole person, and you are key to that equation. If you value every aspect of yourself as a beautiful person without demeaning sexual activity, you can authentically persuade your daughter to consider the same. It helps to not make it so much about the sex, nudity, and partial nudity, but about what she wants in a relationship and what she has to offer.

In extreme situations, you, as the parent, have the right to withdraw phone privileges, just as you have the right to ground the teenager or take away the car keys, especially if the adolescent still lives at home and you are paying for the phone. As with any addict whose substance is removed, you will hear outraged protests, and the teen will act as if she will die without a phone. The two of you, perhaps with an impartial mediator, can create a plan to rebuild responsible phone privileges. Perhaps your teen can regain privileges by doing more chores around the house, by taking care of a younger sibling while you do errands, or perhaps by having planned person-to-person contact with people who need it, such as the elderly or underprivileged children.

## Spending and Shoplifting

As with other addictions, the key point in determining whether there is a spending addiction is to figure out if the spending is getting in the way of close relationships and of functioning well in life. If shopping and spending is a daily preoccupation, especially if it veers into excessive online shopping and credit card debt, then there's a problem. It helps to remember that the longing for the next material thing is a symptom. There's actually an underlying unease that craves something, anything, to make the gnawing feeling go away. Of course, advertisers *want* everyone to get out there and buy the next thing, even if it means standing in line at 4:00 A.M. on Black Friday. Too much spending causes problems in relationships, especially if secrets are kept from others who would be affected by the bills. People who shop addictively get the same kind of high as other addicts. The dopamine flows and the shopper is off to the next store.

Jane Velez-Mitchell offers a checklist that can help in determining whether or not your teen has a problem with too much spending:

- Does shopping hurt you financially?
- Do you shop to escape your emotions?
- Do you imagine that the next purchase will make your life complete?
- Do you buy things to make yourself look important?
- Do you have second thoughts after you take a purchase home?
- Is your closet full of clothing with the tags still on them?
- Are you envious of things that your relatives, friends, and neighbors own?

### ⓔ❗ Alert

As with all the addictions, there are online and in-person support groups to help. Debtors Anonymous helps people overcome the habit of spending more than they earn and shows them how to create a more balanced life.

It is helpful to teach your teen how to distinguish between a true need and a trumped-up want pushed on him by the media or by social pressure. People who base their whole worth as a person on material things end up in a vulnerable position. There are many people around the world who are happy living the simplest of lives. It is humbling to see the joy in human relationships among these wise people who might not know where the next meal is coming from.

In the United States, many homes have more televisions or computers than people. Does it need to be that way? Sometimes less is more. The boomer generation is the first in decades that has not planned particularly well for retirement. Some boomers learned their shopping habits during the beginning of the 1950s and then into the 1960s when the media and advertising came into play as a force in shaping American tastes. Frankly, many boomers would like to continue spending rather than think about being old.

### Why Your Teen Could Be Shoplifting

Some teenagers create an experiential high by getting into competitive games built around shoplifting. Often they do not really need or want whatever is taken, and may even have the money to buy it at the time of stealing. Peer pressure can provoke a teenager to steal, just in order to be a member of the group. In these situations, it helps the adolescent more in the long run if the parent does not bail him out. It is tempting to do so to take away the blight on the family's image, but a better learning experience comes with going through the process of arrest, jail time, and working to repay the value of what was taken.

## Gangs—Preoccupation with Crime

If you watch the news, popular movies, and television shows, it would seem that crime has a lot of appeal to young people. In some urban areas, teenagers are so hungry to belong to a group that they affiliate with gangs in order to have a "family." Some gang rituals can be quite horrendous, requiring that the aspiring member rape or kill someone in order to belong to the tribe. Often the gang member has not had an opportunity to see positive role modeling at home or a chance to foster close relationships with relatives. A certain context has to be present in order for gang membership to look appealing.

 **Fact**

Organizations such as Homeboy Industries and Homegirl Cafe in Los Angeles take in gang members, teach them food preparation skills, send them to farmers' markets to sell the goods, and reap the reward of grateful youth who are off the streets, earning money, and learning a trade that will support them as adults.

As with other addicts, the person who ends up going down this dark road develops a dulled consciousness, performing heinous acts against elderly persons in wealthy neighborhoods who were likely to have cash and expensive possessions at home. Members of the gang would simply overpower the victims, murder them, and take what they could get. This is difficult to fathom for any rational, empathetic person.

## Overeating or Undereating

Some would place the overeating addiction in the substance abuse category, as food is ingested in an addictive way. However, it has such a strong emotional and behavioral dynamic that it is useful to think about it in this category. Like workaholism or being on the Internet, a certain amount of this behavior is needed to survive. In other words, a compulsive overeater cannot go off of food cold turkey and abstain forever. Often the overeater does not know why she overeats. The emotional components are deeply buried, even to the person, but the over or undereating seems to be the solution to feeling uncomfortable in any way. Binging is a secret behavior, one of the few parts of the person's life in which she feels in control and cared for. Overeating has long-term negative consequences, not only physically with associated diabetes, heart disease, and joint problems later in life, but socially as well.

 **Fact**

> Undereating (anorexia nervosa) is a complex, perplexing disorder. More girls than boys have this disorder, going to extremes of exercise, eating very little, eating only one type of food and neglecting other normal nutrients, binging, weighing several times a day, and even re-sisting food if hospitalized for treatment. Sometimes in these cases it is suggested that the entire family undergo therapy.

In anorexia, there is sometimes a component of control pro-voking the destructive aversion to food. For a troubled anorexic teenager, sometimes refusing to eat is the only volitional behavior available to her. It is also a way of making herself the focus of the family, especially the worried parents. Anorexia nervosa is a seri-ous condition; some patients die, as they have a completely dis-torted image of their bodies, feeling fat and continuing to refuse food when they weigh as little as 80 or 90 pounds. In some ways this extreme emphasis on thinness relates to the pressures of the media mentioned in earlier chapters.

## Relationship and Sex Addiction

Unless there are healthy role models in the parents and within the extended family and community, it is a challenge to learn how to form healthy relationships in today's American culture. The divorce rate is high, and teenagers experience a loss of basic secu-rity when the family comes apart, even if they know intellectually that both parents love them. Entertainment and popular culture extol addictive love and finding the meaning of existence in that other person. With the hormones raging anyway, the adolescent years can be tumultuous in terms of forming relationships with significant others.

As with the other addictions, a person who is a love addict goes through enormous mood swings and behavioral aberrations, according to whether or not the object of his affections is interested. The brain chemistry in love addiction is much like that of the other addictions, with huge amounts of dopamine released when all is well and a depressing emptiness when it's not. It sometimes is shared in the rooms of Alcoholics Anonymous that a dangerous trigger for possible relapse is the disappointment of a failed relationship.

**⊕ Alert**

Sex addiction is a driven disorder where the person will risk everything in order to keep the fix available. It *seems* like it's about sex and wanting to be with another person who will provide that, but as with the other addictions, it can be rooted in deeper emotions that momentarily subside when engaged in sex. Sex addicts can spend enormous amounts of money to keep the addiction going, meeting partners at different points during the day to the detriment of work and normal obligations, not to mention relationship losses as significant others discover the hidden addiction.

Sex addiction goes hand in hand with pornography and excessive time on the Internet as meetings are arranged with a stream of anonymous new partners. As with the other addictions, the sex addict craves the high and will go to any lengths to achieve it, engaging in high-risk behavior in order to keep the desired level of excitement.

# CHAPTER 10

# Treatment Options for Your Teen

Once it is apparent that you have to do something with your teenager who seems to be on the way to becoming an addict, it is not easy to think rationally about your choices. More than likely, emotions are running high, and it is a challenge to make good decisions with so much going on. Try to take a few breaths, stay calm, and think about what might be best for your adolescent given your specific circumstances. Most people conventionally think of treatment as inpatient treatment, and that is one choice. Another choice is outpatient treatment. Another choice is therapy with a private counselor who specializes in adolescents. And another choice is the twelve-step approach. Some programs might offer a combination of these approaches, plus a sober-living halfway house as a transition back to mainstream life.

## What to Expect in Rehabilitation Treatment: It's Not One Size Fits All

It will help you to gain some control over your situation if you take time to inform yourself of the range of treatment possibilities in your area. (It is also helpful to look further abroad if you are willing to seek treatment options in another state.) Appendix B gives you some starting points to consider. If you have contacts within the professional community where you live, ask questions and seek referrals about what is available and what is recommended. Keep an open mind and realize that each program will be different. Ask questions to determine whether the treatment facility will mesh with your child's personality, and speak to others who have used a particular facility. Carefully weigh your options.

## Teens Are Not Merely Small Adults

Most professionals in the field do not recommend that an adolescent seek rehab in a program tailored for adults. Teenagers tend not to share openly under these circumstances, and they are likely to be in the minority, trying to fit in as best they can among adults who are struggling with unemployment and child support issues. Teen addicts may have authority figure issues, and if they are strongly outnumbered by people quite a lot older, it can turn out to be an isolating, unhappy experience. Or they may just leave.

## A Checklist for Youth Programs

The book *Inside Rehab* by Anne Fletcher is a valuable resource for parents considering rehab programs for an adolescent, both for a broad overview and for specific points to consider in connection with addicted youth. Fletcher suggests that the parent ask what types of assessment are used in the program being considered and how the program is tailored for teens. You deserve to know the qualifications of the counselors and what types of therapies are offered. If your teenager has other coexisting problems, inquire about how those needs are addressed. How are medications handled, and what is the general philosophy of the program? What would a typical day look like?

You might want to inquire about the staff/client ratio and to what extent the family will be involved. Does the program offer exercise, recreation, creative outlets, individual therapy, and group therapy? Inquire about the rules and the consequences for breaking the rules. Will your teenager have choices, and if treatment falls within the school year, what is the provision for classes? Will credits be transferrable back to your teenager's home school?

Fletcher recommends that you ask whether the sexes are commingled or treated separately and whether residents are divided according to the severity of the addiction. To what degree can the resident mix with the opposite sex? You have a right to know who the other clients might be. You have a right to know how minorities are treated and to what extent they are present in the program. Some programs have a provision for gay clients to have private rooms.

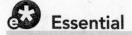 **Essential**

> As a concerned parent, you will want to consider the following points: Will your child be pressured to share deeply personal things in a group session? What will be the extent of communication with the family, and will that be by phone or e-mail? Ask how, and how often, your child will be allowed to be in contact with you. If a personality conflict occurs, can your teen change counselors?

You should also find out about the program's policy toward relapse while in the facility and what education the residents receive to handle possible relapses. In terms of aftercare, find out what you can about follow-up, continued outpatient contact, alumni gatherings, and referrals to community resources.

Find out if the facility takes the residents to twelve-step programs in the community and if there are twelve-step program meetings in house. Is drug testing a part of the program, even after the program is completed? The length of treatment can vary, and you will want to know how long the adolescent's treatment is expected to be and what the deciding factors are for the type and length of treatment.

Fletcher recommends that you boldly ask about the effectiveness of the program. Will it, in fact, meet the needs of your teenager, and why? It might be helpful to talk with other parents whose children have been in the program to determine what their experience has been. If you want, you can ask for the names of other parents who have expressed a willingness to be contacted by people interested in the program.

## Outpatient Treatment

Not every addict needs to be hospitalized; in some cases, outpatient care is quite adequate. Dr. Scott Teitelbaum suggests that parents weigh inpatient versus outpatient treatment with the following thoughtful points:

- Is detox needed, and are intense withdrawal symptoms expected?
- Are there any other medical conditions present that could complicate early treatment?
- Are there any coexisting emotional/psychiatric conditions that require consideration in the treatment plan?
- How much readiness does the adolescent seem to feel? Keep in mind that most addicts deny the seriousness of their illness.
- How great is the relapse potential?
- What is the recovery environment like at home? Are there positive influences for recovery support?

 **Fact**

One of the common complaints about inpatient programs is boredom. Twenty-four hours a day is a long time to be anywhere, and time can weigh heavily on your adolescent unless there is a lot of support for doing fulfilling activities. One advantage of outpatient treatment is that the teenager's life remains somewhat normal with the usual activities with the additional focus of treatment work.

Outpatient treatment does not get as much publicity as inpatient rehab, but in actuality, according to Fletcher, as many as 87 percent of clients under the age of eighteen are treated as outpatients. For teens or young adults involved with the legal system, many localities offer Drug Court. These programs use the legal system to ensure compliance with mandated outpatient treatment. For the most resistant young people, this may be the only way to get them to cooperate in a recovery program.

## Medical Approaches to Adolescent Treatment

Generally, a medical approach is considered when there is the possibility of a severe detox and all the risks that go with that. Withdrawal is the process that the body goes through when the substance or behavior is stopped, and the bodily reaction can be severe. Medical supervision monitors the bodily processes in an effort to keep the client safe. Some hospitals have a detox unit and can refer the addict to an inpatient program after the withdrawal symptoms subside. Sometimes detox can occur on an outpatient basis, especially if the home environment is safe and supportive. The client checks in at the clinic every day. For teenagers with mild to moderate abuse, this can be quite adequate—and is less expensive, as inpatient medical detox can cost as much as $2,000 a day.

Some medically supported detox programs offer medications to alleviate the withdrawal symptoms and support the bodily processes. If this is what you seek for your teenager, take the time to inquire about the specifics in order to avoid re-exposing your child to potentially addictive substances.

Linda Simmons recommends that the following categories of people seek a medically supervised detox program:

- Anyone with a severe, longstanding addiction
- Those addicted to heroin, meth, OxyContin, Xanax, or Vicodin

- The elderly
- Pregnant women
- Those with co-occurring psychiatric conditions
- Those who recently drank excessive amounts of alcohol
- Those with little support in the home environment
- Anyone who has previously experienced severe withdrawal symptoms

There are three FDA-approved medications for alcohol dependence in adults: Antabuse, acamprosate, and naltrexone. These and other medications can be used in treating select patients, but their potential benefits need to be carefully weighed against risks. Bupropion and Chantix can be used to treat nicotine dependence, while methadone, Suboxone, and naltrexone can be used to treat opioid dependence. Other medications find use in mitigating withdrawal, lessening symptoms, and providing a bridge to recovery. However, in considering these options, each individual situation needs to be carefully evaluated by the attending physician.

Most rehab programs for teenagers will have a physician or psychiatrist who is on call as a consulting professional. Whichever way the rehab starts—through the ER, check-in at a rehab center, or a weekend in juvenile detention—if withdrawal symptoms are there, a physician will be in attendance. It is not safe nor wise to allow severe suffering related to drug withdrawal. There is no value in enduring a horrible experience to prevent future relapses.

## Financial Considerations

In recent years more insurance companies have been covering drug and alcohol treatment. If you have this type of coverage, check to verify the amount of copay and whether there will be any delay in the payment. If your family qualifies for Medicaid, ask your chosen facility or outpatient program whether Medicaid is accepted as payment and for what length of time. Most communities have rehab programs that are run on a sliding scale of payment. Ask questions at every step of the way and take notes so you can remember what was said in each conversation.

Some high-end programs with luxurious accommodations cost up to $2,000 a day, and if this is something you're thinking about, really consider the expenditure. Ultimately it will be up to your teenager whether or not she becomes clean and sober. A rehab facility can provide a good environment and educational support, but in the end, it is your adolescent's choices that determine her future as a sober person or one who continues to behave as an addict. In other words, a drastic change in the teenager's perceptual outlook has to occur before the result is a clean and sober individual. The context for that can be in a minister's study, in your own home, at a camp, in a hospital, or in a rehab facility. This is not like buying cosmetics from Amazon. It is not possible to purchase recovery per se; the actual recovery happens within the addict. It may feel like you can buy recovery, and you may want to, but what you are buying is a set of circumstances that you sincerely hope will support your child's own internal processes.

## How to Find a Good Therapist

Sometimes you have exhausted your inner resources and need assistance in coping with teenage addiction. Mental health clinics often offer services at a nominal fee. Social service agencies, as well as marriage and family therapists, may be of assistance. Clinical social workers often work as a part of a team. Certified or licensed drug and alcohol counselors (CDAC, LDAC) are also very involved in dealing with addiction. Psychologists and psychiatrists offer help, but the expense will be greater. When you meet with a counselor for the first time, ask lots of questions and try to determine whether you really feel comfortable with that individual. It's your prerogative to ask the counselor about her level of education, her specialties, and whether she has experience with adolescent addiction and the specific issues you face. Investigate your insurance coverage and determine what documentation you will need for reimbursement.

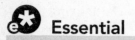 **Essential**

> Damage to the brain can heal with treatment and recovery, but it is slow, and those working with the recovering addict need to understand the parameters of the addict's capability. One counselor noted that if meth addicts were given short, fifteen-minute sessions, they did a lot better than if expected to engage for an hour. Many recovering addicts are quite sensitive to anger and will become more likely to relapse if confronted in an antagonistic manner.

Do not hesitate to shop around a bit and ask for referrals from friends and from addiction and mental health professionals in your life. The fit has to be correct in order for your teenager to make progress. Insurance may or may not cover therapy, but can you place a financial value on mental health for your teenager and your family? Is it equal to a new TV or an upgrade on your car? A luxurious vacation?

In the short term, the therapist will try to tackle the immediate issues connected with the adolescent's addiction. Then, the therapist usually begins to work on a long-term treatment strategy. The long-term strategy can involve looking at some of the underlying causes, risk factors, and patterns associated with using, and giving your teen the skills he needs to function better without escaping into addiction.

### Individual Therapy

The ultimate goal of individual therapy is to help adolescents to unlearn negative patterns of behavior and to learn better ways to relate to others so that the relationships in their lives can be more intimate, enjoyable, and rewarding, along with goal setting and learning new strategies for solving life's problems.

### ❓ Question

**What is the best kind of therapy for a teen addict?**
The success or failure of therapy depends less on the type of therapy used than on the relationship between the therapist and client. In any therapy, patients can learn, maybe for the first time, that they can safely express anger, or any emotion, with their therapists without the risk of rejection or fear that the therapist will stop treating them. Secure and comfortable in the relationship, these teenagers are then able to continue to discuss intimate secrets and painful issues that were locked away and previously not shared with anyone else.

Individual therapy sessions are designed to turn the mirror inward and allow the person to better understand what it is that drives him to addiction, and to help him to find ways to better cope with them.

Individual therapy usually has three stages:

- It begins with the client and therapist going over specific thoughts or feelings in detail.
- The therapist and client work on identifying distorted views.
- The therapist works with the client to entertain new, undistorted ways of thinking and behaving.

Each week the therapist will likely give the client some specific homework assignments.

### Psychotherapy

Another approach to individual therapy is the method originated by Freud: psychoanalysis. Classical Freudian psychoanalytic therapy is not used as frequently today as other styles.

Psychoanalysis based on the psychodynamic model has changed somewhat since the time of Freud, but basically the Freudian model states that emotional disorders are based on inner unresolved conflicts between different aspects of one's psyche—the id, the ego, and the superego—or, more simply, between the conscious and unconscious mind. The goal of individual psychodynamic therapy is to reduce these conflicts, and in doing so, to modify the personality of the individual for the better. It might be possible for this type of therapist to uncover the hidden insecurities precipitating the addictive behavior. The therapist takes a less active role in this form of therapy. He remains fairly quiet and relies on the teenager to reveal increasing amounts of distress buried in her subconscious.

Dreams are an important part of psychodynamic therapy. Freud believed that many subconscious conflicts are revealed in dreams. In this type of therapy, therapist and client will discuss dreams to gain insights into their meaning and what they show about the patient's inner struggles. Psychodynamic therapy can run from one year to two decades. This approach would be the exception rather than the rule in treating adolescent addiction.

## Cognitive Behavioral Therapy (CBT)

The basic idea of cognitive behavioral therapy is to get the teenager to recognize and identify untrue beliefs and negative behaviors, and replace these beliefs and behaviors with healthy, positive ones. The basis of this therapy is that our feelings and thinking play major roles in the way we behave and interact with people and the world around us.

The goal of cognitive behavioral therapy is to get a person to realize that while she cannot control every aspect of her life and the world around her, she does have power over how to interpret and choose to deal with people, events, and objects in the environment.

With addiction, the thought patterns and feelings that cognitive behavioral therapy is trying to change are those of impossible expectations for the self and others along with escape. In order to deal with these destructive thoughts and behaviors, cognitive behavioral therapy begins by helping the client to see her problematic beliefs.

This first stage of the therapy is to get the person to understand how thoughts, feelings, and situations contribute to negative behaviors. This can be a tough process, but when the therapist can break through the client's defenses and gain her trust, the self-discovery and insight that are essential to the treatment process can be achieved.

The second stage focuses on the actual behaviors that are making life miserable for the addict and those around her. This stage can be especially difficult, as the client tends to believe there is nothing wrong with her behavior, and if those around her are taking offense, it's simply because they are too sensitive, out of touch, or even jealous. However, through intense cognitive behavioral therapy, an addict realizes that not everyone shares her worldview and that her actions are harmful.

In the third and last part of the process, the client begins to learn and practice new skills that can be used to get different outcomes in real-world situations. Role-playing, including role reversal, has been shown to be an effective technique. In these role-plays the therapist can get the person to see that there are many ways of relating to people and situations. Specific language will be used in the role-playing to bring about new belief statements and new thought patterns, such as "I can feel angry without drinking." Cognitive behavioral therapy can be a challenging and rewarding method of treatment.

## Perspective of Psychiatrists and Psychologists

Psychiatrists are MDs with a specialty in psychiatry, while psychologists hold a PhD or PsyD in psychology. Both do therapy and conduct research. Most states require that the psychologist do a supervised internship and gain licensure. Psychiatrists have attended medical school and studied further in the areas of assessment, diagnosis, treatment, and prevention of mental illness. Psychiatrists are able to prescribe medications, while in most states psychologists cannot.

Sessions may be shorter with a psychiatrist. Some psychiatrists earn more money prescribing medications than doing therapy. Psychologists are more likely to do testing than psychiatrists. You can expect that a psychiatrist will have a more scientific approach and perspective, and a psychologist will be somewhat broad in perspective. A psychiatrist is more focused on the physical aspects of the brain—chemical imbalance, the actions and interactions of the abused substances, and the drugs prescribed for recovery—and the psychologist with behavioral aspects of addiction. Of course, it is human to think that you know your child best, and that no one else can help your teen the way you can, but the most important thing is that your teenager gets the type of help that you and she want.

 **Fact**

Addiction can be thought of as a defense mechanism for coping with difficult circumstances. A learned behavior can be unlearned, although it will take great effort.

The teenage client has heard admonishments from many sources already and may tend to tune out any professional who also admonishes. The aim is to uncover the roots of the addiction and focus on what is needed to feel loved, cared for, and completely okay without being drunk or spaced out. Some clients, regardless of age, have kept their imperfections secret for such a long period of time that they will stop therapy when the counselor gets close to the core of the matter.

# What Happens after Treatment?

Regardless of which type of treatment you choose, there will be months and years of follow-up. The initial treatment in rehab does not cure the problem of addiction. In some ways it is a time-out for all concerned, to help turn around the Titanic so the addict can start some new behaviors aimed toward a better way of life. Pragmatically there is no way to solve the addiction problem in a month or even ninety days, regardless of how complex and multifaceted the program might be. Addiction recovery is a physical/emotional/mental/spiritual program that requires a lifetime of diligence to arrest the urges and monitor the precipitating factors.

In past times a certain degree of confrontation was accepted as a part of intervention and treatment, perhaps in some way to break through the strong denial of the addict. However, as peer relationships are so important to adolescents, as well as extreme sensitivity to perceptions of the opposite or desired sex, it is now thought unwise to have heavy confrontational sessions in a group setting. Such a setup can embarrass an adolescent to the extent that she might be tempted to skip sessions or leave the program.

There will be some follow-up actions that can vary according to the type of treatment you have chosen. You might expect continuing counseling for the teen and your family, physical checkups, group sessions, drug testing, and twelve-step programs. Depending on the severity of the addiction, you might need to monitor your adolescent's social interactions, Internet and phone use, completed homework, and allowance spending, as all can be lost in the blink of an eye if the teenager is not truly motivated to remain clean and sober.

# CHAPTER 11

# The Twelve Steps Approach

The Twelve Steps approach for recovery from Alcoholics Anonymous has become well known and rather mainstream in recent years. Because of the power and universality of the steps, as well as the fact that the meetings are more or less free (a basket is passed for a voluntary donation), it is a recovery option you should explore for your teen. If your family has experience with the Twelve Steps program, you will already know how to utilize the program to support yourself and your family as your teenager finds his way with his own program.

## History

Alcoholics Anonymous was founded in 1935 by Bill Wilson, a stockbroker in New York City, and his friend, Dr. Bob, a surgeon from Akron, Ohio. Both men were severe alcoholics and could not find any relief through the treatments available at the time. Bill had had medical treatment and had spent time in various sanitarium environments to dry out, but nothing seemed to work. The two of them discovered that if they visited other alcoholics who were trying to get sober, the act of helping and telling their stories had the effect of keeping them sober themselves. Soon the lives of Bill and Bob and their wives, Lois and Anne, were filled with meetings in strangers' living rooms and gallons and gallons of coffee.

**Fact**

Stepping Stones, the historic home of Bill and Lois Wilson in Katonah, a few miles north New York City, is open to visitors who are interested in the founders of A.A. and Al-Anon. You can browse through the books in the bookcases, sit in the kitchen among Lois's teacups, and look through the memorabilia upstairs, which is where Lois had her first Al-Anon office. You can also sit at Bill's desk in his writing cottage, the place where he wrote A.A.'s *Twelve Steps and Twelve Traditions* and *As Bill Sees It*. Lois's flowers grace the pathway and landscaping around the house.

Lois started Al-Anon in 1951 to assist the friends and family of the alcoholics, as it seemed that those people close to the alcoholics had plenty of problems of their own. She used the same Twelve Steps of A.A., adapting the wording slightly to make them suitable for Al-Anon. She used her upstairs as the office for administration, and as the fellowship grew, offices were rented in New York City and a corporate headquarters was built at Virginia Beach, Virginia. Alateen, the companion program for teenagers affected by a family member's drinking, was started in 1957.

## Success Rate

Considering how deeply the Twelve Steps approach is embedded in rehab and recovery programs, it is surprising that there is little literature on the success rates of teenagers who follow the Twelve Steps. The studies that are available tend to focus on the adolescents who finished a treatment program, leaving out those who left the treatment centers. Of those studied, 30 to 40 percent were still abstinent when checked at various points throughout the study. Steve Sussman reported these findings in *Evaluation & the Health Professions*, stating his belief that the figures were overly optimistic because of the dropout factor.

Teenagers who continue to attend Narcotics Anonymous or Alcoholics Anonymous are two to three times more likely to remain clean and sober, especially if they attend two meetings a week. According to Anne Fletcher in *Inside Rehab*, most teenagers do not attend a Twelve Steps meeting, and if they do, they tend to drop out over time. One study shows that of those who were attending meetings at the conclusion of their treatment programs, only one-third remained over a longer period of time. In general, the dropout rate for teenagers is high. Those who attend any treatment program show a dropout rate of about 50 percent during the first ninety days. Adolescents who have an adult take them to their first meeting and introduce them to others in the group tend to have a higher rate of retention.

## Identifying Success Rates

There is no definitive research that shows quantitatively how successful the original Twelve Steps program and other programs compared to those based on the Twelve Steps. Claims range from only 5 percent to up to 90 percent. Of those who stay in Alcoholics Anonymous in a committed manner, the success rate is about 30 percent. As in all treatment programs, many do not stay, and there is no research on why they leave or what their sobriety success might be. According to David Sheff, the whole idea of what success is in recovery is quite subjective. Does it mean sustained abstinence for six months or a year? How are relapses figured in? Do people self-report or are drug tests required? As attendance at A.A. is generally voluntary (except for court-ordered cases), it is easy to see that definitive research would be hard to come by. People come and go in A.A. and all the twelve-step programs.

David Sheff assumes that the situation is one of self-selection. People who attend A.A. and like it tend to stay. Those who stay are more likely to accept the camaraderie, support, and help of the more experienced members. The ones who stay are motivated and tend to become involved in "step work," as well as service within the organization. The step work in the Twelve Steps program involves working on each of the steps in a slow, involved way, sometimes on a specific issue and sometimes overall in a person's life. Sheff observes that no one knows why the general twelve-step programs work at all, and surmises that its success might be due simply to offering a safe place where a troubled person can join others who can understand his problem and are interested in his story. One member said that before A.A. no one had ever listened to her, and she had a strong need to be heard. People listened at the meetings, and her sponsor listened to her challenges and her written fourth-step inventories.

## Specific Groups That Can Help

Alcoholics Anonymous is the oldest and largest twelve-step program, and other groups have adapted its model to various addictions and problems to the point where hundreds of such groups now proliferate, especially in large urban areas. Others that are most related to teen recovery might be Narcotics Anonymous, Cocaine Anonymous, Adult Children of Alcoholics, Al-Anon, Alateen, Crystal Meth Anonymous, Debtors Anonymous, Gamblers Anonymous, Heroin Anonymous, Marijuana Anonymous, Nicotine Anonymous, Overeaters Anonymous, Sex and Love Addicts Anonymous, Smokers Anonymous, Sex Addicts Anonymous, and Survivors of Incest Anonymous. Many of these programs have corresponding programs for the friends and family of the person who is addicted. Attendance at these groups can be enormously helpful in finding information, understanding, and support while helping a teenager through the recovery process. Everyone in the recovery rooms has "been there," and there will be no judgment, no matter what your teen's story may be. Many of these programs are available online and over the telephone.

## Al-Anon Can Help You

Al-Anon is especially helpful for the parents of addicted teenagers, as everyone in the room can empathize with the sadness and futility of seeing a loved one continue on a self-destructive path. Their literature contains a wealth of helpful information about the nature of alcoholism and offers concrete suggestions for how to deal with the troubled person without going crazy yourself. There are parents' meetings in urban areas, where people will absolutely identify with the sorrow and challenges that you face. Members of Al-Anon, as well as the other twelve-step programs, develop very close friendships and talk to each other frequently between meetings, as well as get together for social occasions. Some of those friendships last a lifetime and are sometimes closer than relationships with blood relatives.

# Alcoholics Anonymous for Young Adults

The International Conference of Young People in Alcoholics Anonymous (ICYPAA) was founded in 1958 as a way of assisting young people in A.A. who want and need a special, cohesive group for themselves. There is a large conference each year, moving from city to city, and Alcoholics Anonymous directories will list the young people's groups in each city. If you are interested in this aspect of A.A., a professional can direct you to the right contact and meeting information. It has been found that when young people have their own groups, the sharing is more honest and meaningful. More trust develops as the interests and issues are more likely similar, and the generation gap is not so much in the way. However, young adults are always welcome at regular A.A. meetings.

The young adults meetings were started, and continue, because younger members of A.A. are not always comfortable in the room with so many older people. As building an identity separate from the parents is one of the developmental tasks of adolescence, within the recovery process your teenager may need quite a lot of separateness from you and close relationships with peers. If she asks, though, it might be a good idea to accompany your teen to her first meeting, just to show your support and that you are there for her no matter what during her recovery process.

## Strengths and Weaknesses

As with any spiritual discipline, a variety of opinions exist about whether A.A. is worthwhile. Not surprisingly, those who are actively in the program tend to think highly of it. Some of the strengths of Alcoholics Anonymous are as follows:

- It is spiritual, but not religious. All faiths are welcome, including atheists.
- It is widely available, including online and phone meetings.
- The steps are universally applicable to any type of addiction or problem.
- Belonging prevents isolation and provides fellowship without addiction.
- It is virtually free, asking only for voluntary donations.

Jane Velez-Mitchell praised the twelve-step programs because of the kind of alchemy that arises when like-minded people gather together, tell their stories, and give service to others. It is almost impossible to be a wallflower in a twelve-step program, because the members are sincerely interested in each other. The emphasis on honest self-inquiry without judgment of self or others creates a positive environment for growth and healing.

## Criticism of A.A.

Some don't agree with the A.A. approach. Some say that A.A. levels out individual creativity and uniqueness. Some say it fosters dependency—on the sponsor, the meetings, and even the program itself. Anne Fletcher says in her book *Inside Rehab* that many teenagers are put off by the references to God and Higher Power, tending to rebel against anything remotely religious. Many are fiercely resistant to the first step, which states that the individual is powerless over whichever addiction is the focus of the meeting. It is extremely difficult for a teenager to accept that he can never drink or use again. With his whole life ahead of him, he fantasizes that there will be a time that he can drink like other people. In A.A. rooms, this obstacle is hammered home over and over again, that alcoholics are not like other people, and that they will never be able to drink like other people.

A downside to A.A. and similar meetings—for interested parents, anyway—is that many of the meetings are closed, allowing in the rooms only those who are working on becoming and staying clean and sober. As twelve-step meetings are open to any individual who has that focus, there is no way of knowing what the background is of the various members. The stories of some A.A. members include experience with crime, prison, violence, and homelessness, and you may wonder about the safety of your teenager in such a milieu. Generally everyone is well behaved, but as the addictions cut across all class and socioeconomic lines, so do the people in a twelve-step program. Ultimately this kind of diversity can be enriching, but as a parent, you might want to keep a close watch on the teen's behavior.

## Alert

A study published in the *Journal of Substance Abuse Treatment* in 2011 found that of 127 teens questioned, 20 percent had felt intimidated, threatened, or sexually harassed at least once by an older member. This occurred in Narcotics Anonymous more often than A.A., and there was no difference in the number of incidents reported by boys compared to girls.

Most rehab programs do have twelve-step meetings on the premises, and sometimes residents are driven to meetings in the community. The secretary at each offsite meeting signs off the attendance slip that the rehab attendees bring. Some judges order twelve-step meetings as an alternative to jail or prison. Those attendees also have an attendance record to take back to the judge. For all others attending the meetings, no attendance is taken, although the secretary might note how many people attend each week.

## Generation Gap

Because the first Twelve Steps (A.A.) program has been around for seventy years with others following in the 1970s and 1980s, you might imagine that the rooms are filled with gray-haired, middle-aged, and elderly members. The Twelve Steps approach to life can offer a new freedom and a way to happiness, but younger members might feel pressured and inhibited by the old-timer ways. Sometimes a friendship might arise that fills in a much-needed gap in a grand-fatherly way, and other times the jargon and stodginess can just be annoying. Keep in mind that in most urban areas there are multiple meetings day and night, seven days a week, and if one group is too oppressive, there is always another for you and your teen to try. Meeting schedules are available online as well as in print at the meetings. If your teenager complains about having to sit with "all those old people," help him find other meetings. The steps actually are universal in their application, regardless of the age of the person or the type of situation. One of the Twelve Steps is "Principles above personalities," which encourages those in the meetings to listen to what is said rather than how it is said or who is saying it.

 **Alert**

Parents need to be aware that sponsors in twelve-step programs are not professional counselors. They are individuals who have found a degree of success in their own recovery and want to give back what they have learned. If you are uneasy about the close relationship that develops between your daughter and her sponsor, you can get to know her, as well, and attend open A.A. meetings where you can listen to her share and socialize a bit before and after the meetings.

## Watch Out for Thirteenth Stepping!

What is thirteenth stepping? Thirteenth stepping is program jargon for preying on a newcomer in a sexual way. New people in recovery are extremely vulnerable, and more experienced members of the programs can use that for their own unsavory aims, acting friendly, solicitous, and helpful when they are really just looking for a date or a relationship. Generally people in recovery are cautioned about staying out of relationships for about a year, but the newcomer probably won't be aware of that guideline.

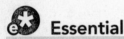 **Essential**

> Old-timers who sincerely have newcomers' best interests at heart will suggest that they only phone or hang out with members of the same sex. Gay newcomers are encouraged to form friendships with straight people of the opposite sex. Usually the honest, experienced old-timers will subtly take on responsibility for the meetings and social interaction, watching for inappropriate flirting and more or less circling the wagons around the newcomer. If out-of-line behavior is noticed, it is stopped.

Although people in twelve-step programs do date each other, it is said in the meetings that it is not a dating service, and friendships of a platonic nature can be something new to explore, after a solid base of not using or drinking is established. For some people in recovery, this is the first taste of intimacy that does not include a sexual relationship. With that discovery, the sober addict's social network dramatically expands, as twelve-step programs are worldwide.

## Common Questions and Concerns

Persons new to the program might wonder if it is religious, as the steps in the meetings frequently refer to God and a Higher Power. Although the steps originated in a Christian cultural context, they are not specifically Christian or any other religion. Bill Wilson was an avid reader and consulted books and people that represented a wide range of philosophies during the development of the steps.

## The Cult Question

Are the twelve-step programs actually cults? You may wonder about this because of the fervor of those who attend, the special jargon that is a part of the programs, and the books and rituals that are fairly uniform worldwide. The online Merriam-Webster dictionary says that a cult is "a small religious group that is not part of a larger and more accepted religion and that has beliefs regarded by many people as extreme or dangerous." Although the twelve-step groups are not an accepted religion, it would be a stretch of the imagination to call them extreme or dangerous.

Other parts of the definition go on to say that a cult is "a situation in which people admire and care about something or someone very much or too much or a small group of very devoted supporters or fans." Although twelve steppers do care about their ideals quite deeply, they do not worship any particular leader or founder.

The twelve-step programs are made up of people who consider themselves equals. In fact, it is somewhat discouraged in meetings to talk of one's profession or to name-drop about famous people and associations, as these references take away from the equality. There is no pressure to do anything in particular in the programs, although members are encouraged to attend frequently, get a sponsor, and study the steps. No attendance is taken, and policies of keeping everything confidential are taken seriously. Most members only know other members by their first names.

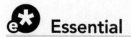 **Essential**

Recovery has to come first in order for it to be successful. During the early years of A.A., Bill and Lois Wilson were virtually homeless, staying with various friends for months and years at a time, as Bill was totally devoted to developing the program.

## What Happens During a Meeting?

Those new to the Twelve Steps program might wonder what happens at a typical meeting. Generally, meetings are held in a public place, such as a church. The meetings are not affiliated with churches; the churches simply rent rooms to the groups. Someone acts as chair of the meeting, reading literature to get things started. Members tell their names and mention whether they're new to A.A. Usually the discussion focuses on a particular topic, or members who are in crisis may have to talk about what is going on. Nobody gives advice. People share what has worked for them and encourage newer members to take phone numbers and feel free to seek support between meetings. Anyone who does not want to speak at a meeting simply declines when asked. A basket is passed for voluntary donations. Meetings generally last about an hour to an hour and a half. Twelve Steps meetings are available all over the world, including on cruise ships, where passengers appreciate being able to ground themselves with fellow members, as there are many temptations for excess in such an environment.

## Recognizing the "Dry Drunk"

You may hear the term "dry drunk" around the Twelve Steps rooms. The dry drunk could be either the teen or a parent. This is the behavior of a person who drank in the past and has stopped, but still behaves in the same ways as before. If he was mean and sarcastic, he will be mean and sarcastic. If he had other challenging character flaws, those are still there in bright colors. The family may or may not notice the bad behavior, as it has become normal for the family to absorb such dysfunction. The alcoholic himself may not know that he is still exhibiting distorted thinking and behaving, believing that everything is great now that he has kicked the habit.

A dry drunk might be going through a grief process, missing the good old days in the favorite meeting places. He might be impatient, grandiose, self-important, and arrogant. He probably believes that he can handle his problems on his own and withdraws from treatment, meetings, and positive associations with peers who could be reflective about what is going on. It can be quite challenging to cope with a family member who seems to be dry drunk. Attending support meetings, such as Al-Anon, will be quite helpful, as your teen will have a roomful of people who perfectly understand. They have gone through the same thing.

## Making Amends

Generally, a sober alcoholic who attends meetings regularly and works with a sponsor does smooth out some of those rough spots, but it can take years. This is true for teen sober alcoholics as well. For example, one diligent member of Al-Anon was so happy when her A.A. husband reached the ninth step and started taking people to lunch and making amends for his past misdeeds. She eagerly awaited her lunch, as truly horrible things had happened during her husband's drinking years. She was not asked to lunch. Finally, her husband said to her that he had so many amends to make to her that it would be an impossibility to name them all. He wanted his amends to be acting better from that point on, which is called "a living amends." She had to be content with that. In terms of teens, the amends could be general or specific, depending on the exact nature of the offenses.

## The Power of Denial

You may become impatient with your teenager who seems to think that she doesn't really have a problem. She might be somewhat flippant and rebellious now that she has been through treatment and attended a few meetings. One of the tenants of the Twelve Steps program is that only the person herself gets to say whether or not she is an alcoholic or addict. Of course, everyone else in the vicinity knows whether she is, but her denial can be very strong. It is necessary for the addicted individual to recognize the extent of her problem and truly want recovery before any significant change can occur.

It is easy to become overly optimistic about all the positive changes that will come with recovery, treatment, and clean and sober living. However, the leopard doesn't change its spots, and the basic personality of the addict will be the same. This can be disillusioning to parents and family who hope for great things. There may be great things in the future for your teenager, but she will still be the very same person, just without the drugs and alcohol.

# CHAPTER 12

# The Baffling Aspects of Addiction

The behavior of the alcoholic or otherwise addicted person seems to defy logic, and unless arrested or controlled, the disease moves forward like a locomotive train. It helps to remember that the addictive person has a different perspective, a different perceptual framework, and although you and the addict might love each other very much, the addict's perspective, at least before recovery, is one of keeping the substance or behavior going. At times you may feel that your teen is a complete stranger. How could this young person that you brought into the world act so illogically and self-destructively? It becomes quite bizarre as you try to enter his world to understand, and you may feel as if you're going crazy.

## Denial and Lying

The classic catch phrase of those experienced in dealing with addicts is that the only time you can be sure an alcoholic isn't lying is when his lips aren't moving. This might seem harsh, but it is often quite true. When dealing with an addict, you often experience feeling offended, insulted, and confused by remarks the addicted person makes. You approach the conversation as if it is a normal human exchange, and in just a few minutes you feel yourself drawn into spiraling confusion. You are not alone. Every person who has had a close relationship with a practicing alcoholic or addict has experienced the same thing.

## Why Would She Act That Way?

A person at the mercy of an addiction has a very different frame of reference. She wants, at all costs, to keep the supply or behavior going. This means that everything else is second priority, including relationships with loved ones. Most of all, she wants to keep you off her back, so that she is free to move forward with the addiction. It's as if her brain and emotions rearrange themselves so she says the right thing to placate you. It may take you a while to discover the pattern of lying and covering up. As much as it hurts, don't take it personally. It's just an aspect of the disease. You will see and hear the utmost sincerity in her voice and manner. That's what makes it so confusing. You want to believe her, but over time you see that there have been endless lies. In some ways, the person is innocent because she thinks what she's saying is true. It *seems* true at the time and is well intended.

For example, a woman met an interesting, attractive man at a recovery center where he said he had become sober and was living a new life. The two dated for some time, and on one occasion she visited his apartment, letting herself in before he arrived, only to find the kitchen floor covered with grocery sacks filled with empty vodka bottles. This was a shock, as he had said that he was sober, and she wouldn't have dated anyone who was not sober. When the man arrived, she asked about the empty vodka bottles in the kitchen, and he said they belonged to his roommate. He didn't have a roommate.

## What You Can Do to Cope

Once you have grasped that lying seems to be more typical than not, you are better prepared to deal with it. It can be extremely disillusioning to assume that the addicted person is lying most of the time, but you have to have that perspective or you will get drawn in over and over again. If there are certain agreements with your teenager that are extremely important, such as being home at a certain time to look after a younger sibling, get that agreement in writing and post it in an obvious place. That way if he starts the double talk with you, you have the proof in writing.

 **Alert**

Experienced people in recovery have some interesting cautionary things to say about dealing with alcoholics and addicts, such as "Trying to make insane behavior sane will make you go insane" and "You can never outsmart an alcoholic. Don't even try."

More often you will simply ignore the things that are said and go more by your teen's behavior. Do your best not to get into long drawn-out arguments, as they will only exhaust you. You need a lot of energy to cope with an addicted person, and futile conversations will not help at all. You can develop a technique of smiling pleasantly at your child, murmuring, "Hmmm" or "You're probably right." In this way you preserve your peace of mind and integrity, and your teen will be left to live with his own conscience.

### Denial

Alcoholics will go to any lengths to prove to themselves and others that they are not alcoholic. They will stop drinking for a time, drink only beer, or drink only on weekends or while on vacation. They will drink only at home or only in bars away from home to prove that actually they do not have a problem, swearing that they can stop any time. It is a part of the disease that the afflicted person believes he does not have it.

Teenagers will swear that they are just experimenting, being sociable, and doing what everyone else does in their crowd, and in the meantime, you notice declining health, failing grades, a crashed car, and a constant tension in your family. It will do you no good to fight the denial because it is a protective mechanism that keeps the disease going for as long as the addict is unable to face the negative consequences and want to do something about them. And paradoxically, it makes no difference how bright the person is. You can argue and argue, and the addict will still say that he has it under control, that it's really not a problem.

Linda Simmons suggests the following checklist to decide whether a person is in denial. Signs of denial are:

1. Refusing to learn the facts about the effects of alcoholism
2. Distorting information about the amount and frequency of drinking
3. Minimizing the significance of his addiction
4. Lying to friends and family about the extent of the addiction
5. Using selective memory, reframing reality to take the emphasis off his addiction
6. Remembering only the good times
7. Wishful thinking regarding the addiction
8. Avoiding conversations regarding his addiction

**Fact**

Alcoholics and addicts may not admit it or show it, but much of the time they suffer from low self-esteem and self-loathing. Because of their defense mechanisms they cover up these deeper feelings, often acting with bravado and arrogant self-assurance. If you can see past that smoke screen and offer your teen occasional sincere praise, it will help the situation, even if she shrugs it off.

Sometimes the cleverness of the alcoholic and addict can turn the situation on you; your teen may make you the problem—the reason she drinks and uses. She may hurl twisted logic at you, claiming that anyone would drink with such a defective mother or father, and if you would just get off her back, she might have a chance in life. This tactic can take you by surprise, but don't fall for it. It is a defense mechanism for displacing the attention onto you so that she and you will not be focusing on her behavior. The addict knows that you suffer and will use that to manipulate you. This dynamic is familiar to those who have been close with alcoholics and addicts, and if you are able to find support groups of such people, you will feel less alone in your struggles.

# Self-Destruction

All the addictions have an element of self-destruction, which is incomprehensible to most people who respect their life and want to continue it. Again, it helps to remember that the aim of the addict is to keep the addiction going. He is always thinking of the next drink, the next hit, or the next game. He has completely lost any thought of long-range plans such as college or having a family of his own. His goals are quite immediate, usually not further than the next hour or the next day.

A gambler who has vowed to his counselor to quit will take his paycheck to a convenience store, cash it, and spend it all in slot machines, $20 at a time. An addicted smoker will lose half a lung, go into rehab to recuperate from surgery, and smoke cigarettes while using an oxygen machine. An addicted shopper will continue to go from store to store, running up credit card debts, as it seems that happiness lies in the next new item. Meth and heroin users subject themselves to dangerous possibilities of explosives and contaminated needles, not caring that the result is probably decline and death.

Jackson Pollock, the famed American abstract painter of the twentieth century, drank heavily throughout his career, much to the despair of his wife and patrons. He continued to work while drunk, but his relationships suffered dreadfully. His wife thought that moving to a house in the country would help and that deciding not to have children, so he could have all her attention, would help, but ultimately he drove himself to destruction and death in a last fast car ride with a female admirer, crashing the convertible and ending his troubled life.

 **Fact**

Various biographies of Jackson Pollock allude to some of the risk factors for alcoholism—a mostly absent father who abandoned the family, lack of male role models, a very close relationship with his teacher/mentor Thomas Hart Benton, who may have had his own agenda for Pollock, and possible clandestine relationships with young homosexuals who got him drunk in order to have their trysts. Such marginality and secrecy contributes to the despair and solace of the bottle.

As hard as it is to accept, there is the element of slow suicide in a serious addiction. That person who is at the mercy of the substance or behavior simply does not value life the way that you do. This is quite difficult to grasp, but if you can, it helps in coping with the experience of seeing a person deteriorate before your eyes, no matter what you do. People do die from their addictions, and if you can face that fact, it gives you a clearer mind when coping with the day-to-day decisions of caring for an addicted person.

### Grieving

You may go through a grief process as you grapple with the reality that you may lose your loved one, needlessly, it seems. There is the loss of the life as you envisioned it for your child, and the loss of the belief that your love would make a difference. A huge disillusionment sometimes accompanies the understanding that much of what you do to try to control or stop the addiction will, in fact, have no impact. With a certain level of acceptance of these cold, hard facts, you regain your energy and peace of mind. Yes, you may lose your child to the addiction; but as much as possible, focus on the good in your life and on positive moments and memories that you have with him. One of the tenets of the twelve-step programs is that each person has a Higher Power, a guiding force that supports and assists that individual throughout his life. When you are distraught with worry and feelings of loss or impending loss, imagine your addicted teenager in the secure, trustworthy care of that force that intends his good, however that may turn out. In fact, some lives sputter out at a young age, and your imploring and pleading will not change that course. It's best for your mental health to focus on the good in your life and let your teenager know that you love him.

## Preying on Those They Love the Most

People at the mercy of addictions can do alarming, quite harmful acts. Drug addicts, especially, seem driven to do whatever it takes to get what they need, including stealing money and objects from you to pawn for the next deal. Of course, you feel deeply betrayed by such misuse of family bonds, but again, this is the disease in action. It's not that your child has stopped loving you; it's just that the addiction is first priority. Take whatever measures seem practical to protect yourself. Change the locks, don't leave cash lying around, and don't take promises of an addict who is asking for a loan "one last time."

In some ways, the addict has a distorted view of love and what people should do who love her. There can be a strong entitlement—that you should give her what she wants, even if it's something self-destructive. As the addict knows you quite well, she can unmercifully push your buttons to get you to turn over the keys to the car, sign a lease to an apartment, or write an excuse for school that you completely realize is fraudulent. There is a part of you that feels hurt and used and another part of you that simply wants to do the expedient thing to end the argument and unpleasantness. Be careful about that, as giving in a few times simply teaches the addict that she can take advantage of you. This is not how to condition a young person into responsible adulthood, which is your ultimate aim in raising a teenager.

## Charm, Charisma, Creativity, and Intelligence

It is difficult to not like an alcoholic or addict. They often have riveting, interesting personalities and can be quite intelligent and entertaining. This type of person sometimes has an edge, a certain style that gets people's attention, sometimes in a positive way. This can be an advantage in business dealings, sales, or entertainment. Imagine Robin Williams in some of his *Mork and Mindy* work and improvisations with Billy Crystal, and this is what a person on cocaine can do. It's as if the brain works differently, for better or worse, and the better part is a kind of debonair charm.

**Alert**

Addiction can take a person's life at a young age, regardless of the degree of genius and talent. Charlie Parker, the noted jazz saxophone player, died from heroin at the age of thirty-four. Even though he had a stellar career for several years, his heroin use eroded his professional life, and he died in the care of a friend, away from family.

It's not always the case, but sometimes alcoholism and addiction are linked with high levels of creativity. Here are some of the people who have struggled with addiction:

- Ulysses S. Grant
- Ernest Hemingway
- Jack Kerouac
- Stephen King
- David Hasselhoff

- Drew Barrymore
- Eric Clapton
- Dick Van Dyke
- Keith Urban
- Johnny Cash
- Elton John
- Elizabeth Taylor
- Judy Garland
- Heath Ledger
- Philip Seymour Hoffman
- Whitney Houston

This list could be much longer, of course. Edith Piaf was on drugs and alcohol most of her adult life, and Hank Williams died in the back seat of a car at the age of twenty-seven from alcohol. It is said that Natalie Wood was perhaps drunk the night she drowned, and William Burroughs wrote his beat literature while drunk.

Kristin Davis of *Sex and the City* admits that she is a recovering alcoholic, and Oprah Winfrey has said that there was a time that she was involved with a cocaine addict and used it herself. However, she believes she was more addicted to the man than to the substance, another instance that indicates that the substance or behavior is a symptom rather than the root problem.

 **Fact**

A University of Iowa study found a link between famous writers and the presence of alcoholism. Examples include Tennessee Williams, Edgar Allan Poe, John Cheever, Raymond Carver, and Eugene O'Neill.

The relationship between creativity and addiction is not clearly understood. Disagreement persists as to whether there is a cause-and-effect link or whether they simply coexist.

# Emotional Immaturity

It is believed that the emotional life of an individual stops maturing at the point that the person starts drinking, using, or doing any addictive behavior. This means that if your son started smoking pot at the age of twelve, when you attempt to get him into treatment at age seventeen, you are still dealing with someone who thinks, feels, and behaves as a twelve-year-old. When he grows into adulthood, marries, and holds a professional job, if he is still using addictively, those in his midst are, in effect, dealing with a teenager in an adult body.

If this fact is known and accepted, it can help in situations of impulsivity, indulgence, and self-centeredness. The person doesn't mean to be that way. He just hasn't evolved past that earlier stopping point. One can think of Michael Jackson, who was able to create a tightly insulated world based on his childhood dreams, wishes, and fantasies, and Howard Hughes, who was able to keep several women, buy a hotel so he could live there unbothered, and pay a physician to keep him supplied with his pharmaceuticals. It is easier to spot this immaturity in its more exotic forms among celebrity figures, but it is actually an everyday occurrence in any family where there is an alcoholic or addict.

# CHAPTER 13

# It's a Family Affair

Alcoholism and the other various addictions are family diseases. Everyone is touched by the behavior of the loved one in dramatic and subtle ways. Without treatment and support, every person in the family feels betrayed, angry, fearful, and neglected. Sometimes the manifestations come out in trying to be a very good person, overcompensating for the problems of the addict. One family member may become a high achiever so that at least one person in the troubled family has some good things to report. Another may become constantly sick, and another may become the scapegoat or the clown, creating a bit of comic relief for the wobbling, sinking ship.

## Coping with the Effects on Nonaddicted Siblings

It is only natural to give your undivided attention to the troubled addict. However, in making that person the sole focus of your resources, both tangible and intangible, you end up doing a disservice to your other children. Yes, it's a blessing that they aren't all in trouble, but there has to be some quality time for the other family members.

When you can, allow some one-on-one time with each of your children. Enjoy some pleasant outings or activities together and encourage them to talk about how they feel about the addicted brother or sister. Be patient and hear them out, including all the negative resentment and feelings of neglect. Those siblings suffer, too, just as you are suffering. In their young, unformed minds, they may feel that they did something wrong to cause the alcoholism or drug problem. Frequently reassure them that their brother or sister is sick, that it is a disease.

It is common for siblings of alcoholics to choose a drinker as a spouse in adulthood because of the deep associations of love. If that brother or sister is highly admired, the charismatic, interesting one in the family, it is almost as if the die is set for what is appealing in a partner. You can counteract this primal force somewhat by making it easy for your other children to have close friendships with healthy children outside the family. If you have children older than the alcoholic, don't let them bail him out, as this prolongs the difficulties of the disease and sets up an enabling dynamic that is unhealthy for the older children.

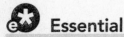 **Essential**

It is absolutely essential that you take care of yourself while so much is going on in your family. It is easy to neglect basic self-care as you tend to emergency after emergency. However, you will soon have nothing to give if you skip your dental and doctor appointments and the activities and friendships that sustain you in a personal way.

Seek out programs in your community for your children to help them cope. Alateen offers support and education for young people affected by another's alcoholism. Some communities offer preteen Alateen groups for those who are very young. An experienced member of Al-Anon is always present to keep the meetings safe and orderly. However, the young people themselves run the meetings. If you have decided to affiliate with a treatment center, the family groups offer education and support for everyone in the family as well as fellowship with others who are going through similar experiences. Even the younger children may have taken on some of the shame and secrecy of covering up for the alcoholic, and it can be tremendously freeing for them to have a place where the truth is spoken and heard.

 **Fact**

Children may draw distorted conclusions about cause and effect, a manifestation of the psychological effects of alcoholism. For example, a young sister may think that brother Billy continues to drink because she was too noisy or keeps forgetting to put away her toys. If you keep the lines of communication open with every family member, you can gently reassure and correct the child. This is especially important if the addict dies. Wrong notions about responsibility can haunt a person, even in adulthood.

## Preserving Your Marriage and Balanced Life

An addicted teenager can put enormous stress on your marriage or other committed relationship. It sometimes seems as if the teenager is determined to destroy everything in the family, including your close alliance with your spouse. There may be times that she pits the two of you against each other, creating dissension and disharmony. As much as you are able, keep that close relationship with the significant other the primary focus. Yes, you will do everything you can to provide a context for the teenager's healing and recovery, but sometimes it comes down to sink or swim. The teenager will have to decide for herself, ultimately, whether recovery is more important for her than the addiction.

Carve out some small pockets of freedom for yourself and your spouse. Indulge in date nights and an occasional weekend getaway. Especially if your teenager is in residential treatment, you can certainly in good conscience enjoy some positive experiences away from the demands of the addict. Some nice dinners, trips, and other activities that you both enjoy are healing for your spirit and your relationship. It is so tempting and insidious to make the addict the family project, but sometimes you have to pull back from that and just be a normal, happy couple.

The teenager may sense the shift in dynamic and act out in defiance. Don't let this outburst deflect you from your plans to enjoy some good couple's time. It's just like a two-year-old having a tantrum in the supermarket because he wants candy. You probably wouldn't give in to the toddler. Similarly, resist the temptation to give in to the addicted teenager. He knows you very well and can have an impeccable sense of timing in terms of bringing chaotic crises into the mix, just as you are ready to take off for a heavenly week at a condo overlooking a beautiful lake. If necessary, appoint someone else as the temporary guardian or crisis manager while you are away. It could be a trusted counselor, a relative, or close friend. Let those professionals who are working with your teenager know that you will be away for a time and who the substitute contact person will be.

## 🔔 Alert

You may need to practice not reacting if and when your teenager attempts to create situations to return the focus to himself. Breathe deeply, hum a little song to yourself, and walk into another room. Leave the house if you need to.

## Strive for Normalcy, in Spite of the Addiction

In an alcoholic family, the norm slides toward despair and constantly accommodating the addicted person. This can happen so gradually that no one really notices. Everybody takes on a particular behavior that seems to keep the wobbling ship afloat, and life limps along. However, this strictly role-bound system isn't good for anyone involved, as patterns are set up, especially for the younger children, who can have their perceptions and later adult lives distorted as a result.

### Fact

Virginia Satir and John Bradshaw brought helpful information about family systems into the mainstream. Bradshaw's books, *Bradshaw On: The Family* and *Homecoming*, have helped many individuals and families in recovery. His books explain, in detail, the effects of the various dysfunctions on family members, especially the typical roles in an alcoholic home.

### Keep a Routine

You have the right to enjoy regular family meals together, whether or not the addict is participating or sequestered in her room. You can enforce family rules for civilized, respectful conversation, even if your resident meth addict is having a violent outburst. As much as possible, keep normal activities going for all the members of the family. Help the other children get to their favorite events and plan gatherings with friends that are for normal events, not for dealing with a new crisis. If necessary, keep a planning calendar in a visible location where everyone can see what is going on and what is coming up. It is very easy to become exhausted and preoccupied with addiction going on, and that's when mistakes and oversights occur.

The more you focus on normal activities for yourself and others in your immediate family, the better you feel, and the more the teenage addict is forced by default to look at her own issues. Each time you react as puppet to the latest crisis or manipulation, her motivation to look at the truth of her life is delayed. Positive role models are important for everyone involved, and the individual members of an alcoholic family have a much better chance for happiness and success if the parents are positive models, individually and together.

Watch out for guilt as you carve out some normalcy for yourself! You may have spent years walking on eggshells and catering to the troubled one. As you take back the reins of focus and control, you may feel as if you're doing something wrong, that you are shortchanging the addict and being self-indulgent at her expense. This is not true. It is more likely that you are starting to let go of an unhealthy obsession with a person whose behavior you cannot control at all, as much as you would like to.

### Strength in Numbers

It helps greatly if you have a group of people who understand what you want to do to create some normalcy—people who will encourage you to create a good life for yourself, no matter what. You might have a therapist of your own who can cheer you on as you take steps to regain or create new plans for yourself—renewed interest in a hobby, classes toward a degree, or participation in something creative that allows healing self-expression.

## How Important Is Your Image?

It is a strong temptation to cover up for the teenage addict, explaining away his absence at family reunions and bailing him out at school and with the police, as you don't want your family name muddied. The truth is often that everyone knows anyway, and it is no reflection on you that your adolescent has a problem. It helps to remember that it is a disease and not a moral issue. You didn't cause it, you can't control it, and you can't cure it. You can set the stage for the addict to seek and follow recovery if the motivation is there, but you can't force that to happen, and it is certainly no reflection on you.

## ⓔ✓ Fact

It takes a huge amount of energy to maintain an image that does not match the facts. When you decide to put less effort into the image, that energy is available to do better things in your life—create experiences you enjoy and make practical decisions about the care and treatment of your addicted teenager.

It is common for parents to live through the accomplishments of their children to some extent, and of course you will be pleased when they are doing well. But it does everyone a disservice if your identity is wholly invested in how well your children are doing. This creates a burden for them. Similarly, it isn't good for anyone in the family if your peace of mind rests on whether or not the addict is in relapse. That's like playing the lottery or building your house on quicksand, a sure way to lose your peace of mind. Create a strong center within yourself that always feels sound, no matter what is going on with the addict. You will find yourself much happier and less reactive to whatever the addict says or does.

Frankly, most people are caught up in the details of their own lives and are not especially interested in the minutiae of others' existence. Keep in mind that your primary concern is your relationship with your own center and higher source. Do the best you can to live an honorable life, and that is enough. If it comes out in the news or community gossip that there is a problem with your addicted teenager, then so be it.

### How to Avoid Denial and Covering Up the Issues

Denial is a strong temptation, not only for the addict, but for you. Such protective thinking is normal, and in some ways it preserves your sanity while you gather your inner resources for what could be challenging times ahead.

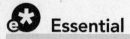 **Essential**

> Denial is a defense mechanism, a reaction to protect oneself from the truth of addiction. Refusing to discuss the subject can be a sign that something is wrong.

Usually, however, the time comes when the stark facts of the situation are laid bare, and you must see the truth. You might experience some shock and elements of the grief process, but things actually start to get better when you face reality and start to make new decisions. Keep in mind that the addiction and your child's behavior are not a reflection on you. You just have a different set of circumstances to work with than you expected—a school dropout, bail money, probation, medical expenses from an accident. When you let denial go, your full decision-making capacity and critical thinking come to the forefront, and you might even feel a sense of relief. There is a part of you that has known all along what is going on, but you chose for protective reasons to keep it filed away. That's only human. Now with the new information about the exact set of circumstances, you can, with help and support, look at options for yourself, your family, and the addicted teenager.

## The Teenager and the Disease Are Not Your Higher Power

Of course, you care deeply about your addicted teenager. That's what parents do—love their children, no matter what. But love can come in many forms. What was appropriate for your child before the addiction may not be working now. It might be the most ultimately loving act to gently pull back and let your teenager have the dignity of her experience. Allow her to experience the consequences of some of her actions and to make choices for her future. She may surprise you, if you take the element of rebellion out of the equation.

It is a part of the adolescent developmental process to individuate, and that can take the form of constantly bouncing against you as a convenient foil. That is normal. If you stop arguing and pushing on the issue of the addiction, the adolescent is forced to look within herself and to others she trusts to see where she wants to go, who she wants to be.

You may have the humbling experience of discovering that all of your time, energy, and resources have gone into the issue of your teenager's addiction. It can be a rude awakening to discover the extent that you have let this issue rule your life. Of course, you care, but making too much of such a project in essence makes that child a little god, and such a misplaced focus does everyone a disservice. It gives too much emphasis to every nuance of the addict's behavior. No one deserves such undue attention, regardless of his or her difficulty. It demeans and trivializes the dignity and importance of others in the family.

As you are able, with help and support, gently pull back and redistribute your attention to your own spiritual life, the relationship with your significant other, your career and hobbies, and your friends and other family members. As you shuffle things around in a healthier manner, you make room for miracles. That unnatural tie is loosened, and there is more room for each person to blossom.

## Maintaining Open Communication

Much of what happens between you and your teenager will depend on the nature of your relationship before the addiction came into your awareness. If you were a good listener, without judgment, you have an advantage. If you are able to ask clear-cut, open-ended questions without recriminations when the answer is not to your liking, you have a further advantage. As much as you can, keep those lines open, even when your adolescent is acting moody and withdrawn. Following are some examples of open-ended questions that can result in more helpful information than closed-ended questions (those with yes or no answers):

- From what you've said and done recently, it seems that you're no longer interested in college. Do you have any ideas about what you'd like to do after school instead?
- The recent DUI resulted in a fine and an increase in your insurance. Any ideas of how we can pay for this?
- I'm curious what you like about your new set of friends.
- I've noticed that you've dropped a lot of the things you used to enjoy. What can I do to help?
- We cannot allow you to continue living at home if you do not work or go to school and continue to practice your addiction. What do you think you are going to do?

## Sanity Savers for You and Your Family

It helps to have a list of things to do when life becomes overwhelming. There will be times when you simply feel at the end of your rope. With practice, you can learn to make the right choice to help you regain your bearings. Following is a list of actions that have proved to be helpful to others:

1. Get some exercise.
2. Call a friend.
3. Attend an extra support meeting.
4. Ask your therapist for an emergency session.
5. Do something creative.
6. Engage more deeply in your spiritual practice.
7. Listen to music you love.
8. Read something uplifting.
9. Take yourself out to lunch.
10. Watch a relaxing, entertaining movie.

Each of these actions will give you a lift, and with repeated use, you will automatically choose one when the going gets tough.

You may discover, as a part of accepting the reality of your teenager's addiction and taking steps to keep your own life on track, that grief is a part of the process. The loss is real, and you may experience emotions of shock, anger, denial, bargaining, and finally acceptance and integration of the new situation. This is normal, and as much as you can, give yourself the time and space to fully embrace each part of the grieving process.

## CHAPTER 14

# The Spiritual Component

Ultimately it becomes much easier to let go of negativity concerning your teenager if you embrace the idea of a spiritual life in a larger sense. Why are you here? Who are all these other beings, and what is the nature of your connection to them? How does a tree nourish itself from sunlight? How does an embryo "know" from the very beginning whether it will be a girl or a boy? These large questions about the nature of life lead one to embrace some kind of spirituality and a sense of a larger power. This can be a relief when dealing with a teenage addict. It gets tiresome being one's own God and having to come up with all the answers yourself.

## New Ways to Think about Spirituality

Sometimes people think that in order to have a spiritual life, they have to join a formal religious institution. They may think that being a part of a church, for example, is the only way to develop a sense of spirituality. If this is a tradition that is comfortable for you, then that is a good path to follow. Some families have been a part of a particular faith for generations, and continuing that bond provides a sense of belonging.

It is said, however, that there are many paths to God, and you might find one that is unique to your personality and system of values. In the United States, religion and spiritual practice have become quite eclectic in recent years, and it is perfectly fine for you to shop around, try some different practices, and see what truly fits.

Instead of associating spirituality with a church, think of it in a broad sense. Where does life come from? How can all the cells in your body know what to do in order to keep you healthy and all your organs functioning? What accident of fate brought you an addicted teenager? Are there lessons to be learned from having such an adolescent in your family? If you think about your personal spirituality as one of choice, a way to create meaning in your life, it can provide you with a profound sense of joy and grounding. No matter what happens with your teenager or anyone else in your life, you will be fine if you have your own well-thought-out system of spirituality.

Some people in the twelve-step groups make the group itself their Higher Power and the steps their blueprint for living. Others develop a sense of something greater than humans that has a guiding hand in the outcome of events, even especially challenging events. Some feel a kinship with Native American beliefs and rituals, feeling a great power in the sun, the moon, the wind, and the forces of nature. If you are an organic gardener, you might feel a higher force in the magic of putting seeds in the ground that result in succulent vegetables that you and your family enjoy.

## Developing Rituals of Meaning

It can be a great comfort to create a spiritual practice that includes various specific rituals. These aspects of a daily routine counter the chaos of addiction in the family, bringing order and ease into daily life.

Some people like to start the day with a meditation. It is calming to decide on the various aspects of this practice and keep them somewhat the same each day, adjusting only if you have an appointment or travel plans that require a change for a day or two. The meditation can be followed by journaling.

## Personal Journaling

Ira Progoff took the practice of journaling mainstream in the 1970s and 1980s with workshops across the United States. It has since become common for people to journal, as it has become an accepted part of spiritual practice.

If you are unfamiliar with journaling, think about some ways you might begin. There is no set way to journal correctly. Perhaps select a notebook for the purpose of journaling. Your local bookstore or craft store will have a wide selection. Choose one that has a design, size, and weight that you like, as it will be a part of your life for many days. Think about whether you want lined or unlined pages. Many like to doodle and sketch as a part of the journaling process.

### Essential

Writing is a gentle way to elicit and order your thoughts. Some traditionalists believe that handwriting pulls more from the part of the brain that stores emotions. Those who have always written at a computer keyboard might prefer to type out entries. Personal preference can be your guide in this choice.

Each day, date the entry and simply let the words flow onto the page. Your writing might include important events of the previous day, strong emotions of the moment, or decisions weighing heavily. You can write down ideas and plans for the coming day or week. Half-baked ideas are welcome! The journal is a place to let seeds of new directions freely scatter on the page.

You can write prayers in your journal, prayers you know from a particular faith, or your own spontaneous conversations. It is a common practice to write blessings for those you worry about or those friends and family members who are experiencing trying times. Write out detailed blessings for people who annoy you! This will free you from the mental obsession of trying to change them.

It is useful to write a daily gratitude list. Focusing on the good is a sure-fire way to move from tension and resentment to relaxation and appreciation. Let the gratitude flow into the journal, and over a period of days, you will find your perfectionism diminishing. Think about the place of prayer in your life and how this can be a part of your daily routine. Some people talk with God while walking in nature or even along a busy urban thoroughfare. Some play a recorded prayer in the car while commuting. Others feel a sense of prayer when listening to certain types of music. It is completely up to the individual to work out a method of communicating with the spiritual guide. If you have a yoga practice, you might experiment with including prayer within some of the resting poses, such as Child's Pose. The physical ease is quite complementary with the spiritual openness that is conducive to prayer.

 **Essential**

Sleepless nights or long waits in a reception room offer opportunities for prayer. Traffic jams, being on hold on the phone, and long checkout lines in a store offer further opportunities for prayer. A creative approach brings richness and depth to your spiritual life.

## Create an Altar

Having an altar in your home is a beneficial way to support your spiritual practice. You might find good ideas in your library or bookstore. A simple table can offer a beginning. Cover it with a cloth that is attractive and appealing to your spirit. Over a period of time, gather objects and photographs that have meaning to you. It is not necessary to have a guru to have a spiritual life, but if someone has been especially inspiring to you, a photo of that person could be a nice addition to your altar.

You may have souvenirs of special times, places, and experiences that made you feel especially close to God. Group those objects in a way that is pleasing to your eye. Incense is an interesting sensory addition and can add to the ritual of spiritual centering. You might want to gather physical representations of material things that you want to manifest in your life, making your altar a sort of three-dimensional vision board.

Some cultures use candles, flowers, and grains to represent the abundance of the earth. You might enjoy putting a few ears of dried corn or a small bowl of rice on your altar to elicit a feeling of gratitude for the abundance of the earth.

Keep your altar clean, and change the arrangement from time to time to keep your response and interest fresh. You might want to include your vision board in your alter arrangement.

## Browse in Bookstores and Libraries

It is invigorating and enjoyable to linger in the spiritual section of your favorite bookish place, tasting some of what is available from the wide range of spiritual disciplines and philosophies. You may find an author that you enjoy and read everything else that person has written. There is nothing to say that you have to accept a particular religion merely because you read books about it.

It can be interesting to explore Zen, Islam, Christian history, Native American shamanism, and Hinduism. Take a look at agnosticism and atheism and make up your own mind about what you believe. It might happen that you develop a personalized spiritual faith that draws bits and pieces from various cultures and various aspects of your own cultural background.

## Dream Work

Many people work with their dreams as an important aspect of their spiritual practice. If you are a person who dreams frequently and remembers your dreams, this may be a way to attune yourself to a course that is informed by your subconscious mind.

There are many dream books available, and you may find them helpful; however, dreams are so laden with images that are specific to each individual that it can be useful to learn how to interpret dreams without running to a dream dictionary. Here are some suggestions for working with your dreams:

1. Keep a journal near your bed so you can write down dreams as you awaken.
2. Write down the dream as you remember it, like a scene or story.
3. Notice any strong emotions as you awaken and remember the dream and write those down.
4. Is the dream one that you have had repeatedly? Note that in your journal.
5. Use the margin of your journal to free-associate from powerful images in your dream. Let the mind be very free in this process and completely true to your background. For example, if there is a woman named Dorothy in your dream, remember all the women you have known named Dorothy and write them down. Note their personalities and significance in your life (including Dorothy from the *Wizard of Oz*!). Was there a spider in your dream? Make a list of your honest associations with spiders—fear, dislike of insects, *Charlotte's Web*, the world wide web of the Internet, whatever comes to mind.
6. Look at the flow of the associations and determine what your deeper self is telling you. It may not be evident right away. It might help to leave it alone for a day or so and see if something occurs to you later.
7. Look back over your dreams as you finish each journal to see what trends are developing in your life.
8. If you have a relationship with a helpful therapist, ask her if she is comfortable helping you with your dream interpretation. Some professionals are well informed and sensitive. Working with a trusted counselor on your dreams can be a fruitful way to determine their meaning and what you might do with the information gleaned.

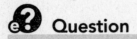 **Question**

**What if I have persistent, repetitive nightmares?**
The subconscious mind is 100 percent efficient in storing information about your experiences and beliefs. Nightmares can be a clearing-out process that occurs after you achieve a place of security and strength. Sometimes nightmares can be a warning about danger in your waking life. Deeply hidden experiences from younger years sometimes come to light first in nightmares, then later in a more linear fashion. Persistent nightmares can be taken to a therapist for help, especially if they continue for months or years.

### God Box

One way to fine-tune your trust in a higher source is to write down concerns on small pieces of paper and put them in a God box. Any box that you choose can be your God box, or you can buy or make one for this specific purpose. The habit of giving concerns to God may be more inviting if the box is attractive and has some type of symbolism for you—perhaps it is a color that you especially like, is covered with shells or gems from nature, or was a gift from a treasured relative or friend.

Small Post-it notes are good for putting worries and issues into the God box. Simply jot down the essence of the situation on the note and put it in the box. Include something about the best outcome for your addicted teenager. After a few weeks or months go by, spend some time reading the notes and see what really and truly has been resolved. This simple practice will help you to trust your Higher Power to a greater degree. If there are any concerns still pending, just keep putting them in the box.

### Spiritual Retreats

Most religious and spiritual groups have periodic retreats during which members come together for a focused time. Often the change in location from the demands of home and work is healing in and of itself. It can be a relief to get away from the dramas of the addicted teenager. Some retreats have a specific purpose; others are more open-ended. They may be tightly structured, or they may offer blocks of free time during which you can rest, meditate, enjoy a library, or socialize with others.

Some retreats offer days of silence, which can be an interesting discipline for people who like to talk a lot! The long periods of quiet inform a person of how much energy is used to express verbally and to listen to others' conversation. What a lot of effort! Silent retreats in the company of like-minded spiritual seekers are quite informative about the nature of the self and the relationship with a higher self.

Retreats are a good place to rest after traumatic happenings or major losses. A retreat can provide a rest from the demands of having an addicted teenager. Meals are usually prepared and served by the retreat organizers, and you are free to heal. Some retreat centers welcome visitors who are on a solo retreat without a structured program to follow. Sometimes professionals are on staff to assist a person individually if therapeutic conversations are desired. Often quiet times in a beautiful setting bring answers from within.

An Internet search for retreats of various types in your specific region will result in many possibilities for exploration. A retreat can be combined with a vacation, making the trip quite rejuvenating and purposeful. If there is a place around the country or world that you have always wanted to see, consider doing a retreat at that location.

## Being in Nature

Time spent in the beautiful outdoors can be a part of your spiritual practice, bringing deep calm and reverence for the processes of life. There is nothing quite like the majesty of redwood trees, the power of the surf, or the delicacy of a finely manicured, formal rose garden. These settings take you away from the daily stresses of personal life and work, making it easier to become attuned to your spiritual nature.

If you like to camp, this is a way to be even closer to the rhythms of the earth, spending longer periods of time away from urban noise and the demands of dealing with an addict. If possible, turn off all your electronic devices and enjoy some freedom from e-mails and texts. Most of those communications probably are not truly urgent.

 **Fact**

The lotus flower has symbolic spiritual meaning in several cultures. In the Buddhist culture, it represents faith, purity, and growth, as the beautiful blossom emerges, seemingly impossibly, from murky mud, flourishing amidst the muddy background. For centuries, thousands of Buddhists have found hope in the shape, color, and mere existence of the miraculous lotus blossom.

If you cannot get away to a quiet place in nature, investigate what is available in your immediate vicinity. A museum might offer a lovely koi pond or herb garden. Even zoos sometimes have authentic areas that are almost like home for the animals.

When you are in nature, notice the sounds and smells of the environment. Thoughtfully go back to some of those basic questions on spiritual matters. What are the plant and animal forms in that place and how are they related to each other? What do the animals eat? How do the plants get their nutrients? What are the cycles of life for the flora and fauna that you are enjoying? Can you re-create some aspects of nature that you especially love in your home or office, perhaps as a part of an altar?

## Meditation

Meditation is one way to develop a spiritual nature and confidence. A Google search for your locale will possibly lead you to groups and teachers who are eager to help others. Churches, yoga centers, and hospitals often offer meditation classes. Be wary of taking perfectionism into the meditation experience, worrying that you're not doing it correctly. Although there are a variety of techniques and meditation philosophies, there is probably not any way a person could meditate incorrectly.

### Getting Started

When beginning meditation practice, try to include the following:

1. Choose a quiet place where there will not be an interruption.
2. Silence all electronic devices.
3. Sit comfortably and close your eyes.
4. Breathe deeply and slowly, feeling the breath move into the body.
5. Relax each section of the body. It might help to contract each muscle and then relax it.
6. Quiet the mind. Notice mental chatter but do not judge it. Let it pass.
7. Aim for a "blank mind" state. Imagine a computer screen that is completely blank.
8. Notice the spaces between the thoughts and words and rest there.
9. After the meditation, thank your higher self for a good experience.

### Meditation Tips

It is a pleasant experience to learn to meditate in a group, and even long-time meditators like being with others who meditate; a different energy arises as individuals calm down and enter into a relaxed state of being together. A calm, focused leader with an attractive voice adds to the quality of the meditation. Some leaders offer a guided meditation with imagery that is very relaxing for the mind and body.

**Fact**

Scientific studies show that when a person meditates, alpha and theta waves increase in the brain. Electrodes attached to the head of the person who is meditating reveal these waves of relaxation and wakeful rest.

If you meditate at home, check that the room temperature is comfortable—possibly a little warmer than you might choose if you are physically active, because the body temperature lowers somewhat during meditation. You might like to have a shawl or soft blanket nearby to wrap around yourself if you become too cool.

Start with a short meditation, perhaps ten minutes, and gradually add a few minutes as you become comfortable with the experience. Some people like to meditate for as long as an hour at a time, as there is a greater chance of experiencing visions, colorful flashes of light, and creative inspirations. It is possible, too, to divide the meditation practice with a portion in the morning and a portion in the evening.

First thing in the morning is a good time to meditate, as it quiets the mind, increasing the possibility for a peaceful day. Similarly, an evening meditation helps the individual become free of the business of the day, making it easier to invite peaceful sleep. It is beneficial to form a habit of meditating at the same time each day, in the same place, for the same length of time, so the body and mind can become conditioned to welcome the quiet state of mind.

Any comfortable chair is satisfactory for meditation. Sometimes people assume that it is necessary to sit with crossed legs on the floor in order to meditate. This is a customary posture for people who come from cultures where it is common to sit on the floor. It is not a prerequisite for meditation, although floor sitting is common in many meditation groups.

Quiet music and a mat or pillow might add to your comfort. Some yoga studios or online suppliers offer special pillows and stools to complement the meditation experience.

### Walking Meditation

If you have tremendous difficulty sitting still during meditation, you might investigate groups that practice walking meditation. The technique is similar to the sitting meditation, but the practitioners quietly walk in a circle within a designated space during a specified length of time, usually forty-five minutes at a time, followed by a seated time of rest.

 **Fact**

Labyrinths for walking meditation are situated in various places around the world, as well as in private locations. Some famous labyrinths include those at Grace Cathedral, San Francisco, California; Land's End Labyrinth, also in the San Francisco Bay Area; and the labyrinth of Chartres Cathedral in France. Many mystics and seekers walk labyrinths as a type of pilgrimage. You could even create a labyrinth in your backyard if you wanted.

## How to Find Kindred Souls

It is stimulating to go to various spiritual centers and listen to speakers, especially when you are dealing with such a difficult problem as an addicted teen. Usually such places are quite welcoming to visitors, and you do not have to commit just because you are there. You might feel more secure visiting a very different kind of spiritual center with a friend who is a member.

Having friends from a variety of different spiritual orientations is an enriching experience. One can learn firsthand the meaning of different rituals and practices and discern the effect in the persons' lives. Are they comforted by their beliefs? Do they seem confident in their lives?

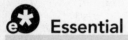 **Essential**

As you build your social network with new spiritual friends, search out those individuals who seem to welcome challenges, as they understand that a person's character flexes and grows with exercise. These people do not react with resentment when life throws them a curve ball. They dig in and put their spiritual practice to work and share what they learn with others along the way.

If you are not Buddhist, it can be exciting to attend a temple on Buddha's Day of Enlightenment. The lanterns, lights, feasts, and sense of celebration convey the joy of Buddha's experiences. Similarly, a non-Christian can attend a Christmas Eve candlelight service in a mainline Christian church and marvel at the candles, the sense of a new beginning, and the mere fact that every person in the congregation seems to know the words to the hymns, joining voices in song.

You might find kindred souls among family groups associated with your teenager's treatment center or in twelve-step rooms where people feel free to share the truth about their situation. If you identify with a person's story, chat with her after the meeting, form a phone friendship, and then ask her to meet for coffee or tea. With a bit of diligence, soon you will have a supportive network in place.

## Overcoming Negative Associations

You might discover that it is difficult for you to continue trying to please a harsh, punitive God—a bearded old man in the sky.

You could write a description of the type of God you believed in starting from early childhood to the present time and see where it stopped feeling right.

### Fact

A December 2009 study of the Pew Research Center's forum on religion found that Americans' religious beliefs and practices do not easily fit into conventional categories. An earlier study revealed that 70 percent of Americans believe in the statement, "Many religions can lead to eternal life."

Part of the maturation process is developing an individual spirituality that is exactly in harmony with deeply held personal values. The result may be the same church as your childhood church, or perhaps not.

It helps greatly to thoroughly examine the nature of your learned beliefs about a deity, death, sin, heaven, and hell. Sometimes childhood experiences with churches and those who worked in the churches or parochial schools leave a harmful residue of resentment, fear, and distrust of all authority figures, including God! It helps to tell a trusted friend, mentor, or therapist about these experiences in order to become free of past associations. There can be challenges if you are subjected to physical punishment in the church or school setting.

For example, in one situation, a woman remembered a time from her childhood when the minister of the church had extramarital affairs with members in the church, causing chaos and confusion among the congregation. She was too young to understand exactly what was going on, but could sense distrust in church gossip. The conclusion was that church leaders are dishonest and untrustworthy. They may say all the good things, but their behavior is not so exemplary. Only through this conscious memory was this woman able to let go of the old association and assess other spiritual leaders on a case-by-case basis.

## Adult Children's Spirituality

Adult children of alcoholics and other dysfunctional parents may have great difficulty accepting a loving God, as the old parental traits are projected onto the spiritual authority figure. It seems that the Higher Power is neglectful, abusive, tricky, too busy, misleading, and in general, downright cruel. This mindset is challenging to unravel because, with that belief, life's experiences tend to appear as self-fulfilling prophecies. This can be most disconcerting, as it seems to prove that God is, in fact, rather cold and cruel.

## ❸ Alert

One modern minister suggested to her congregation that if they do not have an accessible, friendly God, they should fire that one and interview likely candidates. This task does require that a person take complete responsibility for the personal concept of a God. If it's not working in a positive way, get another one.

Over time, however, the willingness to entertain the idea of a loving, generous God will gradually open the door to loving, generous experiences in life. Some, however, cling to bitterness to the end of their days, as it makes the childhood neglect and abuse quite real. Those embittered souls wear their difficulties like a badge of honor and suffering.

In recent decades the news has been full of instances of the abuses of power within some established churches. Sometimes adults remember instances of molestation that had been buried for decades. Along with the challenges of healing from such trauma, the survivors have to decide what they believe about the churches and those who work in the churches.

## Women's Spirituality

Women have a process to go through in determining the place of their gender in a spiritual context. If one affiliates with a conventional church, where much of the power and control is held by men, it is difficult to feel comfortable with the growth process. It sometimes seems that the men have to approve the direction and the women need permission to take any action for their future. This subtle conditioning has to be faced. Some women opt out and seek spiritual centers with female leaders or fashion a personal, eclectic spiritual practice that does not depend upon any particular person. It might bring more of a sense of female spirituality to investigate the Tara figures of Tibetan Buddhism, the female saints of Catholicism, the Greek goddesses, and pagan beliefs concerning goddesses.

# Finding a Higher Self

Most of the major world religions include ideas concerning a deity that the followers worship. It can be stimulating to learn about the beliefs of those religions, not only to understand those rich cultures, but also to inform one's own sense of a higher self.

Ultimately it is a solitary, individual process of figuring out a belief in a divine source. Many are available to teach you *their* way, but this important aspect of adult maturation cannot be borrowed from another. It is genuinely up to each person to work out a comfortable belief, one which provides a secure rudder in the maelstroms of life.

### Questions for Myself

It might help to ask yourself some questions about what you believe or want to believe about a spiritual entity. The following can be a starting point for you to determine your values in this area:

1. Does my God have a gender?
2. Does my God reside in a specific place? Where?

3. Do I believe in angels?
4. Do I believe in animal totems or spirit guides?
5. What do I believe about life after death?
6. What do I think about heaven and hell?
7. Why would God bring me difficult challenges?
8. What is the difference between punishment and consequences?
9. Will I be an outcast if I reject my family's religion?
10. Does my God have form?
11. How does God indicate interest in various aspects of my life?
12. What are miracles and do I believe in them?

## Alert

Persons who grow up in troubled families may have deep-seated resistance to any type of authority, finding it difficult to trust any entity of power. From this background, it is an important challenge to begin to trust a Higher Power, at first with small things, and later with larger, more important aspects of life. It is a gradual process.

# CHAPTER 15

# Emotional Sobriety

Emotional sobriety is the act of keeping a calm, mature state of mind, no matter what is going on. It entails a degree of restraint, so that the individual is able to respond to situations rather than react to them. Emotional sobriety denotes a personality of peace and poise, able to give attention to others but not getting involved in a codependent manner. Emotional sobriety is a worthy goal, as is recovery from any substance or behavioral addiction, as the quality of life is so much better for your teen. Usually in dysfunctional families, everyone needs to regain emotional sobriety.

## The Hole in the Soul

The hole in the soul is the underlying emptiness that precipitates any addiction. Many times the cause is unknown to the addict, as it is easier to reach for the substance or indulge in the behavior that relieves the emptiness. It takes courage to face this void and attempt to deal with it. Many do not, instead switching to another addiction when one is given up. Part of the withdrawal process, aside from the physical symptoms, is looking into the hole in the soul. This can be a very painful process, and it helps enormously to have the close, personal support of others who have gone through the same journey. For the young person facing this precipice, the terror is so great that he may think the only possible outcome will be a nervous breakdown or death. If he has some spiritual beliefs, and the people supporting him have a spiritual life, this is the time for them to draw heavily on those resources.

 **Fact**

In his autobiography, Eric Clapton writes about his early drinking as a teenager, when he thought that holding a lot of liquor would attract girls. When drinking and drugging got in the way of his music performance, a good friend tried to talk with him about his concerns. "At one point he became very emotional and started to cry. You would think that, because I can recall this with such clarity, it had some effect on me, but the fact is, it didn't make the slightest difference. I was hell-bent on doing what I was going to do and really didn't see it as being all that bad." From *Clapton*, by Eric Clapton

## Peace for Yourself

No matter what happens with your teenager, you can weather the storm much more easily if you have a solid grounding within yourself. Work on being at peace with the unknown. It is impossible to predict whether your teenager will embrace recovery and move on to a good, productive life or stay involved with addiction, possibly to a sad, needless death. Of course, you are human and will have expectations and hopes for the best. But truthfully, if you base your emotional well-being on what another person does or does not do, you are doomed.

Work out for yourself a way of mentally and emotionally detaching, so that you have an inner oasis that is always available for respite. As much as possible, believe that your addicted teenager has a Higher Power of his own that is looking out for him.

This spiritual source knows the best for him, and you are free to create a satisfying, peaceful existence for yourself. You may feel, at first, that it is unkind to withdraw your intense attention from the addict and bring it back to yourself, but in actuality that bit of distance gives the addict more room to make independent decisions, uncolored by your interest and preferences. Sometimes the umbilical cord has to be loosened a bit in order for the addict and caring others to independently thrive. Such separation can feel uncomfortable, but the results are worth it. If the two of you are clinging to each other, especially in a negative way, such as enabling or codependency, you both can drown.

### Essential

Kahlil Gibran eloquently describes the concept of loving detachment in his book, *The Prophet*. "Let there be spaces in your togetherness. And let the winds of heaven dance between you . . . Give one another of your bread but eat not from the same loaf . . . And stand together, yet not too near together . . . And the oak tree and the cypress grow not in each other's shadow."

## Ensuring Your Teenager's Serenity, No Matter What

Ultimately it is up to your teenager which direction she goes emotionally, spiritually, and behaviorally. Your example has a great impact on her, and if you are calm and serene, you are being an excellent role model to help your adolescent chart a calm course for herself. You can teach her breathing techniques to calm her body, and offer her the Serenity Prayer, which is well known in Twelve Steps circles. Offer alternatives to work off physical energy—dance, sports, biking, or a workout at the gym.

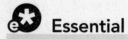 **Essential**

For a person of any age, it is a giant mental step toward serenity to realize that your emotional peace is not contingent on any set of circumstances or the behavior of any other person. You would have to be a saint to have that kind of composure all the time, but it is rewarding and beneficial to work on it in deliberate increments, not dwelling excessively on situations and people that tend to pull you into negative drama and chaos.

If you have a close relationship with your teenager, you may be able to help her detach from friends that seem to bring confusion and unhappiness into her life. Peer relationships are very important to teenagers, so tread lightly here, letting your teen come to her own conclusions about where the negative influences are coming from. Support her if she decides to end an unsuitable friendship or make it less central in her life.

Sometimes when your teenager is completely stuck and frustrated, you can suggest that she make a list of all the things and situations that seem to be problems. Then make two columns to the right of the list, titled "What Can Be Changed" and "What Cannot Be Changed." Have her systematically think about each item and decide whether it can be changed or not. Often a person will be surprised to discover that she is expending a lot of energy trying to change something that cannot be changed!

# The Quiet Within the Storm

As you achieve your own quiet centeredness, you have much to pass on to your teenager about how to be calm, even when seemingly disastrous things are happening. Adolescence is a turbulent time in the best of normal circumstances, with every new skin blemish and unreturned phone call a major crisis. Add addiction to the mix, and there can be a lot of drama. You can't really impart peace of mind to another person, but you can teach him, if he is curious, about how to be less reactive.

When something abrupt and demanding happens, suggest to your teenager that he take a few moments, pause, breathe, and visualize himself as observing the problem, but being slightly apart from it, as if he were watching a movie. He should then take a few more moments and do nothing. With that small time-out, your adolescent gains a few moments of peace, making it possible to decide whether or not to engage in the situation.

Another good technique he can try when friends are especially argumentative and dramatic, trying to create conflict in conversation, is to quietly answer, "Hmmm . . . you might be right." A person who wishes to bicker can't get far in the face of mild agreement. Also, just looking attentive and smiling will sometimes fizzle out a troublesome conversation.

**🅔❗ Alert**

A sure route to self-esteem is to be of service to others, using energy to provide just what another person needs. Your teenager might consider working in a community organic garden, caring for animals at a local shelter, or sorting donations for a women's domestic violence shelter. If he likes physical labor, Habitat for Humanity is a worthy place to do tremendous good.

Encourage your teenager to keep up good self-care—exercise, nutrition, grooming, and caring for his clothing. When an addiction takes over, self-care tends to go out the window, as the substance and behavior take first place. Through treatment and recovery, taking care of the basics does a lot to enhance self-esteem and preserve a sense of dignity.

## Help the Teen Create a Go-To Emergency Action List

Teenagers can be high-energy and wired, feeling that they need to do something right away to take care of a need or situation. This is true when they are experiencing a craving as well. If they are willing to work with you, help to create a plan for action when it seems like the craving is all the matters. Some possibilities might include the following:

- Exercise
- Dance wildly to loud music
- Walk the family dogs
- Clean or organize something in her room
- Chop some vegetables for a future meal
- Do some yoga, tai chi, or martial arts
- Pound a pillow
- Paint a piece of furniture
- Call someone from the emergency call list

The main thing is to use that raw energy in a useful, constructive way so that it is dissipated, and life can return to some semblance of calm. Even a harmless summertime water fight can be fun, if both parties are willing and nothing will be damaged in the environment.

# Realize Clear Mental Choices

It will be of enormous help to your teenager if you are able to teach her some control of her own mind. This will require a close, trusting relationship and perhaps the help of a counselor, but the effort will be well worth it.

### Mistaken Thoughts

One example of a seductive mistaken thought is thinking that a situation is a catastrophe. In psychology, this is called "catastrophizing," a habit of thought and belief that causes chaos and a drain of available energy. One misinterprets a set of circumstances, making it a large emergency, when maybe it's just a happening or occurrence. If your teenager tends to make everything a catastrophe, it helps to suggest a different response.

 **Essential**

One way to de-catastrophize one's thinking is to consciously ask in connection with each riveting event, "Is this a situation, a challenge, or a crisis?" Maybe it's only a situation, and not something to inflate into a giant, dramatic crisis. Help your teenager discern the differences.

Some techniques you could try include:

1. Suggest that your teenager take a step back and detach for a moment.
2. Suggest she breathe deeply and talk to herself in a rational way.
3. If a friend experienced the same thing, what would you say to him?
4. Consider the worst-case scenario, and then think of alternative possible outcomes.
5. Help your teen to push her mind and emotions to be in today in this particular moment.

## Bad or Good?

Labeling events or situations as "bad" or "good" tends to limit constructive thinking and cause knee-jerk emotional reactions, notably negative ones when the verdict is that something is bad. Too much indulgence in negative emotion can shape the personality into something rather dark, pessimistic, and morose. This tendency is often not realized by the adolescent, as each bad situation seems so real and important.

Notice what you feel is good and bad, and try to change your opinion to neutral. For example, you are out for a walk in a busy urban community, and you come upon a traffic accident. Sirens are blaring, fire trucks and paramedics are arriving, and police are setting up roadblocks. Initially, you might label this as a bad situation. Perhaps you might choose to say to yourself, "Help is on the way. The professionals know what they are doing. I'm not involved. I'm going to have a great afternoon." It helps to think about both at the same time. In most dysfunctional families, there is usually some distortion. If one person changes, all have to change.

## Judgmentalism

The habit of being self-righteous and judgmental can be so seductive. It gives the judgmental person a little charge to be a bit better, smarter, more in-the-know than the person he's judging. It is a mental habit to let that judgmental chatter go on and on, without realizing that this type of thinking taints perspective. It does. Someone with this habit of thinking feels superior to others who are making all kinds of mistakes, which, of course, that superior person would not do. One could surmise that such judgments hurt no one if they are not voiced. It's unlikely that anyone thinking this way would be the recipient of a libel or slander lawsuit.

However, this frame of mind locks out many pleasurable opportunities and better uses for brainpower. It wastes time and mental potential to endlessly criticize others, thinking that you always know better in situations that are actually only that other person's business. Judgment and criticism can be a diversion from one's own life, often from an unrealized fear of taking a positive step for one's own good. This is sometimes difficult to recognize, as the judgmental attitude is deeply set from years or decades of practice. Do what you can to gently turn your teenager away from judging and criticizing others, as such attitudes mask the true situation within oneself.

### 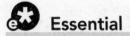 Alert

The seventeenth-century French playwright Molière cautioned against the folly of judging others when he said, "One should examine oneself for a very long time before thinking of condemning others." This seems as true today as it was three hundred years ago!

### Core Beliefs

In order to decide what the focus will be in your teenager's recovery work, you have to know what you're working with. In other words, some archaeological excavation will be necessary in order to determine what is behind some of the difficulties. Your teenager will have to go exploring to look for the core beliefs, the bedrock of his general perception of life and daily events.

Core beliefs are those beliefs that form the foundation of a person's view of self and the nature of life. Generally they are formed in childhood with considerable influence of the family, culture, and surrounding society, including the media.

### Essential

There is much to be gained by looking into the building blocks of your past. The philosopher Socrates said it very well: "The unexamined life is not worth living."

## Negative Core Beliefs

It can be surprising, but many of your teenager's core beliefs might be negative. With the support of you or a therapist, your adolescent might uncover some of the following beliefs:

- "Life is unfair."
- "I'll never get anywhere, so why try?"
- "I'm not lovable."
- "If I can just come up with the right thing, I can fix this situation."
- "Nobody cares what I do."
- "I'm too thin (fat, ugly, stupid, smart, educated, uneducated, clumsy, poor)."
- "This isn't so bad. I might as well settle."
- "I never had the advantages I should have had."

It sometimes helps to journal some of the negative beliefs that shape a person's mental outlook. Journaling pulls from the subconscious mind in a way that may cause beliefs to jump onto the page and surprise you! If your teenager likes to write, suggest that he write down some of the beliefs that come to mind. It's best not to censor. Just let the sentences flow onto the page.

When he discovers particular beliefs that seem especially harmful, start some work to counteract them. You might suggest that he keep a log of times that he notices that belief jumping into his head. Notice the triggering incident, and let the belief separate from the mind. Written or verbal affirmations are powerful for counteracting negative beliefs, as are positive actions that are opposite from the negative belief. Physical action is good because it has a way of harmonizing the mind and body in the new direction, and the new arrangement is stored in the brain, creating a new way to be.

## Positive Core Beliefs

Not all of your teenager's core beliefs will be negative, which is a relief to discover. Undoubtedly your teenager has many positive beliefs that serve her very well. Some of the following may strike a chord:

- "I can learn what I need to know."
- "I'm usually pretty healthy."
- "I understand most of what I read and hear."
- "The police and laws protect me from random, evil people."
- "The forces of life are trustworthy."
- "Life goes on, no matter what."
- "I have a lot to offer."
- "I'm a pleasant person, and people like me."

In your relationship with your teenager, do what you can to reinforce and encourage the positive beliefs, as these are the forces that move one in a productive direction.

## Replace the Addict Friends with an Emergency Call List

It is typical for those succumbing to addiction to gradually replace their usual friends with drug- or alcohol-abusing companions. The recovery process requires that the addict give up these people and the places they frequent. It can be a help to your teenager if the two of you work together to make an emergency call list for her when she is tempted to seek out her former companions. Possibilities for the list are a treatment counselor, minister, twelve-step friends and sponsor, suicide hotline, you and your spouse, and A.A., NA, or Al-Anon information services for meeting information. Help your teenager make a list to keep with her at all times, and help her to enter all the numbers in her cell phone. Also, deleting the drug dealers and associates from the cell phone is important, and maybe even get a new number or block calls from inappropriate sources. Encourage her to use the list and practice being in touch with people so it will be easier to make the call when there is a true emergency.

## CHAPTER 16

# Create Your Action Plan

Most people feel less worried about a big change in life when they know there is something specific that has to be done. For some, assigning a task is the best way to combat anxiety. This may be the case for you as you chart your way through the process of assisting an addicted adolescent. It seems to be that when a person has idle time, the mind tends to run with the worst-case scenario. In order to keep yourself on an even keel and the rest of your life functioning in a balanced way, it will help to have some clear ideas about what you can do to support your recovering adolescent.

## Your Role as a Support Person

You will have an interesting balancing act as the parent of a teenager who has embarked upon recovery. This is a time when adolescents want to be independent and free, yet your teen obviously needs help. It requires clarity and confidence on your part to be aware that you are the mature, decision-making adult. Your teenager may run the whole gamut of emotions and behaviors during the early phase of addiction recovery, from wanting to go out and live completely on her own to crying like a toddler over small things. Emotions can run high for anyone, especially during the withdrawal phase. Early sobriety is quite taxing.

## Hover Close By

At the risk of being too much like a helicopter parent, one who hovers closely over everything, there are certain actions that can be supportive without smothering. First, if your teenager is in a twelve-step program, you can form a relationship with her sponsor. Get to know this person, not to try to get information about confidential conversations, but to form a team in support of the adolescent's progress and well-being. In like manner, if your adolescent is in a rehab program, get to know the counselors and be cooperative with their suggestions. You know your teen, but they know addiction and recovery. Be as open as possible to their input, even if it runs contrary to your usual ways of thinking and doing things.

You and your spouse are the chief decision-makers about what type of treatment and care is the best for your adolescent. Use this book and others to inform yourself about the range of options and make an educated best guess, according to your circumstances and the degree of addiction you are facing. Don't be afraid to ask questions—hard questions, as it is likely that you are handling the cost of the initial treatment, and you have a right to understand what is being said.

Make it clear to your adolescent that you continue to love her quite deeply. Even though adolescents can behave with a lot of bravado, deep down she wants to be loved and cared for, even when she is making a mess of her life. There are times when you might feel angry and sad, but work those out in your own support network without expecting your teenager to take the brunt of your conflicted emotions.

And keep in mind that your top priority is to take care of yourself. As previous chapters have indicated, you have to remain at the center of your life and keep yourself healthy and strong. Otherwise you have nothing to offer.

# Dealing with Cravings

If your teenager is dealing with food addictions, there will be many hot spots to consider—sugar, dairy, and wheat. Your library and bookstore offer numerous resources, if you want to learn more about how each of these functions. Dr. William Davis, author of *Wheat Belly*, provides helpful information on the addictive qualities of foods that contain wheat, setting up cravings for more and more. When you think of the foods that your teenager wants while watching movies or playing games, it's probably not arugula or kale. When you imagine the layout of a typical supermarket, those "foods" in the aisles towards the center of the store are the ones laden with wheat.

 **Fact**

The three basic food types that people most often crave are fat, salt, and sugar. This fact is taken advantage of in the snack aisles in grocery stores and convenience food marts. Those aisles are loaded with soda, chips, cookies, and candy, not celery sticks, carrots, and apples.

In terms of dairy foods, cheese is usually the likely culprit, as it contains casein, a substance, according to some experts, that is akin to opiates. The craving for cheese can be strong, as it can be for ice cream; some of the factors are physical and some are emotional. Some of these foods are so deeply embedded in the cultural collective consciousness that it seems anti-American to pass on them, especially around holidays and family celebrations. You can help your teenager plan something simple to say, if anything, at large gatherings where something unwanted will be served. A comment like "It looks wonderful, but I'll pass for now" or "Everything is delicious. I couldn't eat another bite" will smooth things over in a gracious way.

## The Challenges of Sugar Addiction

Sugar addiction has been in the news for much longer than some of the other food addictions. It is fairly well known that sugar not only contributes to weight problems, but also is a factor in hypoglycemia, chronic constipation, intestinal gas, asthma, osteoporosis, obesity, tooth decay, diabetes, chronic stomach upset, arthritis, headaches, heart disease, and inflammatory bowel disease. When people go off of sugar, the withdrawal symptoms might include anxiety, irritability, anger, restlessness, difficulty sleeping, and a feeling of overwhelming loss. In the United States, many people grow up with a close association between sweets and love. When the sweets are taken away, it feels like a tremendous loss, as if there's no more love. This is especially the case if there has been a dysfunctional family background, and sugary foods were a substitute for love that was not there.

 **Alert**

Cravings can be triggered by damage to the delivery system that moves dopamine from one brain cell (neuron) to the next. Many addicts report they often use substances not to feel high but to feel normal. Their goal is to stop the cravings, and it seems to the addict that he needs the substance in order to survive.

## Support Your Child Throughout Withdrawal

As with withdrawal from any of the addictions, offer your love, presence, and support. If your addicted teenager is hospitalized in order for the symptoms to be monitored, visit as often as you can and bring treats that have nothing to do with the addiction.

Pot smokers are known to have cravings of all kinds and sometimes gain weight as a result of smoking marijuana. If your teenager is going off pot, keep in the refrigerator lots of healthy snacks that will help him get through the cravings.

It is well known in A.A. circles that when one substance is dropped, another craving may come to the forefront. In the old days of A.A. the rooms were filled with smoke, as many of the members turned to cigarettes as they gave up alcohol. Now with smoking being more out of favor, A.A. members always have coffee and snacks at the meetings. The tradition of celebrating each year of sobriety usually occurs in a public way as the sponsor gives the birthday person a cake to celebrate another year of sobriety. This presents an interesting dilemma if your teenager is cross-addicted, not wanting to eat cake but still wanting to celebrate in a social way. It's possible to be a gracious hostess and focus on serving others. No one will notice that she's not eating cake herself.

## What to Do If There's a Relapse

You may feel frightened about the possibility of relapse, but in actuality, relapse is quite often a part of the recovery journey. It does not mean that all is lost, that your teenager is going back to the addictive lifestyle. Many who have achieved long-term sobriety have relapses as a part of their story. The challenge for you is to not make your adolescent's recovery success a badge of achievement for you, obsessively counting the days and months as something good about you. This tendency is human and a hard one to overcome, but the truth is, if you base your well-being on whether or not your teenager has relapses or not, you are stuck with a roller coaster life.

**Alert**

Because of their developmental stage in life, adolescents are at high risk for relapse. Their immature brains are often predisposed to lack of impulse control and poor decision-making. Teenagers with other risk factors, such as a dysfunctional family, dual diagnosis, or learning disability, will need extra help and support.

In the event of a relapse, continue on your calm way, doing your normal daily activities. If your teenager is willing, bring in the support people—counselors, sponsor, sober friends—and ask them to spend time with your adolescent. As much as you can, think about it as a new start, a new beginning. It's not a failure. It's just a turn in the road, and the road goes on. After a bit of time passes, you might talk with your teenager about possible triggers that precipitated the relapse, so that those things can be handled differently in the future. Common triggers for relapse are relationships ending, a death of someone close, or some other major loss. In the future if one of these triggers seems to loom, you can encourage your teenager to spend more time with supportive friends, go to more meetings, and be prepared to ride out the emotions, as uncomfortable as they are.

## In the Beginning

The first six months are the most vulnerable time for relapse. Everything is new, and the recovering teenager has to learn different ways to negotiate his way through life. According to Linda Simmons, some of the most common causes of relapse are as follows:

- Berating/criticizing oneself for having an addiction.
- Preoccupation with the past; remembering the good times while addicted.
- Hanging on to guilt and shame.
- Blaming oneself and others for the problems caused by addiction.
- Overconfidence with early abstinence.
- Self-pity and self-centeredness.
- Pessimism about trusting early successes.
- Sampling of substances or behavior associated with the addiction, even if accidental, such as tasting food cooked in alcohol.

It seems that having one foot in the past is the common denominator for the thinking patterns and behavior that lead to a relapse. As difficult as it is to do so, the teenager seeking recovery has to squarely put the addictive years behind him and move into a new future. It isn't possible to have it both ways.

Linda Simmons suggests that you role-play with the recovering addict to address possible situations that might be problematic as triggers. If you are close with your teenager, this could be beneficial, or it might be best left to a therapist working with your adolescent. Following are some scenarios that could be fruitful for brainstorming:

- What if someone you used to use with calls you up and wants to get together?
- What if you find a hidden bottle of vodka that you forgot about when you threw out your alcohol?
- What if a food addict is invited to a birthday party where sugary cake will be served?
- What if a gambling addict is invited to a Vegas-style fundraiser?
- What if a recovering smoker is invited to a family function where everyone else will be smoking?

### Fact

For someone in fragile, new recovery, it is always good to have a plan of escape, especially when the situation is shaky, providing opportunities to drink or use. One way, if your teenager is of driving age, is to take a separate car. Another is to have an agreement that you or some other responsible adult will be called if she wants to be picked up. If public transportation is an option, make sure your recovering teenager has the fare to get herself home.

# Dealing with the Aftermath

Addiction running through your family may make you feel as if you have been living within a tornado. There can be immense chaos and confusion. However, with effective treatment and follow-up, things do settle down. You may find that you are dealing with a new norm, that things will never be quite the way they were before, and that can be a positive thing. Stark facts come to the forefront, relationships are clarified, and priorities are rearranged. Although there might be hardships, many who recover think in terms of a new beginning, even consider that recovery is when their life actually started.

## Emotional

Support groups and twelve-step programs help immensely with the emotional wreckage of family addiction. Every person in the room has a story to tell, and with quiet attention, you will hear others talking about exactly what you feel. Twelve-step literature is positive and uplifting, and may help alleviate whatever you might be feeling on that day. When an individual within the family recovers, things change for everyone else. The addictions are family diseases, and each person is affected.

Of course, you are happy when the addicted teenager finally agrees to start treatment, but somehow things still feel tense. You may have years of fear, anger, and resentment built up in connection with the teenager's behavior, and it takes time and courage to clean that up. It may surprise you that you don't feel happy all the time, now that your child is sober. Wasn't that what you wanted? Yes, but those buried feelings went underground during the more difficult times, and with the guidance and support of a friend, sponsor, or counselor, you can tease it all out, going through everything that happened, in order to fully participate in a good life now. We know, intellectually, that we only have today, but it is entirely human to hang on to the past in order to have some kind of identity, even if it is negative. Strange, but true.

## Social

Your teenager's social life will have to change as she moves into a recovery lifestyle. During the addiction times, everything was about being with the people who practiced the same addiction. Recall that this is one of the early signs of addiction—a sudden change in friends. As that same group of friends can be a trigger for going into relapse, you will want to do everything you can to encourage new friends, people who are living interesting, vibrant lives. Help your teenager to remain in touch with people she met in rehab. Get to know some of the parents and work out gatherings that will be free of substance temptations. If your teenager is in a twelve-step group, offer to host gatherings at your home where the adolescents can socialize in a safe environment. Be available to drive her to such gatherings in other locations. Twelve-step people are famous for having many events around holidays, as these are often slippery times for a recovering person. Generally, any twelve-step club will have potluck meals and marathon meetings going for hours on holidays. These are friendly events, and family members are welcome. It helps to have a plan, especially on days that are associated with drinking, such as Super Bowl Sunday and New Year's Eve.

## Financial

Depending on what type of treatment you choose for your teenager, the cost can be substantial. Be careful not to let your emotions run away with you, thinking that if you just put enough money into it, the results will be good. High-quality care can have a wide range of fees, so be prudent in looking at all your options and be completely open and honest with your child in terms of what you can handle financially. It's easy to become stressed with this part of recovery, as often you have things to clean up from the addict's misbehavior—fines, increased insurance, attorney fees, and replacement of stolen or damaged goods.

Also, you may find that you are working fewer hours in order to keep up with the responsibilities of being the parent of the addict. If your teenager is working, it can add to his maturity if he is held responsible for some of the financial wreckage he has incurred. You may not want to burden him with all of it, but a frank talk about what can be expected will keep the air clear. If there are medical bills that are impossible to handle, communicate with the hospital or clinic and be up front about the challenges you are facing. Sometimes they have plans that will forgive a portion of the bill.

## Mending Family Relationships

Addiction affects every person in the family. If you have had a suspicion that something is going on with your adolescent, the balance has been off for years. Of course, you want to do what you can to take care of each situation, but eventually the pendulum has to swing back. After you have your teenager situated in whatever treatment program you think is best, give some attention to your significant other. No doubt the sparks have died down a bit considering how much worry there was during your child's addiction. Spend time with your loved one doing normal, intimate things, according to what you enjoy. Taking a hand-in-hand walk along a river, viewing an offbeat foreign film, or having a concert outing to hear an artist whose music forged your relationship can heal those feelings of neglect. You or your partner may feel guilty putting your relationship back into a place of importance, but it is essential to keep this pillar of the family structure strong. This is excellent role modeling for all your children, including the addict.

Make a point to spend quality time with each child. Plan fun activities that have nothing to do with the addicted sibling. Yes, going to family day at the treatment center is important, but it doesn't count as an outing for the other children. Listen attentively to their questions. They may ask life-and-death questions, which you may answer as honestly as possible. "Billy's sick, and we're doing everything we can to see that he has the help he needs." Include some one-on-one time for each child with each parent, as both sexes need both parents to build a solid identity. Be aware of growing interests of each child and offer what you can in terms of extra lessons, visits to a museum, or trips to the bookstore to find books on a new topic of interest. Keep up with your parent conferences to alleviate any concern about the other children falling behind in their schoolwork because of identification with the addicted sibling.

Very young children can be easily entertained with creative ideas like a Backwards Day where everything is done in reverse order. You start with dinner, do the afternoon activities, then lunch, then the morning chores, and then breakfast at night. It can stimulate a conversation about times of the day and why things are done as they are. Another simple activity that is fun for all ages is to fill a wading pool with soapy water, add a bit of glycerin, and play with large rings of all types, even as large as a Hula-Hoop, creating astoundingly large, tough bubbles. Check on the Internet for recipes for outdoor bubble making. Such creative activity is relaxing and expressive for everyone.

# CHAPTER 17

# When to Cut Ties with an Older Teenage Addict

If you have tried everything you know to help your teenager with an addiction and it still continues, you may need to consider letting him go. This may seem like a drastic solution to the family problem, but sometimes it is a realistic measure. It doesn't mean that you no longer love the addict; it simply means that for the good of everyone in the family, including the addict, the time has come for a serious separation. You may come to this conclusion when you fear bodily harm to your family members or when you see the addict make no effort toward recovery.

## Detachment

Detachment means that you let the other person have ownership of her choices, actions, and consequences. You continue to love the person, but without a deep investment in the dramas and problems that often accompany living with an addicted individual. In other words, you make a mental decision to not react, sometimes not even respond, when the addict wants to pull you into the latest addiction-related scenario.

For example, your teenager has been looking forward to taking a trip to visit her cousin in another city. The two of them are close, and she has saved her allowance and earnings from a part-time job in order to pay for the trip. However, when the time arrives, it seems that she spent the money on alcohol and cigarettes and would like for you to pay for her travels. Moving in to take care of poor planning does nothing positive for the child. It is best if you dispassionately say something in a noncommittal way, such as, "Oh, I know you were really looking forward to that trip. Your cousin will be disappointed." Then go on with whatever you were doing in an emotionally neutral manner.

As you detach, the addict may escalate some of the trouble-some behaviors, trying very hard to get a reaction from you. It is human to want to be connected to others, even if it is a negative bond. Remain calm, and if necessary leave the room or even the house until the situation calms down. You have a right to your peace and serenity, no matter what the teenage addict is doing.

## Act of Love

Detachment can be a supreme act of love, as it gives the person the dignity of her own experience. It's not *your* addiction, nor your failure to live up to responsibilities. This concept can take some time to get used to and some practice to get into place. You might think of it as floating above what is happening, seeing the details and being interested but not getting in there to have a part in it, rather like float-ing in a hot air balloon and seeing many interesting things from afar.

In the early stages of practicing detachment it helps to breathe deeply, not say very much, and avoid eye contact with the person trying to pull you into something negative. Keep in mind that by giving undue attention to the problem situation, you are condition-ing the addict to continue that behavior. It doesn't seem like it at the time, as we always hope that each time is the last time that something dreadful happens. It is human to want to do the right thing, to take care of the loved person. But leaving the nest is a necessary rite of passage for most young adults. If the exit is due to addiction causing problems for everyone in the family, the exit might occur a little earlier than you had planned. You can think of this as putting some spiritual space between you and the addict.

**Fact**

> "Detachment is not a wall: it is a bridge across which the Al-Anon may begin a new approach to life and relationships generally." From *Al-Anon: Family Treatment Tool in Alcoholism*

# Damage to Other Members of the Family

The addictions are family diseases, and every person is affected, even if it does not seem so at a casual glance. You, your spouse, and your children are affected in varying degrees, and it takes time to recognize it and heal. Human beings are malleable creatures and able to accommodate all sorts of challenging situations, especially those that develop over time. You might not notice how bad a problem has gotten until something drastic changes, and the negative element is no longer there. There may come that moment when some relief occurs, and you wonder to yourself, "What has been happening? Where have I been?"

Family members feel sadness and tremendous fear with an addict in their midst. Everyone may feel guilty that they didn't love the person enough, that there might have been one more thing that could have taken away the problem. Small children sometimes lapse into magical thinking, believing that if they had made a nicer birthday card, the older brother would have behaved himself and not have had to leave the house.

## Evaluating the Family Nucleus

Everyone in the family needs support. Programs are available in churches, treatment centers, and twelve-step groups. Some meetings provide babysitting for a nominal fee, and the sitters will be recovery-friendly people, understanding that even the smallest ones show symptoms of anxiety, shame, and hypervigilance. Stark realities of jail, bankruptcy, divorce, and hospitalization sometimes accompany the disease of addiction. Each involved person needs courage and wisdom to look at the facts and not internalize any blame and responsibility.

All the family members may intensely want the addict to return to the warm, lovable personality he was before the addiction took hold. Such a longing makes individuals overlook behaviors and patterns, in order to preserve the idea that things might return to what they were before. Linda Simmons suggests the following as a list of signs of family enabling:

- Paying the addict's debts
- Doing his chores
- Excusing the addict's behaviors
- Lying to others about what is really going on
- Forgiving inexcusable, abusive behaviors
- Acting as if bad things didn't happen at all
- Refusing to hold the addict accountable
- Taking over the addict's responsibilities

### ✅ Fact

Recovery requires accountability. At first the addict may resent accountability, thinking it restricts her freedom. Family members may resist holding the addict accountable out of fear that the addict will rebel and the situation will become even worse. However, the truth is that accountability releases all the family members from their fears and frees the addict to pursue her own future.

Roles within the family dynamic can become twisted with the presence of addiction. Young children may take on the jobs of the adults, making certain the food is prepared, laundry done, and bills paid. In bilingual families, children may act as interpreters when speaking to the landlord, bill collectors, or physicians. When roles are segmented in this manner, especially if the imbalance occurs for years, resentments develop. Nobody knows what to do to improve the dynamic, and the addict possibly refuses to do anything, even make his bed or clean up his room. When roles have become rigid and set for years, it might require the drastic measure of removing the addict from the house in order for the situation to become healthier.

Asking the addict to leave does not mean that you are putting him out on the street. Other possible solutions could be living with a different relative or living in a group home. If you have done your homework about these options, you can present the choices to the teenager and set a particular date that the move will occur. Stick to it.

 **Fact**

Manipulation is a hallmark strategy of the addict. Your teenage addict may be very convincing in getting others to help her continue the addiction. Every family member needs to be aware of this strategy and not be taken in. Anyone who feels confused should feel free to talk with others in the family, comparing stories. It is okay to ask the addict direct questions, hold her accountable, and tell her the truth about the consequences. All will be accountable.

It is not possible to force the addict into recovery, but you do have the right to decide who lives in your house and what the conditions are in your house. Many times, insisting that the addict move out brings a sigh of relief from everyone. It doesn't mean that he's gone forever, and visits can still be a part of the dynamic, perhaps on neutral territory outside the home.

# Seeking Spiritual Solace

Asking a child to leave the house when it seems that her sheer survival will be nearly impossible is a radical test of faith. You will need faith in yourself and whatever higher source you believe in to sustain you during the times of loneliness and worry, and you will need faith that some sort of spiritual entity is looking after your troubled adolescent. Lean on your spiritual values and frequently practice whatever rituals bring you to a place of calm. If it feels right to you, stay in touch with kindred souls in your church or seek out more support meetings and forge closer friendships with those who have had similar experiences. When you meditate or pray, imagine your adolescent resting safely in the hands of a spiritual entity that is looking out for her.

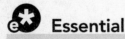 **Essential**

Seek out spiritual literature and books that help you remain spiritually healthy. Be a bit adventuresome and look at material from a variety of faiths. Sometimes something coming from a completely different direction can help you straighten out your own belief system. From the Sufi perspective, writers Hafiz and Rumi wrote wonderful books centuries ago that still are timely in their description of a loving relationship with the Beloved, the God that looks after all things and is always available and interested.

# Love the Person, Hate the Disease

Along with detachment, the idea of loving the person without loving the disease helps family members remain cordial while dealing with the effects of the addiction on everyone. It helps if those with the knowledge remind others in the family that the addict is not behaving in a hurtful way on purpose. It *seems* purposeful and vindictive, but all this is just a ramification of the addictive disease.

**Fact**

> When you become closer with members of your support group and listen to others talk about your very same situations and emotions, you begin to relax and feel at home. The needs that are not met within your own family become met in the new group of people who come together with the common bond of dealing with an alcoholic or addict. Many people in the twelve-step support groups think of the groups as their family and their relatives as the family of origin. It is sensible to go to where your needs are met. A familiar saying in the twelve-step rooms is "Don't go to the hardware store looking for milk."

## Healing Wounds

If every family member has support, encouragement, and empathy, the emotional wounds begin to subside. It helps so much to hear from a therapist, sponsor, or fellow group member that the effects of alcoholism and the other addictions on family members are fairly universal. Each member may have years of anger and disappointment to vent. In the advanced stages of an addicted family, everyone hates everyone else in the family and spends as much time out of the house as possible. All this is salvageable with time, patience, and effort.

When dealing with an addict that you are about to ask to leave, it helps to make a distinction between sympathy and empathy. Sympathy implies overly identifying with the problems of the situation and more or less agreeing that everyone will sink with the addict. Feeling sorry for someone takes away his or her dignity. Nobody really likes to be the focus of someone else's pity. It's demeaning. However, empathy implies that you can imagine yourself in the other person's place and see the various parts of the problem. An empathetic remark to the addict that you are asking to leave might be, "I realize it's scary to think of being completely on your own, but you're nearly an adult now, and I trust that you will figure things out. You're a resourceful person, and I have faith in you."

**Alert**

Painful emotions in regard to hating the disease do not go away if ignored. They merely are repressed and come out later, sometimes in a disrupting way. It is common for children from an addictive family to grow up and choose future mates who are very much like the alcoholic or addict. This pattern can be avoided if the hidden emotions are aired earlier rather than later. It helps a great deal to be in groups of other family members who are recovering, as everyone understands what it feels like.

A pattern that often develops in the emotional dynamic of an addicted family is when the addict is angry or depressed, everyone else becomes angry or depressed. This misguided loyalty feels strangely like love. It takes practice, but each person needs to learn to go on with his or her life, regardless of what the addict is feeling. Ultimately, this frees the addict to take responsibility for his own emotional life. If he has no company in his misery, he might decide to do something about it.

## Savor Small Moments

Regardless of how bad it gets with the addicted teenager, there are always some good times. You may have to be patient and wait awhile, but eventually that little girl you cherished will spring up and surprise you with a cartwheel or a funny poem. Savor those moments, and don't let them get lost in the whirlwind of deciding what to do with an addict. Sometimes just acting as if things are normal will create an atmosphere of normalcy. Maybe there's a special dish that your teenager likes to cook with you. Make the time to do that and enjoy the camaraderie around sharing the kitchen. Present her meal with pride to others in your family and pretend that you are a normal family for an evening. You are creating memories to hold fast in your heart, and possibly for her, too, although you may never know.

If you have banned your daughter from the house because of serious addiction, remain open to phone calls and news about her life. Listen to the small details, respond to her jokes, and make small talk about what she had for lunch and what she thinks about something recent in the news. Act as if it is a normal conversation and be happy that your addict is alive and cares enough to call. If you have an address to mail her something, do so from time to time, but not as a way of caretaking or enabling. Maybe send along some colorful nail polish and a gift certificate for dinner at her favorite restaurant. If you see something that reminds you of her or hear a song that you enjoyed together, write her a little note, describing how that memory feels to you. Addicts may act as if they are not at all interested in family relations, but deep down they are. They have just lost the skill to keep up a relationship in the effort it takes to keep a substance problem going.

# CHAPTER 18

# Healthy Self-Care for You and Your Family

At some point during your teenage addict's treatment and recovery, you will discover that you and other members of your family require attention and care. A helpful counselor or friend in a support group might point this out, as it is easy to lose your compass when trying very hard to help an addicted person. Perhaps for years the focus has been solely on the alcoholic and addict, draining other family members of their individuality and true selves. It is quite easy to become enmeshed with the addicted person, but luckily the process can be reversed, especially if the addict is in treatment at a location outside the home.

## Strive for a Balance

We all know that it is ideal to live a balanced life, but what does that mean, and how can you do it? The first step is to accept the fact that your life is and has been out of balance for some time because of the demands of addiction in the family. It doesn't mean that you were wrong or bad for giving the troubled person most of your time and energy; it just means that it is time to rearrange the components of your existence so the addict and her needs do not dominate.

Think for a moment about the parts of your life—health, loving relationships, work, finances, spirituality, and creative expression.

**Alert**

> At times, reaching a balance will entail unloading outdated fantasies and illusions about people, situations, and expectations. Sometimes immature romantic notions have to fall by the wayside in order for everyone in the family to thrive. You may not be a Hallmark family, but you have worthy, unique characteristics that can be celebrated.

## Health

If you have become overly stressed in the course of attempting to manage someone's problems, then it is likely your health can use more attention. Do what you can to catch up on your checkup appointments and to intelligently modify your nutrition, exercise, and de-stressing activities.

## Relationships

Of course you love the addict, but it may be time to rebuild relationships with others who love you, mending bonds that have eroded because of lack of attention or shame around the problems in your family.

## Work

If you have a career, has it suffered because of the demands of dealing with addiction? Arriving late, forgetting appointments, taking personal calls during business hours, and overall being tired and preoccupied a lot of the time—if this describes you, you have a lot of company among others whose lives have been affected by alcoholism or other addictions. As with the other aspects of your life, take an honest look at how you have been functioning and consider what you can do to improve your work life. Some people in recovery take a lower-level job during the early years of getting better in order to have more energy for that important effort.

## Finances

If your work has suffered, it is likely that that decline plus the expenses of treatment for your teenager will require that your finances undergo an overhaul. It may be necessary to cut back on customary expenditures and look at additional sources of income in order to balance the scales. Addiction is expensive. There are losses that occur before recovery and investment in treatment and recovery.

## Spirituality

Many people who have dealt with family addiction find that they have spiritual repair work to do. Some have become so angry with God that they have turned their back on anything that seems remotely related to religion or spirituality. If God allowed such devastation to happen to a teenager and her family, then what kind of God is that? It is human to feel anger, loss, disillusionment, and lack of trust in whatever spiritual entity you believe in under those circumstances. Usually, with time and the support of others, there is a way back to some kind of faith, perhaps a larger faith that includes drastic change and healing for every person in the family. Some people in the twelve-step rooms say that they are grateful to have an alcoholic relative. This can be alarming to a newer person who would like nothing more than to *not* have such a problem. But relatives of addicts often feel blessed that alcoholism and addiction brought them and others in the family to a spiritual life that offers sustenance, no matter what happens with the addict.

### ✺ Essential

Gratitude is an important aspect of healthy spirituality. If a person is truly grateful for most parts of life, even the challenges, a spirit of grace usually follows. It is helpful to write a gratitude list each day in order to focus on the good things of your life. Simple blessings like food, clothing, and shelter can go on the list, as can your awareness of the beauty in your environment.

## Creative Expression

Creative expression, whether it is as a profession or an avocation, delightfully rounds out your life. If you neglected such things because of all your time and energy going to the addict, it is time to reclaim this part of your life that brings so much pleasure to you and others who enjoy your particular creative pursuit. Perhaps you grow beautiful roses, excel at fly-fishing, play the piano, or delight in sleuthing in genealogy.

Make a point of carving some time out each week for the thing that makes your heart happy. Override any guilt you might feel about this and forge forward, as the world needs what you have to express. Your family needs to see you happy, and it is better for the addicted teenager to have happy parents. It is unhealthy for any one individual to have power over the dynamic in a family. When you take the ball back into your own court, the addict has no choice but to focus on her own difficulties and make some decisions for change.

## Rekindle Hobbies and Interests

It is tempting to give up everything and put your own interests aside when the needs of the addict are so real and urgent. However, the overall health of the family improves when you are able to maintain your normal pursuits, hobbies, and interests. You may not have noticed them slipping away, as the sacrifices for the addict can be gradual. Think back to the period of time before you became concerned with the troubles of the addict, and remember how you spent your spare time. Recall what you most enjoyed and bring those activities back into your life, perhaps gradually at first.

If you draw a blank about what you even like to do, recall your favorite pastimes as a child, and try some of those. Perhaps you used to like to sketch animals. Consider spending an afternoon at the zoo with your drawing pad. It is impossible to feel anxious and sad when your focus is on creating the lines and shapes you see. Perhaps you enjoy the craftsmanship of vintage clothing. Seek out the local flea markets and quirky shops to see what they might offer.

As you set the example for rekindling the parts of your life that make you happy, you set an excellent example for other family members to do the same. If your spouse enjoys golfing, then time can be made for that. Your other children may want to explore ceramics, martial arts, or dinosaurs. Encourage them to do what they enjoy, and as much as you are able, offer to drive them to where those activities take place. A family outing with a picnic basket to a concert in the park can be fun for everyone, relaxing and healing. Many such cultural offerings are free, and you can find out about them by scanning the local newspaper calendar section and picking up fliers at your favorite coffeehouse.

Taking care of your own growth and development through recreation sets a good example for the addict, although at first she may act petulant and try to lure you away. When she achieves sobriety and clean recovery, she will have much time on her hands, and it is good for her to know that healthy people can have a good time without being drunk or high.

Pursuing recreation and hobbies is therapeutic because it gives your mind a break. You are momentarily freed from the stress and problems of the addict, and your brain and body are able to regenerate and heal. It is difficult to think about two things at the same time, and if your passion is sufficiently engrossing, you will find yourself setting aside thoughts of the teenage addict, if only for a little while.

### ✅ Fact

Self-discovery is a marvelous adventure. With trial and error you may discover that you love sushi, Middle Eastern food, and organic gardening. You may enjoy collecting needlework that reminds you of your grandmother and discover that you enjoy climbing, maybe even rock climbing. A part of the process of learning about yourself is learning what you don't like. In dysfunctional families people sometimes take on the interests of others out of misguided loyalty. You may decide that you don't like classical music, steak, or garish Christmas lights.

If you don't even remember or know what you are interested in, you are not alone. Many family members come to support groups and realize that, after years of preoccupation with others' needs and preferences, they do not even know their own! If your parents were alcoholics or otherwise addicted, it is possible that you learned at a young age to set aside your own wants and desires in order to take care of the more needy people. It can take some time to learn what you like, but with a bit of trial and error, not worrying too much about the results, you can discover some pastimes that bring you happiness, regardless of what is going on with the addicted teenager. This separate focus, apart from addiction, gives your life depth and meaning, and you deserve that.

## Exercise, Meditation, Social Connections

Are there sports and exercise pursuits that you enjoyed in the past and have set aside? Now might be the time to try them again. Decide if you like to work out solo or enjoy the company of others in a group. Most cities have a parks and recreation department program that offers classes at a nominal fee. It might be interesting to try tai chi, yoga, or water ballet. Many enjoy the physical and social exertion of dance. People in their fifties and older have trained for marathons and found it marvelously fulfilling. Exercise is not only good for your body; it releases endorphins and helps to alleviate and prevent depression.

### Meditation

Like enjoyable recreation and hobbies, meditation gives your mind a rest. The negative preoccupations subside, and a deeper calm moves into your mind and body. There is no right way to meditate. Sometimes community centers, yoga studios, or churches offer meditation groups. The community college or adult education sector of your local school system might have classes. There are different varieties with different accompanying rituals, according to the part of the world from which they came. It might be interesting for you to investigate Zen or Hindu traditions of meditation, and you will likely find books on the topic at your local library or bookstore.

YouTube offers meditations and visualizations of all kinds, some with lovely music, photos, and guided narrative to follow. If you fear that you have a short attention span and simply cannot sit still for any length of time, note the length of the video and choose a short one. Sometimes online sites associated with well-known personal growth advocates, such as Oprah Winfrey, Deepak Chopra, and Eckhart Tolle, offer a series of meditations. Meditation gets easier with practice and familiarity. Occasionally you might get a flash of a good idea to help you solve a problem—the name of a person who could refer you to a good treatment center for your teenager or a book you remember that someone recommended. If you live in an urban area and are interested in twelve-step meetings, some of those have a meditation time included in the meeting.

## Social Connections

Many people who have had close experiences with an addict or alcoholic feel stunted in their social skills. Unfortunately, the dynamic in an addicted family can become so distorted that family members may have forgotten how to talk with and listen to each other. It is said that sometimes the mantra for an alcoholic home is "Don't talk; don't trust; don't feel." You may feel that when you go out into the world, you have a brand on your forehead that broadcasts how bad things are at home.

Social skills are easily relearned or learned for the first time, if you came from a background that discouraged close connections outside the family. This is often the case when there are problems in the family. If you have decided to participate in support groups, these people are likely to have a lot in common with you, and you can practice being friendly. Simply look at the person next to you, extend your hand, and introduce yourself. Then do the same with the person sitting on the other side. A good open-ended question is "How's your day going so far?" Or if it is someone you have seen repeatedly and you are aware of a particular challenge he has, you might ask, "How's it going with your job search?" Then listen.

So many think that conversation is waiting for your turn to jump in, but often attentive listening will give you important clues about what you can talk about. Ask for more details, and say back to the person what you heard. This might seem odd, but it reassures the other person that you really care about what she says, and she can correct you if you have made a wrong conclusion or assumption from what was said.

 **Fact**

The fellowship aspect of recovery is a marvelous bonus for active involvement in family aftercare, church support groups, or twelve-step programs. The emotional bonds are deep because of the common challenges, and lifetime friendships can arise. When you travel or move to a different city, you can always find a fellowship and make friends right away.

Little by little you may find yourself more interested in people outside your family, people who have a lot to offer in terms of fun, activities, and exploration. If you are a bit brave and courageous, marvelous surprises can come into your life. One woman in a twelve-step group was just starting to learn of her interests and small short-term goals, and she shared that she had always wanted to ride an elephant. A gentleman in the group talked with her after the session ended and told her he knew of a zoo that had elephants to ride, and he offered to treat her to an afternoon of elephant riding. A friendship was born.

As your social skills heal, you will find yourself offering conversation to others who are at the beginning point of recovery. It may surprise you that after a few months of healing for yourself, you can greet and exchange pleasantries with a newer person who has been silent for several weeks. You may never know how much those lives are touched by your friendliness and courtesy.

## Support Groups

There are many kinds of support groups, and it will be good for you and your family to search until you find something that has a good fit. If your teenager is in a treatment facility, it is likely that there is a family group designed to help you. Hospital programs generally have family support as a part of the treatment, and sometimes this extends to the outpatient phase of recovery. If you are affiliated with a church, this can be an avenue to find people who understand what you are going through. There are twelve-step programs for each of the addictions, behavioral as well as substance, and many of these programs have meetings for the friends and partners of addicts as well.

 **Alert**

As with the addict in new recovery, watch out for the temptation to think that you have reached a point where you no longer need support. It seems logical that once the addict is clean and sober your problems are over, but this is not true. There are many threads to untangle, and it may take years to get to a place of deep understanding about the nature of addiction and your part of the puzzle. Support groups allow you to thoroughly examine where you are in the picture and what you can do to create a good life while still remaining a loving parent to the addict.

Sometimes the YMCA offers opportunities for families in recovery, and you might find community education classes that supplement what you are learning about the addiction diseases. This is also a great way to make new friends. Numerous online support groups are available to help people associated with recovery, and almost all of these are free. The method of communication could be by conference telephone calls or by e-mails between members. These options are quite helpful for people in isolated areas or who have a complex schedule to work around.

## Therapy for Yourself

There are many kinds of therapies and therapists available, and you have a right to look for a good match for your value system and unique set of needs. In particular, when you have an initial consultation (and please do take the time to do this), ask specific questions about the therapist's knowledge and experience in terms of alcoholism and addiction. As surprising as it is, some therapists have little knowledge about alcoholism beyond the average person's. This can be quite confusing when you want to talk about some of the effects of drinking or using and the therapist says, "But hasn't he stopped drinking now?" Those close to the disease understand that the effects go on even after the drinking and using have stopped.

The most important thing in choosing and working with a therapist is that you like the person. You must feel at ease and in a situation where you can trust, in order for you to benefit from the therapy. It helps both you and the therapist if you are clear about your goals. This will prevent months of expensive muddling along, not knowing where you are headed. Ask yourself if you look forward to the sessions and if the therapist makes you feel inferior in any way. This should not be the case, as the relationship is a collaborative partnership to help you forge some new understandings about your life. If you feel that the therapist is not working out, give reasonable notice and make your exit. Therapists also go through feelings of loss when they lose a client, so if you wish, say in a few sentences what you feel as the partnership nears its end.

# Prescription for Isolation and Shame

Isolation is a common side effect of addiction in the family. The family system pulls inward in order to cope with the stress of the disease, and outside ties fall away. This can happen so gradually that you might not notice it, but you may realize that you have stopped inviting people over, and you have stopped accepting invitations to outside events.

You are not alone in this tendency, although you may feel quite unique in your isolated life. Little by little, as you join helpful groups and expand your recreation activities, the isolation will subside. You don't have to be a social butterfly to have a happy life, but it is helpful to remain connected to others outside the family, even for a few pleasant exchanges with a barista or a bank teller. If you frequent your local library for books and special events, you will find that the librarians are usually quite conversational and pleasant. Most of the twelve-step programs offer phone lists with the names and phone numbers of the members. You can use these to remain in touch throughout the weeks between meetings. E-mail communication is helpful if you aren't especially talkative or have a busy work schedule without a lot of time to be on the phone. Sometimes the best antidote for loneliness is to call up someone you know and ask how that person is doing. Such generous outreach will brighten both of your days.

### Fact

Shame can dissipate when it is shared with others in a safe environment. This can be an enormous catharsis for those who have harbored dark secrets for decades. Once an atmosphere of trust is felt in a group situation, the rewards are great for courageously talking about those feelings and incidents that have been hidden in the attempt to preserve a personal or family image. Usually everyone in the group will identify with what is said, and intimate bonds are deepened.

Shame is an insidious emotion that is sometimes confused with guilt. Guilt indicates that you feel that you have done something wrong, and shame indicates that you *are* something wrong. This emotion, especially if unrealized, does harm to your self-esteem, making it difficult to live a thriving life with your needs at the forefront. Unfortunately, shame is a strong part of the family dynamic when alcoholism or addiction is present, as the addicted one is driven to blame others, making them feel ashamed for having needs and wants of their own.

If a child is subjected to this, it can take years to undo the damage, eventually realizing that every person has a right to individual wants and needs. In some twisted addicted families, children are shouted at and even told that they were a mistake, that the parent's life would not have turned out so badly if the child had not been born. Of course, this is the disease talking, but it can take a while to silence those inner voices. Journaling can help unearth hidden shame as well as sharing specific memories and situations with a twelve-step sponsor or a therapist.

# CHAPTER 19

# Alternative Treatment Approaches

Conventional treatments, such as counselors and support groups, are not the only avenues to recovery. It is said that there are many paths to God, and the same can be said for the road to recovery. If you remember that the root problem in addiction is the hole in the soul, it becomes easier to take the focus off the specific problematic substance or behavior. Go deeper into embracing activities that provide meaning to life and spiritual, possibly creative, sustenance. Sometimes a family's specific ethnic origins may make an alternative route more appealing.

## Music

In virtually every culture, music has an important place in expressing individual and group values and aims. It provides individual and communal experiences of unity and expression, releasing pent-up emotions that inhibit the immune system and healing. For example, when Eric Clapton suffered from the death of his four-year-old son, he struggled with unexpressed sorrow for several years and finally wrote and performed the song "Tears from Heaven." He never expected it to be of interest to anyone but himself, though it struck a chord with a wide audience, as most everyone has experienced some kind of deep loss.

**Alert**

No particular talent is required to participate in and enjoy music therapy. The credentialed music therapist is trained to observe and work with a wide range of cognitive and emotional conditions, tailoring the sessions to match the abilities and interests of the teenagers. Adolescents might experience improvisation, note reading, and theory instruction, all in a safe environment, free from the ridicule of their peers.

Drumming groups have proved to be helpful and appealing for recovering teenagers. The communal effort and conversation between instruments is relaxing and healing for the addict who has become isolated with the addiction. It is said that young people crave structure and ritual, especially if they come from environments that do not offer those aspects of an orderly life.

Drumming groups provide a set time, place, set of instruments, and rhythms to improvise that provide security, as well as release of stress. Drumming requires active participation, a good balancing effect for a teenager who had succumbed to a passive addictive life. Dr. Michael Winkleman of the American Public Health Association found in his studies that drumming enhances theta waves in the brain and synchronizes the brain wave patterns. It alleviates self-centeredness and provides a way for those with a secular orientation to sense a Higher Power.

The Internet site AlcoholRehab.com cites the following benefits of music therapy as a supplemental component of recovery from alcoholism:

- Music purges destructive emotions.
- Music helps to manage stress, a big help for highly stressed, newly sober teenagers.
- Music alleviates boredom, which can be a trigger for relapse.
- Performing in a group alleviates loneliness when the addict misses the drinking and using friends.

- Music can be a good introduction into meditation, when the individual is not yet ready for a formal practice.
- Music enhances concentration and heals long-term memory function.
- Music helps to counteract depression.

## Fact

Thamkrabok is a Buddhist temple in Thailand that offers music therapy to people who want to recover from an addiction. The program draws upon the healing powers of music. The monks at Thamkrabok even have constructed a recording studio at their temple.

Music is a part of almost every world culture, and it is interesting that the parts of the world that are not as economically prosperous have strong healing cultures associated with music, such as Africa and parts of Asia and South America.

Music therapy can have a marvelous balancing effect in a media-driven society where it seems that one has to be a star or nothing. Children from a young age catch the celebrity bug and follow their favorite musicians, and everyone forgets that anyone can make music. The stars do not own all the expressive capabilities.

## Sports

Participating in sports, whether as part of a structured recovery program or as a separate activity, can aid teens in recovery from addiction. Learning to have fun without drugs and alcohol is part of the process for teenagers in recovery, and participating in sports is a beneficial way to structure time, connect with others, and create a healthier body and release of endorphins in the brain. Sports usually take place outdoors, which connects the adolescent to nature. Activities such as backpacking, white-water rafting, rock climbing, and learning survival skills help the addict restore self-confidence, social skill, responsibility, and an integrated life of exercise and good nutrition. Sports programs, if accredited, might be covered by insurance and generally are from three weeks up to two years in length.

## Important Life Skills

Crossroads Academy, an alternative high school in Utah, has a philosophy that leisure skills are necessary to a happy, sober life. At Crossroads, therapy and academics are closely integrated with fishing, scuba diving, basketball, racquetball, hiking, backpacking, paintballing, skateboarding, and skiing. The staff focuses on sports skills that enhance lifelong enjoyment with the belief that the focus on learning the technical skill is beneficial in the short term, and having a pleasurable activity for a lifetime makes addiction less attractive. Students are not expected to excel in sports, and they are invited to work out in a gym if that is what they prefer.

A National Institute of Health article indicates that the types of programs that emphasize sports for recovering teenagers often fall into the category of residential treatment communities. In other words, the philosophy behind these types of boarding-school arrangements is that a twenty-eight-day program (typical for many rehab programs) is simply too short for the emotional, mental, and behavioral restructuring required to retrain the adolescent to live a sober life. Some of the features of treatment communities for adolescents might include the following:

1. Treatment focuses on behavior, the emotions, and developmental tasks.
2. Adolescent programs are less confrontational than adult programs.
3. The emphasis is on education rather than work.
4. Adolescents have little say in the management of the program.

5. Staff members provide considerable supervision and evaluation.
6. Coexisting conditions, such as learning disabilities and ADHD, are assessed and managed.
7. Family therapy is well integrated into the program, and if family members are not available, social workers, probation officers, and other adult friends may participate in family therapy. Visiting the treatment community may be a challenge if it is far away from the parental home.

 **Fact**

Synanon was one of the first treatment communities, established in 1958 in Santa Monica, California, by Chuck Dederich Sr., and was active until 1989. This community focused first on drug rehabilitation and later expanded to holistic living and a full sense of recovery and service. Jazz musician Art Pepper credits Synanon for his recovery from heroin and describes the experience in detail in his book *Straight Life*. People who had the Synanon experience generally speak highly of it and remain in touch with each other. Some have gone into various businesses together or started their own recovery communities.

These types of learning communities generally have a staff that is a mixture of counselors who have gone through recovery themselves and consulting professionals, such as medical doctors and psychologists. Generally a nurse is present to monitor medications. The rules are somewhat strict in this type of recovery community, primarily in an effort to prohibit contraband drugs and alcohol and undue sexual activity.

## Mindful Meditation

Meditation and deep breathing help the recovering teenager achieve quiet and peace of mind, a way to get in touch with the soul and the spirit, making the addictive substances and behaviors less appealing. Marianne Marcus published an article for the National Institute of Health in 2009 indicating that one of the major challenges for the recovering addict is managing high stress levels. Meditation is a good method of managing stress, and some alternative recovery programs are based on that premise.

Mindfulness meditation, derived from Buddhist Vipassana traditions, was first used in the West in the 1970s to manage pain and mental health disorders. In recent years, it has found its way into recovery and treatment for various addictions. Marcus makes the following points about the features of mindfulness meditation for adolescents in recovery:

- The mind is trained to stay in the present moment.
- Mindfulness acknowledges the constant stream of thoughts, emotions, and bodily sensations, but the meditator learns not to react to them.
- The person meditating learns to control the point of attention.
- Meditation encourages deliberate, intelligent behavioral choices.
- Mindfulness is easily combined with other types of therapies.
- Treatment communities where everyone practices meditation provide a safe separation from the triggers and temptations of life on the outside.

Meditation is a useful technique for the recovering adolescent, as it teaches her that she need not give in to impulses, one of the difficulties of the addictive personality. With practice, a meditator is able to experience a whole range of thoughts and desires without taking action on them. An important aspect of meditation is to be aware of thoughts and feelings but to not judge them. This can be of enormous help to a teenage addict who tends toward constant self-criticism. Some relapse prevention programs using meditation have reported a decrease in the incidence of relapse when the participants meditated regularly.

Meditation is suggested in the twelve-step programs, although there is no pressure to do it in any particular way. Each member is encouraged to pray and meditate regularly as a way to be close to the Higher Power and to determine what direction the Higher Power is guiding the individual. Often it is said in twelve-step meetings that prayer is asking God for something, and meditation is listening to the answer. Such quietness is often contradictory to the typical nature of an addictive personality, and when learned can bring deep peace and serenity. Some recovery programs provide a combination of meditation and yoga, bringing in the physical component and conscious use of the muscles and energy.

## Nutritional Therapies

The substance addictions are notorious for leaving the addict malnourished and ill. Sometimes in the end stages of alcoholism the alcoholic has completely stopped eating, relying solely on the alcohol for sustenance. According to Linda Simmons, nutritional therapy in the treatment of addictions is designed to restore the body's balance of amino acids, essential fatty acids, vitamins, and minerals. The body has to have proper nutrition to enable it to naturally produce norepinephrine, serotonin, and endorphins, the chemicals that regulate mood and behavior. Vitamin C is thought to be helpful in moderating the physical and emotional symptoms of withdrawal. There is a also a study about chronic marijuana users that shows that taking 500 mg of the nutritional supplement N-acetylcysteine (amino acid) twice daily can reduce cravings for the drug.

Alcoholics, amphetamine addicts, and heroin addicts may suffer from hypoglycemia, leading to difficulties of depression, anxiety, and panic attacks. Nutritionists may suggest niacin, chromium, and magnesium after detoxification. Addiction harms the nervous system, the liver, and the digestive tract, and specific nutrients can assist in restoration. The B vitamins are often defi-cient in those who abuse sugar, caffeine, alcohol, and drugs, and potassium deficiencies are common. If nutrition therapy is a con-sideration, search for a professional who has experience working with recovering addicts and alcoholics, as he will understand the various ramifications of your teen's recovery.

# Service and Work

Service is a large part of all the twelve-step programs, and as soon as a newcomer has a bit of sobriety, she is given a task to do—making coffee, greeting newcomers, passing out books, or putting away chairs. Such responsibility and the belief that some-one thinks she can do something worthwhile is good for the self-esteem of the newcomer, and some of the service positions require talking with others, which is good for drawing the newly sober person out of isolation.

For example, if the job is that of literature enthusiast, it entails talking to newer people about pamphlets and books and what each offers, and the literature enthusiast usually ends up reading all the literature, which is a personal bonus. Members who are in twelve-step programs for a number of years sometimes progress in service responsibility to positions as delegates, attending state and national conferences where organization business is managed. Such responsibility and growth is a personal, and sometimes pro-fessional, bonus for the member.

Homeboy Industries and HomeGirl Cafe in Los Angeles has found that providing former gang members and addicts with meaningful employment, as well as guidance with housing and finances, creates miracle after miracle, as lives are restored to functionality and dignity. Similarly, the Fresco market in the city of Hermann, near Los Angeles, makes a practice of hiring ex-addicts who are newly clean and sober, mentoring them into a useful career in the store. The manager prides himself on the successes of his protégés, and the workers are deeply grateful to be on their way to a normal life. Framed photographs with their personal stories are prominently displayed in the supermarket for the customers to view.

## Equine Therapy

Being around animals tends to lower a person's heart rate and blood pressure, decrease stress levels, increase endorphin levels, and provide a sense of calm and well-being. Equine therapy combines the advantages of being around animals with the benefits of being outdoors, close to nature.

Equine therapy is the use of horses in a therapeutic setting and has been shown to be of great benefit to addicts who have lost their way in terms of life priorities. In this type of therapy, usually combined with other therapies, the recovering teenager spends time with the horse every day, feeding it, grooming it, and exercising it. The adolescent learns how to put the saddle on the horse and may learn how to ride the horse, although that is not always the case. Some horses in equine therapy programs are too old or injured to be ridden.

Working with horses increases the adolescent's sense of self-worth and provides a different focus. It can be a new experience for the teenager to feel the horse's trust and unconditional love. Horses are very sensitive, and the adolescent gets feedback on the effects of his moods, anger, and tendency to act out in an erratic way. This is useful for a teenager who has learned to tune out much of what is said to him in the way of criticism and recriminations. Once the bond with the horse is formed, the adolescent wants to preserve that good relationship, creating a fresh motivation for straightening out his motivation and behavior.

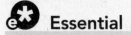 **Essential**

Control is often an issue for those in addiction recovery and their family members, as the addiction spins everyone out of control. A drug rehab patient at the Hazelden facility in Minnesota was ruining her relationships by bulldozing over everyone most of the time, and she found that when relating to her horse in the equine-assisted therapy, controlling had a negative effect on the horse. As she highly valued that relationship, she backed off and learned to do so with people as well, forming a healthy relationship with a Higher Power to guide her in all her dealings with others.

Caring for a horse requires structure and a regular schedule, something that probably was missing in the addict's life. Horses are gentle, intelligent animals, yet they have clear boundaries and will not allow the caretaker to lead them into illogical or dangerous places. This healthy relationship can be a beginning for the addict re-learning how to have relationships. According to one equine therapist, this type of recovery work is excellent for people who tend to intellectualize too much, burying their emotions until they are inaccessible. Working with horses allows those emotions to emerge and run their course. Equine therapy programs are conducted by certified equine therapists.

## Expressive Arts Therapies

Many addiction recovery programs, both inpatient and outpatient, include components of dance, drama, poetry, writing, movement, and visual arts such as painting and ceramics. The creative arts therapies serve many valuable purposes in treating addicted teenagers. First, they provide a relaxed atmosphere in which the adolescent can reconnect with his inner self, begin to understand an identity apart from the addiction, and explore a personal spirituality. Second, the arts have a way of drawing from the subconscious mind, allowing the artist to express difficult and perplexing emotions. Not everyone is highly verbal, and highly introverted teenagers can have an outlet with recovery programs that include the arts. And third, because many addicts have lost the ability to feel pleasure and enjoy life, the arts can begin this deeper type of rehabilitation, giving the addict something to live for besides the next drink or high.

The visual arts allow the recovering addict to express ideas and feelings that are complex and mostly inaccessible, adding to his self-confidence and sense of fulfillment. Those participating in the visual arts can feel a strong empowerment because of the control of the medium and what goes on the canvas. Creation is a marvelously uplifting experience, one needed by the addict who has been struggling against the forces of addiction.

## Dance

The New Dawn adolescent treatment centers in California offer dance and movement therapy, which is especially beneficial for those undergoing treatment for eating disorders. Eating-disordered individuals often have a distorted image of their bodies, and dance and movement experiences do much to assist in learning the true expressive nature of their physical selves. Dance therapy offers structured exercises, as well as freestyle dancing, and the leaders are generally certified dance therapists.

## Poetry

Charles Gillispie mentions in his article from the *Journal of Poetry Therapy* (2001) that writing poetry in collaborative groups in a treatment center is an excellent way to facilitate communication and deeper bonds among the participants. One of his activities, called Round Robin, entails each person saying a spontaneous line, going around the circle, with one member acting as scribe. Discussion ensues, and various meanings are teased out, although he noted that in such a group activity for adolescent girls, they were not as concerned about interpretation as they might have been in a school setting. Various behavioral traits came out in the poems, as with those who continually talk "drug talk," bringing the subject back to alcohol or marijuana. One in the group expressed violent ideas, and others in the group mentioned that they were afraid of her the day she moved into the center, as she had broken a vase against the wall.

### ✅ Fact

At Paradigm Malibu in California, recovering teenage addicts have the opportunity to explore family relationships in drama therapy sessions. These sessions are led by a certified drama therapist. Emotions can run high, but the leader sets guidelines and parameters, such as no touching, so that no one gets hurt emotionally or physically. This work is similar in some ways to the Gestalt method in conventional therapy, where the client speaks to an imaginary person sitting in an empty chair.

# CHAPTER 20

# Maintenance: A New Norm

Everything is different in addiction-free living. You, your teen-ager, and others in the family may feel slightly disoriented for a time. It is difficult to realize, but if you have been living with addiction for a few years, patterns became set without anyone really noticing them. Gradually, new ways of living for your recovering adolescent and the rest of the family are embraced. Your hope is to set a healthy family stage where the newly sober teenager can lay a new foundation and start a new life.

## A Routine for Healthy Sobriety

Treatment centers have a specific routine that everyone follows, giving the recovering residents a feeling of security and some control over small aspects of their lives. Such structure prevents the newly recovering person from wandering off into daydreams, boredom, and longing for the more exciting times of using and abusing. You won't be able to duplicate the schedule of the treatment center, nor should you try, but a definite plan for each day and week makes life easier for everyone.

Some families have a large calendar available in a communal area, perhaps the kitchen, where each person is able to see what is going on for each family member. Appointments are noted, as are classes outside of school and leisure plans that involve everyone.

You might want to note birthdays, paydays, and dates of bills due. Probably your teenager will have a planning calendar of her own to keep track of homework assignments, therapy appointments, and work to do before each therapy session.

Offer to spend time with your teenager to look at her calendar and schedule, perhaps every Sunday evening, in order to avoid missing something that needs preparation and advance planning. This may feel awkward and uncomfortable for both of you, as she likely didn't plan a lot during the addicted times, and you weren't as involved in the daily activities of her life. If you can work through the awkwardness, she will be able to learn some skills that will help throughout her life, never being at the mercy of whims or forgetfulness.

Do what you can to encourage a balanced life for your teenager—fun, spirituality, friendship, education, exercise, healthy meals, family time, and creative time. This balance will help her maintain a sobriety-friendly life now and in the future. As with any child, your ultimate goal is to raise a self-sufficient person who is able to function as an adult on her own. It might have been necessary to take a few steps backward in terms of dealing with the addiction and recovery, but the basic movement is still forward. If you have an attitude of faith, your teenager is likely to follow your example.

## Cultivating Self-Discipline

In new sobriety you may instill a daily routine for your teen, but over time, the goal is to inculcate self-discipline so that the structure is internalized. This process may take months or even years, especially if the teenager used and abused substances and behaviors for an extended time period. Even though the body may be relatively grown up, the emotional maturity has likely lagged behind. Patience is in order. Speak calmly and firmly but never condescendingly, as that's offensive, no matter the age of the individual.

## Let Them Take the Lead

Bit by bit, let your teenager establish some skill and credibility with internalized self-discipline. It can begin with small chores at home—making the bed every day, emptying the dishwasher, doing her own laundry. School is more or less the job of a teenager, and as she does better remembering and doing assignments, you can back off a bit with your help. At first you might want to be in touch with teachers, guidance counselors, and therapists, but gradually that checking can diminish as your teenager takes more and more responsibility for herself.

If your adolescent squandered money on the addiction, gradually rebuild some good habits with her finances. Spend some time each week or month on her budget. Help her understand the concepts of living within her means and adjusting her expenditures according to her allowance or amount of money earned from chores or a part-time job. Such practical skills will serve her for a lifetime, and it is time well spent to learn the basics of budgeting, saving, planning, and maintaining a checking account.

Clothing these days does not require a lot of care, but the basics of laundry, storing in a closet or chest of drawers, ironing, and mending require time in order to present a good appearance. If you have been the family maid in the past, it is time to redistribute the tasks so that each person is relatively self-sufficient, including the recovering teenager. Maintaining clothing takes some time, and with your encouragement your teenager can learn to apportion a part of each evening or weekend to planning the outfit for the next day.

If car maintenance is a part of your teenager's responsibility, factor in the time and money to take care of those things. At the very least, whoever uses a family car should return it with gas in the tank and washed at regular intervals. Any trash from meals out should be removed, and in general, the car should be returned in the same shape it was when borrowed. If your teenager has earnings, it would be prudent to expect some responsibility in paying the insurance. If there have been fines and an increase in the cost of the policy because of your teen's misconduct, such repayment can be allotted over a period of time.

## Rewards Within the Family

There is much to learn for everyone in the family in treatment and recovery. If each family member is actively involved in therapy and group work, it will be easier to keep the focus on the present, letting go of the resentments and chaos of the addicted months or years. Help everyone catch the addict doing good things and compliment such efforts in the right direction. Even the smallest children can learn to say something nice from time to time. This requires that each person give up the idea that the addicted teenager is a scapegoat, rebel, or villain. Each family member can work to reinforce each other to look for the good.

Little by little, even the small children can be taught to say a good word now and then to the addict. Maybe it could be something small, like complimenting how nicely she has folded the laundry. This good step helps the addict to feel better about doing small things for oneself. This basic goodness enhances how the entire family gets along.

## Forgive and Forget

There is a misconception that forgiving others means that you condone their bad behavior and are ready to resume the relationship with the bad times behind you. This is not necessarily the case. You do not have to accept your child's bad behavior in order to move forward with forgiveness. It can be a matter of redirecting your attention to other people and situations so that your child is not constantly on your mind. This mental feat can be a bit tricky but reaps tremendous rewards of freedom, as it takes a lot of energy to remain angry with someone—especially your teenager.

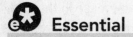 **Essential**

Resentment is a harmful emotion, damaging relationships, your general perception of people and life around you, and possibly your health. It is said in the twelve-step programs that "resentment is like swallowing poison, expecting the other person to die." One way to prevent resentments is to have fewer expectations of others, just letting them be who they are.

In order to reach the place of forgiveness, it can be helpful to write out a list of your resentments, in detail, and share it with a partner or trusted friend. The mere act of letting another person in on the sordid happenings takes away some of the power of the past. Another useful method is to say out loud or to write out specific forgiveness for those who have mistreated you, including your child struggling with addiction. If you decide to do this verbally, it is a good way to pass the time while driving. It takes many repetitions to reach the belief that it actually is possible. An example of such a statement could be, "I forgive _____ for _____. That person is free, and I am free." This kind of work done over a period of weeks or months brings peace and acceptance. Once you have done your mental clearing work, it will be possible to relate to your teen on a more positive note. One of the ironic truths of life is that overall, those people that you have resented for so long have no idea that you have harbored years of anger. Most likely, your child has no idea as well.

## Diligence Without Helicopter Surveillance

There's a fine balance between supervision and smothering. The need for supervision runs counter to the teenager's need to grow into independence. Your monitoring of her every move will possibly feel insulting and intrusive to her need to sprout wings of her own. However, the presence of addiction, treatment, and recovery has altered the situation to a certain extent. This new element gives you the right to be more a part of your teenager's daily activities than you might have been without the addiction.

Try not to be dogmatic or dictatorial in your new role, striving more for neutral, loving consistency. Remember that adolescents crave structure, and you can provide that. You are the loving container within which she can feel safe and thrive. Keep it firm with a neutral, no-nonsense attitude, and your teenager may come around to appreciating the care and attention you are giving to creating a good environment for her new recovery life. Do your best not to be accusatory or punitive in your questions and comments. It will help if you take a deep breath before checking, and minimal eye contact may help the situation. Imagine you're going over the contents of a memo with a coworker, and not much emotion is invested. When you can maintain this type of neutrality, you are able to save your energy. Possibly you and your teenager are tuned into each other's voices and body language, and you may experience times of manipulation when the teenager wants to go back to the old ways. Enlist the help of your spouse or other trusted relative if there is no spouse, in clear, honest conversations about the new rules and how you plan to enforce them. Gradually loosen the constraints, but only after your teenager has proven trustworthy in the new behaviors.

## Hang with New Peers

An important part of your teenager's ongoing sobriety will be to stay away from the previous friends who were a part of the drinking and drugging time period. Teenagers can be very susceptible to triggers associated with the addiction times, and simply seeing those people or being in those places could be enough to motivate a relapse. It is not entirely possible to prevent a relapse, but you do have a certain degree of control over whom your teenager spends time with. You can say who is invited into your home, and you can say when your adolescent has use of the car and require clear information about where he is going.

Your rules may have to be a little tighter than you both were accustomed to before treatment and recovery, but you have to believe that it is for his own good. There can be a great deal of reporting and checking in, so that your newly recovering teenager is not at the mercy of too many environmental temptations. It might not be fun to police the situation, but in truth, trust has been lost in many ways, and it takes time to regain solid footing.

Encourage your teenager to continue relationships with those he met during rehab, and get to know the parents, if that is convenient and comfortable. As much as possible, create a context for a sober, thriving life. Aftercare is important, and if continuing groups and therapy are available for you and your teenager, avail yourself of them, as it is a wise protection from the temptations of the previous peer group.

## Genuine Hope for New Beginnings

It is important to recognize that it is possible to maintain sobriety throughout one's life, and to continue to grow as a human being without the influence of illegal or addictive substances. It is also important to recognize your teen's frailties as she continues on with her alcohol- and drug-free life. There will be ups and downs, as everyone has their flaws, but sobriety is absolutely attainable with the appropriate tools and effort.

As the alcoholic or drug abuser in the family begins to heal, so does everyone else in the family. It doesn't all have to occur at the same time, but eventually healthy relationship will begin to form in place of destructive ones. Don't give up on your teen or yourself.

# Appendix A:
# Those Who Have Been There

This section features interviews and case histories of people who have traveled a road similar to yours. In many of the stories, the subjects have overcome significant obstacles when dealing with addiction. The struggles presented in these case histories are real, but many also highlight examples of when intervention, treatment, and support networks do work—and when recovery is possible. The names have been changed and identifying details altered in order to protect the anonymity of those whose stories are told.

## Danielle

Danielle is married with two children. One, a son, was a model child—quiet and well behaved. The other one, Amy, was troubled and problematic from about age eleven, when after an argument with her mother, she pulled a kitchen knife on her. It seemed that Amy always wanted to be the queen bee, manipulating her parents to get what she wanted. As she moved into her teens, she threatened suicide many times and made a couple of actual suicide attempts.

A counselor that the family was seeing suggested that they call her bluff and not react. The suicide threats and attempts stopped, but Amy started having trouble in school. She ran away several times. She would get into verbal altercations with her dad, bang her head repeatedly against the wall, and the police would threaten to arrest the father, as he was very angry about the situation. The Department of Family Services was called in several times, and Amy was sent to an alternative school, where, according to Danielle, she learned to smoke and picked up some other bad habits from the other students. When Amy was at home, other members of the family slept with their doors locked.

For a time, Amy lived with an older female friend in an environment where there was a live-in boyfriend and drinking and alcohol. She became addicted to chaos. The family took her to two different psychiatric hospitals, and she had sessions with a psychiatrist, who also prescribed medication. It is the mother's opinion that she learned more bad behavior in these facilities.

By the time she was sixteen, Amy was sneaking out at night to meet boys she liked, mostly bad boys. Her father called the police one of those times, and she was placed in a juvenile detention center where she learned more bad habits. The family went to court and the state appointed a guardian to look after the interests of the girl. She lived in a group home for about a year, an experience that had a positive effect. The facility taught responsibility and regular attendance in school, and she did well.

At this time she had one goal in life—to get pregnant—which she did at about age seventeen. She finished high school before the child was born. She lived with the father of the baby for about two years. He became a police officer and became abusive in the relationship, so she left. She started college but met another man, became involved with him, and dropped out of college. The father of her child took custody because the new boyfriend had a background of prison and drugs. Amy became pregnant by this boyfriend, married him, and had another child.

Amy claimed she had been smoking since age twelve and drinking since age fourteen. Her parents did not know about these activities. She seemed inclined toward risky behavior, even smoking throughout all three of her pregnancies, and she has been easily overwhelmed by too much stimuli and too many choices. In terms of family background, Amy's father is a sober alcoholic. His father was an alcoholic, a military man who moved frequently, requiring that Amy's father change schools every year. He learned not to be close to people. He favored the son, as the son was so well behaved. Danielle's mother is bipolar.

As she matured, Amy took more responsibility for her life choices and for being a good parent to her children. Amy is now in her thirties, works as a certified nursing assistant, and is involved in the care of all three of her children. She is somewhat calmer and no longer feels the need to numb her feelings with alcohol and drugs, but she does continue to smoke. The family is hopeful that as she matures, some of the difficulties will level out, making it easier for her to regulate her life. It was the recovering from addiction to chaos that led her to develop a real life of her own, a growing result of evolutional maturity.

## Andy

Andy is a single parent who is also a lesbian, and has raised her son alone since his infancy. She was in the military and learned the profession of respiratory therapy, which she practiced after leaving the military, along with occasional jobs as a translator, as her family is from Puerto Rico and she is fluent in both Spanish and English.

She managed very well on her own, keeping up with her job and raising her son until he reached high-school age, when he started to get into trouble with drugs and alcohol. Andy was active in Al-Anon by this time, as she had an on-again, off-again relationship with an alcoholic woman that brought stress and conflict into her household, even though the two never lived together.

Toward the end of high school, her son was arrested for a series of credit card crimes and ended up in prison. This was devastating to Andy, as she adored her son and had done everything within her power to be a good mother for him. She focused on her own life while he was away, visiting only occasionally, as the prison was far from her home and the security system for visiting was so tight it made her feel like a criminal as well. Mostly she stayed in touch by mail and went on with her own recovery and professional life.

In prison the son finished his high school with a GED and regularly attended twelve-step groups that were offered inside the prison, helping him to gradually grasp the idea of recovery and think that maybe he could create a new life for himself after he had served his sentence. After his release, he spent more time with his girlfriend, who became pregnant. Although he was still young, he decided to get married and start living the life of a responsible man.

His wife went to college and got a degree in nursing, and he worked as an information technology assistant, mostly self-taught. The two of them juggled schedules with two jobs, a baby, and then soon another baby, with the help of both mothers who pitched in as babysitters when needed.

As Andy looks back, it seems that the time he spent in prison was a turning point for her son. It was a great blessing that he was able to detox in prison and receive the support and education of the recovery programs that are offered there. The families have good, solid lives now, and she is deeply grateful.

# Lonni

Lonni, a grandmother and great-grandmother, has the dubious honor of raising her great-grandchild because of her granddaughter's drug addiction. She, of course, loves the child, but didn't expect to be raising a two-year-old when she herself was moving into her sixties. Her son, the father of the young mother, is busy with his life, and is interested in the situation but doesn't have the time and resources to be of practical, consistent help.

The granddaughter has been troubled and problematic throughout her teen years—missing school, drinking, and then getting into drugs. The pregnancy was unwelcome, but she decided to have the child, even though she is immature and unable to provide for the baby. The great-grandmother has stepped in to become the custodial caretaker, along with her husband, a real estate broker. They have the time and means to care for the child.

The granddaughter has been arrested and is currently on probation, but is irresponsible about staying in touch with her probation officer. She eludes the regular check-ins and frequently disappears, sometimes showing up at her father's house and sometimes hanging out with friends who are using drugs.

Lonni is frequently distraught over the granddaughter's behavior. Her granddaughter lies, promises to visit the child and doesn't show up, and greatly inconveniences everyone involved. It is difficult for Lonni not to be angry a lot of the time, as the erratic behavior of the granddaughter impacts everyone's lives. It becomes a major accomplishment when Lonni and her husband hire a sitter and get away for a quiet, companionable evening, as much of their existence is turned upside down by the presence of the baby and the chaotic behavior of the granddaughter. Despite the challenges that her granddaughter creates, Lonni finds it quite difficult to imagine completely cutting her off, as she would like for her to have a relationship with her child. Like many parents and guardians of children with addictions, Lonni finds comfort and support in Al-Anon, a twelve-step program for people who have been affected by someone's drinking. If your child is drinking, finding a local Al-Anon meeting can be a huge support for you. You will meet other parents who are going through similar situations and can offer their experience, strength, and hope.

# Terry

Terry has three children, two girls and a boy, rather close together in age. The two girls were always more trouble than the boy, who was a high achiever and did rather well in most aspects of his life. Terry is Mexican American, and her parents were hard-working, second-generation people, spending most of their waking hours working in order to provide a good material existence for their children. Terry recalls that the family atmosphere was cold and nonloving. There was a very high emphasis on appearances and doing well. She recalls going to parochial school every day hoping that there were no wrinkles in her uniform.

Terry married rather young, mostly to get away from her parents and to have a life of her own. She married a white man from Iowa, thinking that would be the solution to her problems. There were cultural differences in the relationship that neither person expected. Terry's conventional, conservative Catholic background tremendously clashed with the laid-back, casual personality of her husband. Even the patterns of when and how often to visit relatives caused conflict. Then everything got worse. It turned out that he was a drinker and drug user. He died while his children were teenagers.

All three of the children drank in high school and continued to do so in their twenties and thirties. Although the boy was able to control his drinking enough to run a successful business, the girls floundered, going from profession to profession, relationship to relationship, never completely finding a mature, satisfying niche. The older girl had difficulties with depression and has been in and out of mental health facilities. The younger girl seems to have the most problems, exhibiting the strongest elements of the alcoholic personality—deceit, manipulation, irresponsibility, and refusal to make healthy decisions about her life.

For years, Terry blamed herself for many of the children's problems, including alcoholism. However, she realizes that she did not have enough information to help her children when they were young, and that they made their own choices as adults. She has found recovery for herself in the Al-Anon twelve-step program and does the best she can to focus on her own happiness while loving her children. Being able to understand that her children's addictions are not all her fault, and that she must detach from their unhealthy behavior to live a fulfilling life, has given her peace of mind and happiness.

# Donny

Donny is a transgendered person who came from a highly troubled and dysfunctional family. He realized during his middle-school years that there was something wrong with his body, that somehow he was really a boy, although he had been born a girl. His Italian parents were violent with each other, and beat their children—Donny, his two brothers, and his sister. The family came from a wine culture, and annual grape stomps were a family ritual.

During Donny's teen years the tension from his dysphoria and the family violence caused him to act out, drinking with friends and practicing risky behaviors. He did not have a clear-cut sense of identity and had no knowledge yet of people who go through the transgender experience. He felt the most comfortable with gay people, and in retrospect, he assumes that most people in his family and friendship circle assumed that he was lesbian. He didn't have enough knowledge about his actual situation or any information about what his choices might be. All these tumultuous concerns were mixed with the normal angst of adolescence, making him ripe for a tendency toward alcohol and drugs.

So much violence in the home set a pattern for Donny, and during his young adult years, there were many altercations with the police, landlords, and romantic partners. The ER became his home away from home. Donny relocated to San Francisco, where he allied himself with transgendered friends and professionals who helped him to start the transition process. All along the way, there was drinking and partying with whoever would accept him as a person. Because of his violent childhood, he had no censoring discernment regarding who was safe and who was dangerous.

Upon reflection, Donny is able to see that the mold was cast during childhood. It was probably destiny that he became a drinker, and later an abuser of prescription drugs, as he had no role models whatsoever for handling difficult emotions and conflict. He learned in his family that angry, violent outbursts were the only way to have any impact, creating a life of confusion and turmoil.

His role models were not positive. His father was a violent, somewhat shady man with connections to the Italian mob, someone who had no qualms about dishonest business practices or using people to his benefit. Donny's mother was a beautiful, rather passive woman who had married her husband because of a teenage pregnancy. She was an incest survivor at the hands of an uncle and felt powerless to do anything about the unhealthy forces and practices in her home and family.

As he settled into his transsexual transition, Donny found recovery from alcohol in the Alcoholics Anonymous twelve-step program, and was able to moderate the use of prescription drugs on his own. He enjoys a functional life, mostly with twelve-step and LGBT friends, dates, and is active in various political causes. He is so grateful that he survived his various challenges that he wrote a book about his experiences, and is attempting to have it published.

## Betty

Betty has two children, a boy and a girl. Her parents had mental problems, and her father was a drinker. She married a man who turned out to be very controlling and dictatorial, making it difficult for her to have friends or any authority over her children. Her husband was addicted to pills, especially Dexedrine (an amphetamine), and had mental problems. Betty eventually got a divorce, as she was unhappy and unable to have any experiences of her own within the marriage.

Both of the children used pot and alcohol in their teens. The girl, a few years older than her brother, started at about age fourteen, spending a lot of time with a male who influenced her to use pot.

Betty remembers that once the boy's mother called to see if the daughter was at home and could tell her where her son was.

The girl had tucked a stuffed animal in bed to make it look as if she was asleep. Betty's daughter and the male friend ditched class a lot, and the girl was expelled from school. Betty took her to a mental health agency, but the helpful effects were not long lasting. Through her father's influence, the daughter was able to transfer to a different high school, from which she graduated.

The daughter was able to attend community college and go on to earn two master's degrees, but she was unable to work. She didn't use drugs or drink while she was in graduate school, as she was worried about the effects on her brain. After graduating she started using again, primarily pills, and her father supported her financially, which Betty can see in retrospect weakened the daughter's confidence and initiative.

Betty relates that at one time while she and her husband were still together, the family went into therapy. She gained strength and started countering some of the husband's power moves, and he stopped the therapy. Betty somewhat blames herself for her children's difficulties, feeling sad that she had no role models for loving relationships and didn't really know how to connect with people, including her husband and children. Her childhood home was rather cold, and at one point in her childhood, she remembers that her mother paid a friend to have Betty live with her, so she was free to pursue her own interests.

The daughter is now living in another state with infrequent communication with Betty. She is living and working in a Salvation Army and is clean and sober, as she cannot stay there if she is using and drinking. She is unable to get work and is frustrated because she does not have a useful credential, in spite of having two graduate degrees.

Betty has found solace and support in the National Alliance on Mental Illness (NAMI), an organization that provides help to those coping with family members who have mental illness. She recently finished a seven-week class with NAMI and also spends considerable time with her hobby of photography, occasionally taking on freelance jobs and photo shoots.

# Jennifer

Jennifer and her husband had one daughter who was an outgoing and social girl. The high school their daughter attended was known in that city to be the "drinking school." The girl sometimes would join her friends to do homework together after school, and the parents didn't suspect that anything was amiss, although their daughter seemed unhappy. The parents did what they could to support and help, eventually transferring the girl to a private liberal arts high school where the child flourished, developing her talent for abstract painting, culminating in a senior show at the time of her graduation. The daughter went to college for a year to study graphic arts and then went to a college in San Francisco, where she graduated with a degree in art.

Jennifer relates that only in retrospect, as the daughter told more of her stories, did the true picture become apparent. It was at summer camp that the child took her first drink, and she loved it. She had been drinking for years since that first time. The homework group was actually a drinking group that did some homework, and in college she was heavily enmeshed with a drinking and drugging crowd.

After college, the daughter went back to her hometown and lived in her parents' basement. She continued to drink and get into financial trouble until the parents intervened, explaining to her that she could continue down her self-destructive path or she could start recovery. She elected to try recovery, and attended A.A. meetings, achieving as many as three years of sobriety at one time. She relapsed and started over several times. ·

Jennifer and her husband are now divorced. Her ex-husband was and is a daily pot smoker, and Jennifer no longer wanted that to be a part of her life. She suspects that her ex-husband started his daughter on pot to "help wean her from alcohol." Jennifer is adopted but researched her birth family and found no history of alcohol or drug abuse. Her ex-husband had numerous aunts and uncles who were alcoholic, and a sister who is an alcoholic. His father was a gambler.

Jennifer had therapy for several years to cope with the addictions of her husband and daughter and has attended Al-Anon for support. The daughter has always worked, although the expenses of her on-and-off addictions keep her on the edge financially. Currently, she has a boyfriend and is happy, although she still struggles with her weight and considers herself a social drinker.

# Alissa

Alissa and her husband have three boys, and one exhibited problems during his teen years. During his junior-high years he wouldn't do his homework, and Alissa sat with him to help him complete the assignments. He could do the work if she read the assignment to him out loud. She wonders in retrospect if he had a learning disability.

In high school the son wanted to play baseball, but his father thought it was too dangerous, so the son went into music. He wrote songs, formed a band, did some tours, and signed with a record company for a recording, and was functioning pretty well. Alissa learned years later that he was drinking and doing drugs— everything except heroin, according to him. He had a car accident in a borrowed car and decided not to drive any more after that, as he didn't want to have difficulties with the law.

The son moved out when he was eighteen. The family owns rental properties, so he moved into one of those and worked in a restaurant that the family owns. The family had a savings account for his college tuition, but he was not interested in college, and the parents gave him access to the money. During the time he worked in the restaurant he ranted at Alissa every day, and she put up with it, as he seemed to calm down afterward. She says that she covered things up a lot, trying to preserve a good family image.

In terms of family history and the genetic component, Alissa's husband was adopted, so it is unknown whether there is addiction on that side of the family. Her husband drinks three beers a day, having cut back from their early married years when he drank a twelve-pack a day. On Alissa's side, her maternal grandfather was an alcoholic who committed suicide at age fifty. Two of her maternal uncles are heavy drinkers. On the paternal side, there was an uncle who wrote bad checks and spent a lot of time in prison. A paternal aunt was addicted to morphine.

At the present time, the son is living in a basement apartment in the family home. He is not working, but seems to have created enough of a life for himself with his music and artistic pursuits that he enjoys himself. His parents monitor his medication for schizophrenia, and he is allowed five beers a day. He listens to music and plays a lot but doesn't record or write anything down. Alissa mentions that he had therapy at one time but gave that up, as the therapist wouldn't prescribe the medication that he wanted. Alissa has been open with the other two sons about the genetic component of the brother's difficulty. The two brothers have not, as yet, married and had children. Alissa herself finds solace in Al-Anon, her church affiliation, reading, and helping with the family businesses.

## Steve

Steve's daughter started having problems with anorexia nervosa when she was in high school. Steve sought out Al-Anon, even though the child's difficulty was not alcohol, and he was welcomed into the meetings. He was frantic, as his daughter was of average height, and her weight was veering down into the 90-pound range. He was afraid she was going to die.

Sometimes he was so overwrought with emotion when he shared in the meetings that he could barely breathe and put together sentences. He received much warm support and was able to calm down after a few months. He described how things were in his family. Every meal was a battleground, trying to get the girl to eat, and every family member focused on what she put into her mouth and what she left on her plate. It was a nightmare for all concerned.

With the help of his support network, he investigated treatment options for his daughter and decided on hospitalization. He felt sad about this, as it felt that he was incarcerating her, and that he had failed in some ways. However, the hospital staff had specialized knowledge to guide anorectic patients back into normal eating and normal perception. The daughter had body dysmorphic disorder (BDD), a mental illness that causes a person to be preoccupied with perceived flaws in his or her physical appearance. She always felt that she was fat. She also felt unloved, and thought that the only way to get attention was to not eat.

Little by little, the girl responded to treatment and started gaining weight. After she left the hospital, she continued with outpatient treatment, and the whole family was in therapy for months, as the dynamics had to change.

Steve is now a relaxed, less obsessed parent, and proud of his daughter, who is studying interior design at the local community college. She still lives at home in order for the family to be able to afford her education, but the mealtimes are no longer battlegrounds. Steve is quite happy that his daughter and the entire family survived the ordeal; he continues to attend Al-Anon, as it helps him remain calm, no matter what challenge comes into his life. He is completely grateful for the eating disorders program at the local hospital.

## Alice

Alice grew up in what seemed like a normal family at the time, but in retrospect, two parts of her family dynamic dramatically impacted her. Her father was an alcoholic, and one of her grandfathers was obsessed with the weight of each person in the family, especially the women. This undue attention on her physicality caused her to vacillate between gaining weight and losing weight. A male gym teacher had an important influence on her, praising her when she was thin and criticizing the overweight girls in front of an entire class. All these pressures resulted in several years of bulimia and becoming overweight.

A turning point was the unfortunate death of her father, only in his late forties at the time. Alice had experimented with alcohol and drugs, but felt the dangers were too great in terms of what she saw as the devastation in her father's life. With the help and support of her mother and sister, she got treatment in a hospital program for eating disorders. She lived with her sister at the conclusion of that program, as she needed guidance and daily mentoring about what were normal, three square meals a day. Both her mother and her sister attended family therapy sessions during follow-up aftercare treatment. Her condition stabilized. She was able to finish her GED and get a good job in a bookstore.

Alice is in her twenties now, happy with her job, addiction-free, and able to maintain a normal weight for her height and body type without going to either extreme of losing or gaining unnecessarily. She has allowed her innate creativity to flourish, supplements her bookstore job with modeling stints, and has published a book about her recovery experience.

# Polly

Polly and her husband, an alcoholic, had two sons, both of whom had some problems with alcohol and drugs during the high-school years. Polly chose to get a divorce from her husband, as it seemed that his alcoholism was progressing, and it was too much for her to deal with, along with her own career and raising the children.

One of the sons got into trouble with the law and ended up in prison, where he completed his GED and participated in the prison's twelve-step program. He went through detox in prison and was medically monitored for his safety. Upon his release, he married and had a son, whom Polly observes carefully, as she understands the genetic component of the disease. The little boy's father has done fairly well maintaining his sobriety with the help of Alcoholics Anonymous, although he has had relapses. He has become a responsible family man.

Polly has been in Al-Anon for decades, and the support of the Twelve Steps program allowed her to make the decision to leave her husband and support her sons through their recovery process. She is now retired and does a great deal of service for the fellowship, holding various leadership positions and representing groups at the regional levels.

# Jessica

Jessica had a seven-year relationship with a man who she realizes in retrospect was and is probably an alcoholic. They were engaged, planning to be married, and the relationship ended.

The young man was not a drinker in high school, but he enlisted in the military right out of high school and began drinking at that time. According to Jessica, if an alcoholic's emotional development stops at the time he starts drinking, she was having a relationship with a perennial eighteen-year-old.

Jessica recalls that during the earliest years of their relationship, he would be sober or dry for a period of time and then go out with a buddy and get thoroughly drunk. He always said that he did not have a drinking problem and could stop at any time. During the course of their relationship, he generally did not hide the drinking, but Jessica noticed that it increased over that time. Toward the end, he would get a large soda, drink part of it, and fill the container with rum.

Lying was a part of the fiancé's behavior from the beginning, although it took time to become evident. During the final months of the relationship, Jessica noticed many calls to a particular girl who lived in a nearby town. There were numerous very long calls when Jessica was out of town for her work. When she confronted him about the calls, he said, "I didn't make those calls. I don't even know who that is." One day his phone was lying on the kitchen counter, and an incoming text beeped. The phone was turned on, so Jessica read it, and it was an erotic text from the same person.

He had financial difficulties fairly consistently, getting frequent payday loans to tide himself over. At one point, Jessica paid off several thousands of dollars of payday loans, telling him it was a dealbreaker if he got one more loan. He got one two months later. Soon after that he had the household mail stopped because a check had bounced, and he didn't want Jessica to know about that. She was starting to realize the seriousness of his various addictions, and they seemed to get worse.

He ended the relationship saying he was unhappy and wanted to be on his own. He seemed to need a bit more freedom. In three months he begged to come back, saying that he made a terrible mistake and wanted to "get her back." It has been almost two years since the relationship ended, and he still calls her the love of his life and says he would do anything for the relationship to start again.

At one point, he attended A.A. for several months, trying to prove that he could stop drinking. During that time, his mother frequently offered him drinks, saying that she'd like him to have just one "to keep her company." These days he socializes a lot with drinkers, favoring young women that he can rescue, take home, and keep out of trouble. Most of his close friends are married women. He apologizes to Jessica for some of the things that he did wrong during the relationship, but never owns up to his deeper addictions that created difficulties. He habitually blames others when he's in trouble and continues to show a lack of responsibility in many aspects of his life, although he is a good worker and always has a job.

He is aware that Jessica attends Al-Anon and assumes that she goes because of all the things he did. He thinks that because she continues to take part in Al-Anon there is a chance that he can resume the relationship because she's still there, "talking about him." He doesn't understand that twelve-step programs are spiritual blueprints for a good life, not just a way of coping with an alcoholic. He still acts as if Jessica is the love of his life, and in time, he will be with her again.

## Louise, Frank, and Maria

Louise and Frank adopted their daughter Maria when she was only two. Maria's older half siblings were placed with relatives when her biological mother, who was a methamphetamine addict, had the children removed by child protective services. For years, Maria seemed to make a great adjustment to their home, doing well in school and taking gymnastics. Maria was accepted by the extended family on both sides, but had some counseling related to her adoption as her different ethnic background made for some emotional confusion when she was in middle school. However, in her sophomore year, Louise and Frank began to notice Maria's grades dropping, and there were unexcused absences from classes that showed up on her final report card.

That summer, they faced several shouting matches and noticed that Maria spent more time in her room away from them. When the call came at 2 A.M. that Maria had been arrested during a raid at a teen party, they had no idea she had even left the house. On direction from the court, Maria attended classes about substance abuse. However, when that ended, Louise and Frank were now monitoring the situation more closely, and soon discovered Maria was sneaking out of the house and missing school again. They took her to a substance abuse counselor, but Maria refused to return, saying she had no problem. Soon, Maria was caught stealing from their bank account, and they filed charges themselves against her. Maria was court ordered to attend substance abuse counseling, had regular drug testing, and spent time in community service for missing school periods.

This gradually allowed Louise and Frank to see their daughter returned to her normal self. They have been thankful that she has proceeded on to college, and is still substance-free.

# Alex

Alex was a longtime member of Al-Anon who came into the program during the Alateen years, especially focusing on the effects that his mother's alcoholism had on him and his closest brother. He learned through other people's stories how to take the focus off his mother's behavior and to put the emphasis on his survival with his father and brother. He shared continually how, as his mother retreated into alcoholism, he focused on good meals out in restaurants with his dad and brother.

He learned to take the fixation off trying to get his mother to stop drinking. He knew that it was a family disease and that he had little to do with it. As a highly intelligent man, he learned to incorporate the ideas of the program into his own life. He began to see that some of his own vulnerabilities came about because of his wish to escape his mother and her drinking patterns.

As his life went on and he became older, he continues applying the ideas of Al-Anon into the various escapades of his life. For example, as his brother became older, he became more and more dependent upon Alex for solutions to his life's difficulties, looking for money and various solutions to his quandaries. Alex chose to share, moment by moment, all the experiences with the brother. Bit by bit people could help him see his progress as he moved through the plan of his life.

Alex began to understand that Al-Anon applies to everything in one's life. The effects of a disease like alcoholism are more or less permanent, but his ways of handling the effects of the disease are ongoing and adaptable.

# Liza

Liza has a son who became involved with drugs and alcohol when he was a teenager. She was aware of substance abuse problems, as she had decided to divorce the son's father because of his own addiction issues. As a single mother, her life was quite busy, keeping up with breadwinning responsibilities and looking after her own mother, who was becoming elderly and needing more attention. Liza stayed in close touch with school counselors and offered to take her son to Alateen, so that he would see that his was not the only family with challenges. He was resistant to most everything that she offered.

The son did graduate from high school; by this time he was bringing unsavory characters into the family home, and Liza started to feel that her own house was unsafe. She was concerned not only about her son's increasing addiction, but also about possible theft and opening herself up to a lawsuit if something dreadful happened on her premises and a parent considered her liable.

Liza had been active in Al-Anon for years in connection with her husband's problems and had continued as the son's addiction came to the surface. With the support of friendships and solid meeting attendance, she gathered the strength to insist that the son leave her house.

She shared for a few years about how hard it was to have an addicted son on the streets in a large city, but she stuck with it, sometimes feeling guilty and sometimes confident that she had done the right thing to take care of herself. She was always open to phone calls from her son, and their relationship was warm enough that he did call her every few months. If he needed money for the next meal, she would drive to any section of the city that had a reputation for drug use to spend a little time with him, have a meal with him, and leave him with a little spending money. Usually his requests were simple. Once he asked for a spare pair of warm, dry socks.

Liza's son found recovery on his own, and she is not sure of the details of where, how, and with whom he became clean and sober. She's simply glad that a miracle occurred in her family. The son is now working and lives in his own apartment, completely self-supporting, and grateful for his mother's continued support and detached love. Although there were times when Liza's confidence wavered, she feels in retrospect that letting him go was the best that she could do for both of them. Without her hovering over him with too much worry and negative attention, he was forced to face the realities of life both with the addiction and without.

# Julie

Julie's son was a well-behaved boy, but she worried about his drinking during his teenage years. Alcoholism was new to Julie, as there was no alcoholism—at least, none that was evident—on either side of the family. She worked hard to encourage her son to do the right thing and expended considerable effort to keep the family challenge secret from friends, neighbors, and relatives outside the home. The son was a good student and never got in trouble with the law.

Finally, Julie and her husband decided to place the boy into a residential treatment center, and he was sober during that time and for several months afterward. When there was a relapse, the family decided to try a different treatment center, and the pattern was repeated. The counselors suggested that he attend A.A., even though he was younger than most of the members. With A.A., his attitude and confidence increased, and his lengths of sobriety became longer.

Julie found help and support in Al-Anon and learned not to blame herself for the son's alcoholism. Her son is now a grown man with a marriage and a child. He has many years of sobriety behind him and attends A.A. regularly. Julie was quite honored and flattered when he invited her to attend an open A.A. meeting where his birthday was celebrated. He publicly thanked her for her loving support for so many years.

# Appendix B:
# Helpful Websites

### Al-Anon Family Groups
1600 Corporate Landing Parkway
Virginia Beach, VA 23454
757-563-1600
*www.al-anonfamilygroups.org*
For helping families recover from a family member's problem drinking.

### Parents Anonymous
250 West First Street
Suite 250
Claremont, CA 91711
909-621-6184
*www.parentsanonymous.org*
For strengthening families, breaking the cycle of abuse, and helping parents create safe homes for their children.

### Adult Children of Alcoholics
P.O. Box 3216
Torrance, CA 90510
562-595-7831
*www.adultchildren.org*
Twelve-step organization to help persons who come from alcoholic and other dysfunctional families.

### Alcoholics Anonymous
P.O. Box 459
New York, NY 10163
212-870-3400
*www.aa.org*
The Twelve Steps organization that helps people stop drinking.

### National Alliance on Mental Illness (NAMI)
3803 N. Fairfax Drive, Ste. 100
Arlington, VA 22203
703-524-9094
*www.nami.org*
This organization helps people with mental illness and family members of the mentally ill.

### Overeaters Anonymous
P.O. Box 44020
Rio Rancho, NM 87174
505-891-2664
*www.oa.org*
This twelve-step organization helps people who eat compulsively.

### Debtors Anonymous
P.O. Box 920888
Needham, MA 02492
800-421-2383 (United States only)
*www.debtorsanonymous.org*
Twelve-step organization to assist persons who use unsecured debt compulsively.

### Gamblers Anonymous
P.O. Box 17173
Los Angeles, CA 90017
626-960-3500

*www.gamblersanonymous.org*

This twelve-step organization helps people stop compulsive gambling.

### Emotions Anonymous

P.O. Box 4245

St. Paul, MN 55104

651-647-9712

*www.emotionsanonymous.org*

This twelve-step program helps people find emotional sobriety.

### Families Anonymous

701 Lee Street

Des Plaines, IL 60016

800-736-9805 (United States only)

*www.familiesanonymous.org*

This twelve-step program assists family members who are coping with other family members who have behavioral or drug issues.

### Nar-Anon Family Group

P.O. Box 2562

Palos Verdes Peninsula, CA 90274

310-547-5800

*www.nar-anon.org*

### National Institute on Drug Abuse

Office of Science Policy and Communications, Public Information and Liaison Branch

6001 Executive Boulevard

Room 5213, MSC 9561

Bethesda, Maryland 20892-9561

301-443-1124

*www.drugabuse.gov*

**Substance Abuse and Mental Health Services Administration (SAMHSA)**
1 Choke Cherry Road
Rockville, MD 20857
800-729-6686
*www.samhsa.gov*

**Behavioral Health Treatment Services Locator**
800-662-4357
*www.findtreatment.samhsa.gov*

**Outofthefog.net**
*www.outofthefog.net*
This site assists those who are coping with a friend or family member who has various psychological disorders.

**Drug Strategies**
*www.drugstrategies.com*
For guidance on effective drug treatment programs.

**National Stepfamily Resource Center**
*www.stepfamilies.info*
For information about stepfamily relationships.

**Parents Without Partners**
*www.parentswithoutpartners.org*
For information about single parenting.

**The Successful Parent**
*www.thesuccessfulparent.com*
For information about parenting adolescents.

**ParentsTalk**
*www.parents-talk.com*

For help with a difficult child and other parenting information, plus dialoguing with other parents.

### Thirdworldpapa.com

*www.thirdworldpapa.com*

An eclectic modern blog on many aspects of relationships.

### Noslang.com Drug Slang Translator

*www.noslang.com/drugs/dictionary*

Street slang for drugs.

# Appendix C:
# Additional Resources

## Recovery/Treatment Facilities

The following list is for reference, and no particular endorsement is implied.

### Mayo Clinic
Men, women, and adolescents
507-284-6150
Arizona, Florida, Minnesota
*www.mayoclinic.org/chemical-dependency*
Chemical dependency treatment, intensive inpatient and outpatient treatment programs, addresses coexisting mental health conditions.

### Remuda Ranch
Women, adolescent boys and girls
800-445-1900
Arizona and Virginia
*www.remudaranch.com*
Inpatient and residential programs for anorexia, bulimia, and other eating disorders and related issues.

### Visions Adolescent Treatment Centers
Adolescents
818-889-3665
California
*www.visionsteen.com*
Residential center for substance abuse and behavioral disorders. Other issues such as mental health, eating disorders, cross-addictions, low self-esteem, anger management, and family dysfunction are addressed.

### Newport Academy
Teenage girls
949-887-0242
California
Long-term inpatient treatment for substance abuse and co-occurring disorder treatment.
*www.newportacademy.com*

### Miami Behavioral Health Center and Spectrum Programs
Children, youth, adults, and elderly
305-757-0602
Miami Dade and Broward Counties
*www.banyanhealth.org*
Crisis intervention, psychiatric services, substance abuse inpatient, outpatient, residential, and detox treatment.

### Father Martin's Ashley
Women and young adults age 18–25
800-799-4673
Maryland
*www.fathermartinsashley.org*
Detox and inpatient drug and alcohol treatment center.

### Hazelden

Men, women, and youth age 14–25

800-257-7800

Minnesota, New York, Illinois, Oregon, and Florida

*www.hazelden.org*

Minnesota, Oregon, and Florida offer residential treatment centers for women. Specialized rehab programs for drug addiction and alcoholism. Provides publishing, researching, and professional education opportunities.

### Caron Treatment Centers

Adults, young adults, and adolescents

610-743-6532

Pennsylvania

*www.caron.org*

Inpatient and outpatient treatment for drug and alcohol abuse and psychiatric/psychological disorders

### Clearbrook

Men, women, and adolescents

570-823-1171

Pennsylvania

*www.clearbrookinc.com*

Detox and rehab treatment programs for alcoholism and/or chemical dependency.

### White Deer Run

Men, women, and adolescents

814-816-6198

Pennsylvania

*www.whitedeerrun.crchealth.com*

Inpatient detox, residential rehabilitation, mental health residential treatment, intensive outpatient, outpatient with individual or group and family therapy.

### Cumberland Heights

Men, women, and adolescents

615-352-1757

Tennessee

*www.cumberlandheights.org*

Detox, inpatient, and outpatient holistic treatment center for drug and alcohol abuse.

### Brattleboro Retreat

Men, women, adolescents, and children

802-258-3719

Vermont

*www.brattlebororetreat.org*

Inpatient and partial hospitalization for mental health and addiction treatment.

# Appendix D:
# Teen Drug Slang Glossary

Adolescent language changes constantly, so some of these terms, a sampling gleaned from WebMD and *The Everything® Health Guide to Addiction and Recovery*, may no longer be in use. You will never be able to completely keep up with your teenager's slang, but at least she knows that you're not completely in the dark.

**A-bomb**
Marijuana cigarette with heroin or opium

**Acid**
LSD

**Air blast**
Inhalant

**Angel dust**
PCP

**Antifreeze**
Heroin. Synonyms are brown sugar, dope, junk, and smack.

**Author**
Doctor who writes illegal prescriptions

**Bag man**
Person who transports money or drugs

**Barbies**
Depressants

**Bikers coffee**
Methamphetamine and coffee

**Breakfast cereal**
Ketamine. Also called Special K and Vitamin K.

**Brown sugar**
Heroin. Synonyms are antifreeze, dope, junk, and smack.

**Buttons**
Mescaline

**Channel**
Vein into which a
drug is injected

**Coke**
Cocaine. Also called crack,
nose candy, and snow.

**Cotton**
OxyContin

**Crack**
Cocaine. Also called coke,
nose candy, and snow.

**Crank**
Methamphetamine. Also
called glass, meth, and speed.

**Dexing**
Drinking cough syrup to
get high. Synonyms are
robotripping or robodosing.

**Do a line**
To inhale cocaine

**Dope**
Heroin. Synonyms are
antifreeze, brown sugar,
junk, and smack.

**Factory**
Place where drugs are
packaged, diluted,
or manufactured

**Fall**
Arrested

**Forget pills**
Rohypnol, a date-rape drug.
Also called roche and roofies.

**Freebase**
To smoke cocaine

**Glass**
Methamphetamine. Also
called crank, meth, and speed.

**Graduate**
Completely stop using drugs
or progress to stronger drugs

**Gym candy**
Steroids

**Honey**
Currency

**Ice**
Crystal methamphetamine

**Juggler**
Teenage street dealer

**Junk**
Heroin. Synonyms are antifreeze, brown sugar, dope, and smack.

**Meth**
Methamphetamine. Also called crank, glass, and speed.

**Meth monster**
Someone who becomes crazed when on methamphetamine.

**Miss Emma**
Morphine

**Nose candy**
Cocaine. Also called crack, coke, and snow.

**On ice**
In jail

**Pepsi habit**
Occasional use of drugs

**Potato chips**
Crack cut with benzocaine

**Raspberry**
A girl who trades sex for crack or money to buy crack

**Rave**
All-night parties designed to enhance hallucinogenic experiences

**Robotripping, robodosing**
Drinking cough syrup to get high. Also called dexing.

**Roche**
Rohypnol, a date-rape drug. Also called forget pills and roofies.

**Roofies**
Rohypnol, a date-rape drug. Also called forget pills and roche.

**Runners**
People who sell drugs or connect buyers and sellers

**Sam**
Federal narcotics agent

**Score**
Purchase drugs

**Server**
Crack dealer

**Shooting gallery**
Place where drugs are used

**Smack**
Heroin. Synonyms are antifreeze, brown sugar, dope, and junk.

**Smurf**
Cigar dipped in embalming fluid

**Snow**
Cocaine. Also called crack, coke, and nose candy.

**Special K**
Ketamine. Also called breakfast cereal and Vitamin K.

**Speed**
Methamphetamine. Also called crank, glass, and meth.

**Swallower**
Person used as a drug courier

**Syrup heads**
Users of over-the-counter cough suppressants

**Tester**
Person who is given a drug early in the day, spreading the word about its availability

**Thoroughbred**
Drug dealer who sells pure narcotics

**Tracks**
Row of needle marks on a person

**Tussin**
Short for Robitussin

**Tweaker**
Crack user who looks for drugs on the floor after a police raid

**Vitamin K**
Ketamine. Also called breakfast cereal and Special K.

**Vitamin R**
Ritalin

**Weight trainers**
Steroids

**White lightning**
LSD

**X**
Ecstasy

**Zombie**
PCP or a heavy user of drugs

# Appendix E:
# Recommended Books and Pamphlets for Teens

Aretha, David. *Cocaine and Crack*. (Berkeley Heights, NJ: Enslow Publishers, Inc., 2005).

Aretha, David. *Methamphetamine and Amphetamines*. (Berkeley Heights, NJ: Enslow Publishers, Inc., 2005).

Carroll, Marilyn. *Cocaine and Crack*. (Springfield, NJ: Enslow Publishers, Inc., 1994).

Green, Carl R. *Nicotine and Tobacco*. (Berkeley Heights, NJ: Enslow Publishers, Inc., 2005).

Jeffrey, Laura S. *Marijuana = Busted!* (Berkeley Heights, NJ: Enslow Publishers, Inc., 2006).

Manley, Claudia B. *Crack and Your Circulatory System* (New York, NY: Rosen Publishing Group, Inc., 2001).

Monroe, Judy. *LSD, PCP, and Hallucinogen Drug Dangers*. (Berkeley Heights, NJ: Enslow Publishers, Inc., 2001).

# Index